DATE DUE

BLACK AMERICAN WOMEN
FICTION WRITERS

Writers of English: Lives and Works

BLACK AMERICAN WOMEN FICTION WRITERS

Edited and with an Introduction by

Harold Bloom

CHELSEA HOUSE PUBLISHERS
New York   Philadelphia

Jacket illustration: Jacob Lawrence (b. 1917), *Forward (Harriet Tubman* theme, 1967) (courtesy of the North Carolina Museum of Art, Raleigh, Museum Purchase Fund).

CHELSEA HOUSE PUBLISHERS

Editorial Director Richard Rennert
Executive Managing Editor Karyn Gullen Browne
Copy Chief Robin James
Picture Editor Adrian G. Allen
Creative Director Robert Mitchell
Art Director Joan Ferrigno
Production Manager Sallye Scott

Writers of English: Lives and Works

Senior Editor S. T. Joshi
Series Design Rae Grant

Staff for BLACK AMERICAN WOMEN FICTION WRITERS

Assistant Editor Mary Sisson
Editorial Assistant Scott Briggs
Picture Researcher Ellen Dudley

© 1995 by Chelsea House Publishers, a division of Main Line Book Co.

Introduction © 1995 by Harold Bloom

Printed and bound in the United States of America.

First Printing

1 3 5 7 9 8 6 4 2

Library of Congress Cataloging-in-Publication Data

Black American women fiction writers / edited and with an introduction by Harold Bloom.
    p. cm.—(Writers of English)
    Includes bibliographical references.
    ISBN 0-7910-2208-0.—ISBN 0-7910-2233-1 (pbk.)
    1. American fiction—Afro-American authors—History and criticism. 2. American fiction—Afro-American authors—Bio-bibliography. 3. American fiction—Women authors—History and criticism. 4. American fiction—Women authors—Bio-bibliography. 5. Women and literature—United States. 6. Afro-American women in literature. 7. Afro-Americans in literature. I. Bloom, Harold. II. Series.
PS374.N4B57 1994
813'.009'9287'08996073—dc20   94-5887
[B]   CIP

◼ Contents

◪ User's Guide

THIS VOLUME PROVIDES biographical, critical, and bibliographical information on the fifteen most significant black American women fiction writers. Each chapter consists of three parts: a biography of the author; a selection of brief critical extracts about the author; and a bibliography of the author's published books.

The biography supplies a detailed outline of the important events in the author's life, including his or her major writings. The critical extracts are taken from a wide array of books and periodicals, from the author's lifetime to the present, and range in content from biographical to critical to historical. The extracts are arranged in chronological order by date of writing or publication, and a full bibliographical citation is provided at the end of each extract. Editorial additions or deletions are indicated within carets.

The author bibliographies list every separate publication—including books, pamphlets, broadsides, collaborations, and works edited or translated by the author—for works published in the author's lifetime; selected important posthumous publications are also listed. Titles are those of the first edition; variant titles are supplied within carets. In selected instances dates of revised editions are given where these are significant. Pseudonymous works are listed but not the pseudonyms under which these works were published. Periodicals edited by the author are listed only when the author has written most or all of the contents. Titles enclosed in square brackets are of doubtful authenticity. All works by the author, whether in English or in other languages, have been listed; English translations of foreign-language works are not listed unless the author has done the translation.

The Life of the Author
Harold Bloom

NIETZSCHE, WITH EXULTANT ANGUISH, famously proclaimed that God was dead. Whatever the consequences of this for the ethical life, its ultimate literary effect certainly would have surprised the author Nietzsche. His French disciples, Foucault most prominent among them, developed the Nietzschean proclamation into the dogma that all authors, God included, were dead. The death of the author, which is no more than a Parisian trope, another metaphor for fashion's setting of skirt-lengths, is now accepted as literal truth by most of our current apostles of what should be called French Nietzsche, to distinguish it from the merely original Nietzsche. We also have French Freud or Lacan, which has little to do with the actual thought of Sigmund Freud, and even French Joyce, which interprets *Finnegans Wake* as the major work of Jacques Derrida. But all this is as nothing compared to the final triumph of the doctrine of the death of the author: French Shakespeare. That delicious absurdity is given us by the New Historicism, which blends Foucault and California fruit juice to give us the Word that Renaissance "social energies," and not William Shakespeare, composed *Hamlet* and *King Lear*. It seems a proper moment to murmur "enough" and to return to a study of the life of the author.

Sometimes it troubles me that there are so few masterpieces in the vast ocean of literary biography that stretches between James Boswell's great *Life* of Dr. Samuel Johnson and the late Richard Ellmann's wonderful *Oscar Wilde*. Literary biography is a crucial genre, and clearly a difficult one in which to excel. The actual nature of the lives of the poets seems to have little effect upon the quality of their biographies. Everything happened to Lord Byron and nothing at all to Wallace Stevens, and yet their biographers seem equally daunted by them. But even inadequate biographies of strong writers, or of weak ones, are of immense use. I have never read a literary biography from which I have not profited, a statement I cannot make about any other genre whatsoever. And when it comes to figures who are central to us—Dante, Shakespeare, Cervantes, Montaigne, Goethe, Whitman, Tolstoi, Freud, Joyce, Kafka among them—we reach out eagerly for every scrap that the biographers have gleaned. Concerning Dante and Shakespeare we know much too little, yet when we come to Goethe and Freud, where we seem to know more than everything, we still want to know more. The death of the author, despite our current resentniks, clearly was only a momentary fad. Something vital in every authentic lover of literature responds to Emerson's battle-cry sentence: "There is no history, only biography." Beyond that there is a deeper truth, difficult to come at and requiring a lifetime to understand, which is that there is no literature, only autobiography, however mediated, however veiled, however transformed. The events of Shakespeare's life included the composition of *Hamlet,* and that act of writing was itself a crucial act of living, though we do not yet know altogether how to read so doubled an act. When an author takes up a more overtly autobiographical stance, as so many do in their youth, again we still do not know precisely how to accommodate the vexed relation between life and work. T. S. Eliot, meditating upon James Joyce, made a classic statement as to such accommodation:

> We want to know who are the originals of his characters, and what were
> the origins of his episodes, so that we may unravel the web of memory
> and invention and discover how far and in what ways the crude material
> has been transformed.

When a writer is not even covertly autobiographical, the web of memory and invention is still there, but so subtly woven that we may never unravel it. And yet we want deeply never to stop trying, and not merely because we are curious, but because each of us is caught in her own network of memory and invention. We do not always recall our inventions, and long before we age we cease to be certain of the extent to which we have invented our memories. Perhaps one motive for reading is our need to unravel our own webs. If our masters could make, from their lives, what we read, then we can be moved by them to ask: What have we made or lived in relation to what we have read? The answers may be sad, or confused, but the question is likely, implicitly, to go on being asked as long as we read. In Freudian terms, we are asking: What is it that we have repressed? What have we forgotten, unconsciously but purposively: What is it that we flee? Art, literature necessarily included, is regression in the service of the ego, according to a famous Freudian formula. I doubt the Freudian wisdom here, but indubitably it is profoundly suggestive. When we read, something in us keeps asking the equivalent of the Freudian questions: From what or whom is the author in flight, and to what earlier stages in her life is she returning, and why?

Reading, whether as an art or a pastime, has been damaged by the visual media, television in particular, and might be in some danger of extinction in the age of the computer, except that the psychic need for it continues to endure, presumably because it alone can assuage a central loneliness in elitist society. Despite all sophisticated or resentful denials, the reading of imaginative literature remains a quest to overcome the isolation of the individual consciousness. We can read for information, or entertainment, or for love of the language, but in the end we seek, in the author, the person whom we have not found, whether in ourselves or in others. In that quest, there always are elements at once aggressive and defensive, so that reading, even in childhood, is rarely free of hidden anxieties. And yet it remains one of the few activities not contaminated by an entropy of spirit. We read in hope, because we lack companionship, and the author can become the object of the most idealistic elements in our search for the wit and inventiveness we so desperately require. We read biography, not as a supplement to reading the author, but as a second, fresh attempt to understand what always seems to evade us in the work, our drive towards a kind of identity with the author.

This will-to-identity, though recently much deprecated, is a prime basis for the experience of sublimity in reading. *Hamlet* retains its unique position in the Western canon not because most readers and playgoers identify themselves with the prince, who clearly is beyond them, but rather because they find themselves again in the power of the language that represents him with such immediacy and force. Yet we know that neither language nor social energy created Hamlet. Our curiosity about Shakespeare is endless, and never will be appeased. That curiosity itself is a value, and cannot be separated from the value of *Hamlet* the tragedy, or Hamlet the literary character. It provokes us that Shakespeare the man seems so unknowable, at once everyone and no one as Borges shrewdly observes. Critics keep telling us otherwise, yet something valid in us keeps believing that we would know Hamlet better if Shakespeare's life were as fully known as the lives of Goethe and Freud, Byron and Oscar Wilde, or best of all, Dr. Samuel Johnson. Shakespeare never will have his Boswell, and Dante never will have his Richard Ellmann. How much one would give for a detailed and candid *Life of Dante* by Petrarch, or an outspoken memoir of Shakespeare by Ben Jonson! Or, in the age just past, how superb would be rival studies of one another by Hemingway and Scott Fitzgerald! But the list is endless: think of *Oscar Wilde* by Lord Alfred Douglas, or a joint biography of Shelley by Mary Godwin, Emilia Viviani, and Jane Williams. More than our insatiable desire for scandal would be satisfied. The literary rivals and the lovers of the great writers possessed perspectives we will never enjoy, and without those perspectives we dwell in some poverty in regard to the writers with whom we ourselves never can be done.

There is a sense in which imaginative literature *is* perspectivism, so that the reader is likely to be overwhelmed by the work's difficulty unless its multiple perspectives are mastered. Literary biography matters most because it is a storehouse of perspectives, frequently far surpassing any that are grasped by the particular biographer. There are relations between authors' lives and their works of kinds we have yet to discover, because our analytical instruments are not yet advanced enough to perform the necessary labor. Perhaps a novel, poem, or play is not so much a regression in the service of the ego, as it is an amalgam of *all* the Freudian mechanisms of defense, all working together for the apotheosis of the ego. Freud valued art highly, but thought that the aesthetic enterprise was no rival for psychoanalysis, unlike religion and philosophy. Clearly Freud was mistaken; his own anxieties about his indebtedness to Shakespeare helped produce the weirdness of his joining in the lunacy that argued for the Earl of Oxford as the author of Shakespeare's plays. It was Shakespeare, and not "the poets," who was there before Freud arrived at his depth psychology, and it is Shakespeare who is there still, well out ahead of psychoanalysis. We see what Freud would not see, that psychoanalysis is Shakespeare prosified and systematized. Freud is part of literature, not of "science," and the biography of Freud has the same relations to psychoanalysis as the biography of Shakespeare has to *Hamlet* and *King Lear*, if only we knew more of the life of Shakespeare.

Western literature, particularly since Shakespeare, is marked by the representation of internalized change in its characters. A literature of the ever-growing inner self is in itself a large form of biography, even though this is the biography of imaginary beings, from Hamlet to the sometimes nameless protagonists of Kafka and Beckett. Skeptics might want to argue that all literary biography concerns imaginary beings, since authors make themselves up, and every biographer gives us a creation curiously different from the same author as seen by the writer of a rival *Life*. Boswell's Johnson is not quite anyone else's Johnson, though it is now very difficult for us to disentangle the great Doctor from his gifted Scottish friend and follower. The life of the author is not merely a metaphor or a fiction, as is "the Death of the Author," but it always does contain metaphorical or fictive elements. Those elements are a part of the value of literary biography, but not the largest or the crucial part, which is the separation of the mask from the man or woman who hid behind it. James Joyce and Samuel Beckett, master and sometime disciple, were both of them enigmatic personalities, and their biographers have not, as yet, fully expounded the mystery of these contrasting natures. Beckett seems very nearly to have been a secular saint: personally disinterested, heroic in the French Resistance, as humane a person ever to have composed major fictions and dramas. Joyce, self-obsessed even as Beckett was preternaturally selfless, was the Milton of the twentieth century. Beckett was perhaps the least egoistic post-Joycean, post-Proustian, post-Kafkan of writers. Does that illuminate the problematical nature of his work, or does it simply constitute another problem? Whatever the cause, the question matters. The only death of the author that is other than literal, and that matters, is the fate only of weak writers. The strong, who become canonical, never die, which is what the canon truly is about. To be read forever is the Life of the Author.

▨ *Introduction*

LIKE RALPH ELLISON, Zora Neale Hurston will be remembered for one novel, though *Their Eyes Were Watching God*, despite its aesthetically achieved pathos, is not of the eminence of *Invisible Man*. And yet it clearly is a permanent book, remarkable in its kind. One way of seeing its splendor is to read it side-by-side with Hurston's allegorical and satiric narrative, *Moses: Man of the Mountain*, an admirable attempt to do something astonishingly difficult, which is to appropriate biblical narrative as an essentially cheerful paradigm for African-American experience. As a biblical allegorist, Hurston largely fails precisely where William Faulkner frequently succeeds (although not in the dread disaster of *A Fable*). Faulkner's language in *Light in August* and its companion works is marked by the controlled exuberance that the biblical analogue demands, and Faulkner is very skilled in taking up a consistent rhetorical stance in regard to his narrative and its characters. The language in *Moses: Man of the Mountain* is very uneven, and frequently gives the effect of distracting Hurston from the Exodus pattern she seeks to follow. I am uncertain, as I finish the book, precisely where the novelist stands in relation to figures she dislikes, Miriam and Aaron in particular. Perhaps Hurston tried to do too much in the one book, but more likely her primordial vitalism made her distrust the transcendental element, without which the Exodus story lacks coherence and weight.

Yet turning back to *Their Eyes Were Watching God*, directly after rereading Hurston's *Moses*, vividly demonstrates again the superb vitalism that transfigures Hurston's portrait of Janie Crawford. It is true that sometimes the language falters or mounts up too high for its subject, but the rhetorical stance of exuberant identification is unwavering. From the folklore that preserved an African gnosis, Hurston quarried one of the classic versions of an American Gnosticism, exalting the spark or pneuma that condenses what is best and oldest in Janie, a divinity that is no part of creation and that has the strength to outlast all the disasters of love and sleep that make up our Fall:

> When God had made The Man, he made him out of stuff that sung all the time and glittered all over. Then after that some angels got jealous

xi

and chopped him into millions of pieces, but still he glittered and hummed. So they beat him down to nothing but sparks but each little spark had a shine and a song. So they covered each one over with mud. And the lonesomeness in the sparks made them hunt for one another, but the mud is deaf and dumb. Like all the other tumbling mud-balls, Janie had tried to show her shine.

The jealousy of the Angels is an ancient Gnostic motif, but Hurston stirs it to an immediacy quite her own. *Their Eyes Were Watching God* finally may be seen as heretical wisdom literature, the precise and perfect expression of the formidably heterodox personality who created it.

—H. B.

⬙ ⬙ ⬙

Maya Angelou
b. 1928

MAYA ANGELOU was born Marguerite Johnson in St. Louis, Missouri, on April 4, 1928. Her life has been both remarkably varied and occasionally grim (she was raped at the age of eight by her mother's boyfriend), and she has won greater critical acclaim for her several autobiographical volumes than for her poetry and drama. She attended public schools in Arkansas and California, studied music privately, and studied dance with Martha Graham. In 1954–55 she was a member of the cast of *Porgy and Bess*, which went on a twenty-two-nation world tour sponsored by the U.S. Department of State. Some of her songs were recorded on the album *Miss Calypso* (1957). Later she acted in several off-Broadway plays, including one, the musical *Cabaret for Freedom* (1960), that she wrote with Godfrey Cambridge.

In addition to these artistic pursuits, Angelou held a variety of odd jobs in her late teens and early twenties, including streetcar conductor, Creole cook, nightclub waitress, prostitute, and madam. She has been married twice: first, around 1950, to a white man, Tosh Angelos (whose surname she adapted when she became a dancer), and then, from 1973 to 1981, to Paul Du Feu. She bore a son, Guy, at the age of sixteen.

When she was thirty Angelou moved to Brooklyn. There she met John Oliver Killens, James Baldwin, and other writers who encouraged her to write. While practicing her craft, however, she became involved in the civil rights movement. She met Martin Luther King, Jr., was appointed the northern coordinator of the Southern Christian Leadership Conference, and organized demonstrations at the United Nations. She fell in love with the South African freedom fighter Vusumzi Make, and they left for Egypt, where in 1961–62 Angelou worked as associate editor of the *Arab Observer*, an English-language newspaper in Cairo. She broke up with Make when he criticized her independence and lack of subservience to him.

In 1963 Angelou went to Ghana to be assistant administrator of the School of Music and Drama at the University of Ghana's Institute of African Studies. In the three years she was there she acted in several additional

1

plays, served as feature editor of the *African Review*, and was a contributor to the Ghanaian Broadcasting Corporation. Returning to the United States, she was a lecturer at the University of California at Los Angeles and has subsequently been a visiting professor or writer in residence at several other universities.

Angelou's first published book was *I Know Why the Caged Bird Sings* (1969), an autobiography of the first sixteen years of her life; a tremendous critical and popular success, it was nominated for a National Book Award and was later adapted for television. Two more autobiographical volumes appeared in the 1970s, *Gather Together in My Name* (1974) and *Singin' and Swingin' and Gettin' Merry Like Christmas* (1976), along with three volumes of poetry. While writing several more dramas, she wrote two screenplays (directing one of them and writing the musical scores for both) and several television plays (including a series of ten one-hour programs entitled *Blacks, Blues, Black*). She also continued to pursue her acting career and was nominated for a Tony Award in 1973 for her Broadway debut, *Look Away*. She was appointed a member of the American Revolution Bicentennial Council by President Gerald R. Ford in 1975.

In the 1980s Angelou solidified her reputation with two more autobiographies, *The Heart of a Woman* (1981) and *All God's Children Need Traveling Shoes* (1986), along with several more volumes of poetry. The peak of her fame was perhaps achieved when in 1993 she composed a poem, "On the Pulse of Morning," for the inauguration of President Bill Clinton. Angelou's latest prose work, *Wouldn't Take Nothing for My Journey Now*, a collection of essays and sketches, also appeared that year and, like most of its predecessors, was a best-seller.

Maya Angelou, who has received honorary degrees from Smith College, Mills College, and Lawrence University, currently resides in Sonoma, California.

▨ *Critical Extracts*

MAYA ANGELOU   There was shuffling and rustling around me, then Henry Reed was giving his valedictory address, "To Be or Not to Be." Hadn't he heard the whitefolks? We couldn't *be*, so the question was a waste of time. Henry's voice came out clear and strong. I feared to look at him. Hadn't he got the message? There was no "nobler in the mind" for the Negroes because the world didn't think we had minds, and they let us know it. "Outrageous fortune"? Now, that was a joke. ⟨. . .⟩

I had been listening and silently rebutting each sentence with my eyes closed; then there was a hush, which in an audience warns that something unplanned is happening. I looked up and saw Henry Reed, the conservative, the proper, the A student, turn his back to the audience and turn to us (the proud graduating class of 1940) and sing, nearly speaking,

> "Lift ev'ry voice and sing
> Till earth and heaven ring
> Ring with the harmonies of Liberty . . ."

It was the poem written by James Weldon Johnson. It was the music composed by J. Rosamond Johnson. It was the Negro national anthem. Out of habit we were singing it.

Our mothers and fathers stood in the dark hall and joined the hymn of encouragement. A kindergarten teacher led the small children onto the stage and the buttercups and daisies and bunny rabbits marked time and tried to follow:

> "Stony the road we trod
> Bitter the chastening rod
> Felt I the days when hope, unborn, had died.
> Yet with a steady beat
> Have not our weary feet
> Come to the place for which our fathers sighed?"

Every child I knew learned that song with his ABC's and along with "Jesus Loves Me This I Know." But I personally had never heard it before. Never heard the words, despite the thousands of times I had sung them. Never thought they had anything to do with me.

On the other hand, the words of Patrick Henry had made such an impression on me that I had been able to stretch myself tall and trembling and say, "I know not what course others may take, but as for me, give me liberty or give me death."

And now I heard, really for the first time:

> "We have come over a way that with tears
> has been watered,
> We have come, treading our path through
> the blood of the slaughtered."

While the echoes of the song shivered in the air, Henry Reed bowed his head, said, "Thank you," and returned to his place in the line. The tears that slipped down many faces were not wiped away in shame.

We are on top again. As always, again. We survived. The depths had been icy and dark, but now a bright sun spoke to our souls. I was no longer simply a member of the proud graduating class of 1940; I was a proud member of the wonderful, beautiful Negro race.

> Maya Angelou, *I Know Why the Caged Bird Sings* (New York: Random House, 1969), pp. 177–79

ERNECE B. KELLY   Miss Angelou confidently reaches back in memory to pull out the painful childhood times when children fail to break the adult code, disastrously breaching faith and laws they know nothing of; when the very young swing easy from hysterical laughter to awful loneliness; from a hunger for heroes to the voluntary Pleasure-Pain game of wondering who their *real* parents are and how long before they take them to their authentic home.

Introducing herself as Marguerite, a "tender-hearted" child, the author allows her story to range in an extraordinary fashion along the field of human emotion. With a child's fatalism, a deep cut ushers in visions of an ignoble death. With a child's addiction to romance and melodrama, she imagines ending her life in the dirt-yard of a Mexican family—among strangers! It is as if Miss Angelou has a Time Machine, so unerringly does she record the private world of the young where sin is the Original Sin and embarrassment, penultimate. ⟨. . .⟩

Miss Angelou accommodates her literary style to the various settings her story moves through. She describes a rural vignette which is "sweet-milk fresh in her memory . . ." and a San Francisco rooming house where "Chicken suppers and gambling games were rioting on a twenty-four hour basis down-stairs." Her metaphors are strong and right; her similes less often so. But these lapses in poetic style are undeniably balanced by the insight she offers into the effects of social conditioning on the life-style and self-concept of a Black child growing up in the rural South of the 1930's.

This is a novel about Blackness, youth, and white American society, usually in conflict. The miracle is that out of the War emerges a whole person capable of believing in her worth and capabilities. On balance, it is a gentle indictment of white American womanhood. It is a timely book.

Ernece B. Kelly, [Review of *I Know Why the Caged Bird Sings*], *Harvard Educational Review* 40, No. 4 (November 1970): 681–82

SIDONIE ANN SMITH   Maya Angelou's autobiography, like ⟨Richard⟩ Wright's, opens with a primal childhood scene that brings into focus the nature of the imprisoning environment from which the self will seek escape. The black girl child is trapped within the cage of her own diminished self-image around which interlock the bars of natural and social forces. The oppression of natural forces, of physical appearance and processes, foists a self-consciousness on all young girls who must grow from children into women. Hair is too thin or stringy or mousy or nappy. Legs are too fat, too thin, too bony, the knees too bowed. Hips are too wide or not wide enough. Breasts grow too fast or not at all. The self-critical process is incessant, a driving demon. But in the black girl child's experience these natural bars are reinforced with the rusted iron social bars of racial subordination and impotence. Being born black is itself a liability in a world ruled by white standards of beauty which imprison the child *a priori* in a cage of ugliness: "What you looking at me for?" This really isn't me. I'm white with long blond hair and blue eyes, with pretty pink skin and straight hair, with a delicate mouth. I'll try again. The black and blue bruises of the soul multiply and compound as the caged bird flings herself against these bars:

> The Black female is assaulted in her tender years by all those
> common forces of nature at the same time that she is caught in
> the tripartite crossfire of masculine prejudice, white illogical hate
> and Black lack of power.

Within this imprisoning environment there is no place for this black girl child. She becomes a displaced person whose pain is intensified by her consciousness of that displacement:

> If growing up is painful for the Southern Black girl, being
> aware of her displacement is the rust on the razor that threatens
> the throat.
> It is an unnecessary insult.

If the black man is denied his potency and his masculinity, if his autobiography narrates the quest of the black male after a "place" of full manhood, the black woman is denied her beauty and her quest is one after self-accepted black womanhood. Thus the discovered pattern of significant moments Maya Angelou superimposes on the experience of her life is a pattern of moments that trace the quest of the black female after a "place," a place where a child no longer need ask self-consciously, "What you looking at me for?" but where a woman can declare confidently, "I am a beautiful, Black woman."

> Sidonie Ann Smith, "The Song of a Caged Bird: Maya Angelou's Quest After Self-Acceptance," *Southern Humanities Review* 7, No. 4 (Fall 1973): 368

ANNIE GOTTLIEB   *Gather Together in My Name* is a little shorter and thinner than its predecessor; telling of an episodic, searching and wandering period in Maya Angelou's life, it lacks the density of childhood. In full compensation, her style has both ripened and simplified. It is more telegraphic and more condensed, transmitting a world of sensation or emotion or understanding in one image—in short, it is more like poetry. (Maya Angelou published a book of poems, *Just Give Me a Cool Drink of Water 'Fore I Diiie*, in between the two autobiographical volumes.)

"Disappointment rode his face bareback." "Dumbfounded, founded in dumbness." "The heavy opulence of Dostoevsky's world was where I had lived forever. The gloomy, lightless interiors, the complex ratiocinations of the characters and their burdensome humors, were as familiar to me as loneliness." "The South I returned to . . . was flesh-real and swollen belly poor." "I clenched my reason and forced their faces into focus." Even in these short bits snipped out of context, you can sense the palpability, the precision and the rhythm of this writing. ⟨. . .⟩

In *Gather Together in My Name*, the ridiculous and touching posturing of a young girl in the throes of growing up are superimposed on the serious business of survival and responsibility for a child. Maya Angelou's insistence on taking full responsibility for her own life, her frank and humorous examination of her self, will challenge many a reader to be as honest under easier circumstances. Reading her book, you may learn, too, the embrace and ritual, the dignity and solace and humor of the black community. You will meet strong, distinctive people, drawn with deftness and compassion; their blackness is not used to hide their familiar but vulnerable humanity any more than their accessible humanity can for a moment be used to obscure their blackness—or their oppression. Maya Angelou's second book about her life as a young black woman in America is engrossing and vital, rich and funny and wise.

> Annie Gottlieb, "Growing Up and the Serious Business of Survival," *New York Times Book Review*, 16 June 1974, pp. 16, 20

FRANK LAMONT PHILLIPS   Maya Angelou begins the second book of her autobiography, *Gather Together in My Name*, with a brief history of Black American thought and culture after the second World War; it is not a precise history, certainly not history as viewed coolly and through statistics. It is not even "accurate," but viewed from the vantage of almost 30 years, as one might hear it on the streets: biased, authoritative, hip, almost wildly funny, like certain urban myths. It seems right, and if this is not history as it was, it is history as it should have been. ⟨. . .⟩

Maya Angelou is not the stylist that Himes is, nor a Richard Wright. She manages, however, a witty poetic flow (intensely more successful than in her book of poems, *Just Give Me a Cool Drink of Water 'Fore I Diiie*) that is sometimes cute, sometimes lax, often apt. The events of her life make interesting if somewhat lurid reading: an unwed mother, she is unlucky in love; she becomes a prostitute, enduring every nadir of fortune, her motherly instincts intact, her ability to adapt to adversity functioning.

Miss Angelou has the right instincts, that mythomania which one who is given to prattling about his life seems to possess. She applies it cannily, preserving the fiction that one can recall and, from a distance, whole conversations and surrounding trivia—as if she were a reel of recording tape, consuming for later regurgitation a problematic life. Further, she is schooled in situation ethics, licensing them retroactively to cover her having been a prostitute, making it seem almost enviable that she pulled it off so well.

It can also be said that Miss Angelou possesses an ear for folkways; they spawn abundantly in the warm stream of narration, adding enough mother wit and humor to give the events a "rightness." To some extent she is coy, never allowing us a really good, voyeur's glimpse into the conjugal bed that several male characters enjoy with her; rather, she teases. And though the author is never mawkishly sentimental, she shows herself to have been, like most of us, silly, only more so than many of us will admit. Yet she is proud. She stumbles, falls, but like the phoenix, rises renewed and wholly myth.

Frank Lamont Phillips, [Review of *Gather Together in My Name*], *Black World* 24, No. 9 (July 1975): 52, 61

ALLEN PACE NILSEN   Last fall, Maya Angelou came out with a highly acclaimed third part of her autobiography. Entitled *Singin' and Swingin' and Gettin' Merry Like Christmas*, it does not need to be read as a continuation of the other two volumes, *I Know Why the Caged Bird Sings* and *Gather Together in My Name*, although people who have read those books will be especially interested in the new one.

Besides the always present Angelou zest and style, a value of the book is that it covers the period of her life when she made the transition from being part-time clerk in a record store to being "somebody." The part of the book that fascinated me the most was the recounting of her tour as a featured dancer in *Porgy and Bess* when it played in Italy, France, Greece, Yugoslavia, and Egypt. Because of the cast of characters, Angelou's keen sense of observation, and her lively writing, this is no ordinary travelogue. For readers who have a harder time getting into poetry than into prose, this book might make an exciting introduction to Angelou's poetry.

Allen Pace Nilsen, "A Roundup of Good Books," *English Journal* 66, No. 6 (September 1977): 87–88

SONDRA O'NEALE   Unlike her poetry, which is a continuation of traditional oral expression in Afro-American literature, Angelou's prose follows classic technique in nonpoetic Western forms. The material in each book while chronologically marking her life is nonetheless arranged in loosely structured plot sequences which are skillfully controlled. In *Caged Bird* the tenuous psyche of a gangly, sensitive, withdrawn child is traumatically jarred by rape, a treacherous act from which neither the reader nor the protagonist has recovered by the book's end. All else is cathartic: her uncles' justified revenge upon the rapist, her years of readjustment in a closed world of speechlessness despite the warm nurturing of her grandmother, her grand-uncle, her beloved brother Bailey, and the Stamps community; a second reunion with her vivacious mother; even her absurdly unlucky pregnancy at the end does not assuage the reader's anticipatory wonder: isn't the act of rape by a trusted adult so assaultive upon an eight-year-old's life that it leaves a wound which can never be healed? Such reader interest in a character's future is the craft from which quality fiction is made. Few autobiographers however have the verve to seize the drama of such a moment, using one specific incident to control the book but with an underlining implication that the incident will not control a life.

The denouement in *Gather Together in My Name* is again sexual: the older, crafty, experienced man lasciviously preying upon the young, vulnerable, and, for all her exposure by that time, naïve woman. While foreshadowing apprehension guided the reader to the central action in the first work, Maya presses the evolvement in *Gather Together* through a limited first-person narrator who seems to know less of the villain's intention than is obvious to the reader. Thrice removed from the action, the reader sees that L. D. Tolbrook is nothing but a slick pimp, that his seductive sexual refusals can only lead to a calamitous end; that his please-turn-these-few-tricks-for-me-baby-so-I-can-get-out-of-an-urgent-jam line is an ancient inducement for susceptible females, but Maya the actor in the tragedy cannot. She is too much in love. Maya, the author, through whose eyes we see a younger, foolish "self," so painstakingly details the girl's descent into the brothel that Black women, all women, have enough vicarious example to avoid the trap. Again, through using the "self" as role model, not only is Maya able to instruct and inspire the reader but the sacrifice of personal disclosure authenticates the autobiography's integral depth.

Sondra O'Neale, "Reconstruction of the Complete Self: New Images of Black Women in Maya Angelou's Continuing Autobiography," *Black Women Writers (1950–1980): A Critical Evaluation*, ed. Mari Evans (New York: Anchor Books/Doubleday, 1984), pp. 32–33

CHRISTINE FROULA   Mr. Freeman's abuse of Maya ⟨in *I Know Why the Caged Bird Sings*⟩ occurs in two episodes. In the first, her mother rescues her from a nightmare by taking her into her own bed, and Maya then awakes to find her mother gone to work and Mr. Freeman grasping her tightly. The child feels, first, bewilderment and terror: "His right hand was moving so fast and his heart was beating so hard that I was afraid that he would die." When Mr. Freeman subsides, however, so does Maya's fright: "Finally he was quiet, and then came the nice part. He held me so softly that I wished he wouldn't ever let me go. . . . This was probably my real father and we had found each other at last." After the abuse comes the silencing: Mr. Freeman enlists the child's complicity by an act of metaphysical violence, informing her that he will kill her beloved brother Bailey if she tells anyone what "they" have done. For the child, this prohibition prevents not so much telling as asking, for, confused as she is by her conflicting feelings, she has no idea what has happened. One day, however, Mr. Freeman stops her as she is setting out for the library, and it is then that he commits the actual rape on the terrified child, "a breaking and entering when even the senses are torn apart." Again threatened with violence if she tells, Maya retreats to her bed in a silent delirium, but the story emerges when her mother discovers her stained drawers, and Mr. Freeman is duly arrested and brought to trial. ⟨. . .⟩

Maya breaks her silence when a woman befriends her by taking her home and reading aloud to her, then sending her off with a book of poems, one of which she is to recite on her next visit. We are not told which poem it was, but later we find that the pinnacle of her literary achievement at age twelve was to have learned by heart the whole of Shakespeare's *Rape of Lucrece*—nearly two thousand lines. Maya, it appears, emerges from her literal silence into a literary one. Fitting her voice to Shakespeare's words, she writes safe limits around the exclamations of her wounded tongue and in this way is able to reenter the cultural text that her words had formerly disrupted. But if Shakespeare's poem redeems Maya from her hysterical silence, it is also a lover that she embraces at her peril. In Angelou's text, Shakespeare's Lucrece represents that violation of the spirit which Shakespeare's and all stories of sleeping beauties commit upon the female reader. Maya's feat of memory signals a double seduction: by the white culture that her grandmother wished her black child not to love and by the male culture which imposes upon the rape victim, epitomized in Lucrece, the double silence of a beauty that serves male fantasy and a death that serves male honor. The black child's identification with an exquisite rape fantasy of white male culture violates her reality. Wouldn't everyone be surprised, she muses, "when one day I woke out of my black ugly dream, and my real hair, which was long and blond, would take the place of the kinky mass that Momma wouldn't let me straighten? My light-blue eyes were going to hypnotize them. . . . Because I was really white and because a cruel fairy stepmother, who was understandably jealous of my beauty, had turned me into a too-big Negro girl, with nappy black hair, broad feet, and a space between her teeth that would hold a number two pencil." Maya's fantasy bespeaks her cultural seduction, but Angelou's powerful memoir, recovering the history that frames it, rescues the child's voice from this seduction by telling the prohibited story.

Christine Froula, "The Daughter's Seduction: Sexual Violence and Literary History," *Signs* 11, No. 4 (Summer 1986): 634–37

MARY JANE LUPTON   *All God's Children Need Traveling Shoes* opens by going back in time to Angelou the mother, who anxiously waits at the hospital following Guy's car accident. In an image that parodies the well-fed mother of *The Heart of a Woman*, Angelou compares her anxiety over Guy to being eaten up:

> July and August of 1962 stretched out like fat men yawning after a sumptuous dinner. They had every right to gloat, for they had eaten me up. Gobbled me down. Consumed my spirit, not in a wild rush, but slowly, with the obscene patience of certain victors. I became a shadow walking in the white hot streets, and a dark spectre in the hospital.

The months of helplessly waiting for Guy to heal are like fat, stuffed men, a description that evokes memories of Reverend Thomas, who ate Momma Henderson's chicken, and of Mr. Freeman, who ate in Vivian Baxter's kitchen and raped her daughter. Guy's accident has an effect similar to the rape; Angelou retreats into silence. She is a "shadow," a "dark spectre," a Black mother silenced by the fear of her son's possible death.

Guy does recover. Their relationship, which like the autobiographical form itself is constantly in flux, moves once again from dependence to independence, climaxing in a scene in which Angelou learns that her son is having an affair with an American woman a year older than herself. Angelou at first threatens to strike him, but Guy merely pats her head and says: "Yes, little mother. I'm sure you will." Shortly afterwards Angelou travels to Germany to perform in Genet's *The Blacks*. Guy meets her return flight and takes her home to a dinner of fried chicken he has cooked for her. Then, asserting his independence, he announces that he has "plans for dinner."

Reading between the texts, we see Angelou alone again before a plate of chicken, as she was at the conclusion of *The Heart of a Woman*. In the *Traveling Shoes* episode, however, the conflicting feelings of love and resentment are more directly stated:

> He's gone. My lovely little boy is gone and will never return.
> That big confident strange man has done away with my little boy,
> and he has the gall to say he loves me. How can he love me? He
> doesn't know me, and I sure as hell don't know him.

In this passage Angelou authentically faces and records the confusions of seeing one's child achieve selfhood, universalizing the pain a mother experiences when her "boy" is transformed into a "big confident strange man" who refuses to be his mother's "beautiful appendage."

Mary Jane Lupton, "Singing the Black Mother: Maya Angelou and Autobiographical Continuity," *Black American Literature Forum* 24, No. 2 (Summer 1990): 272–73

DOLLY A. McPHERSON   Through the genre of autobiography, Angelou has celebrated the richness and vitality of Southern Black life and the sense of community that persists in the face of poverty and racial prejudice, initially revealing this celebration through a portrait of life as experienced by a Black child in the Arkansas of the 1930s (*I Know Why the Caged Bird Sings*, 1970). The second delineates a young woman struggling to create an existence that provides security and love in post–World War II America (*Gather Together in My Name*, 1974). The third presents a young, married adult in the 1950s seeking a career in show business and experiencing her first amiable contacts with Whites (*Singin' and Swingin' and Gettin' Merry Like Christmas*, 1976). The fourth volume (*The Heart of a Woman*, 1981) shows a wiser, more mature woman in the 1960s, examining the roles of being a woman and a mother. In her most recent volume, Angelou demonstrates that *All God's Children Need Traveling Shoes* (1986) to take them beyond familiar borders and to enable them to see and understand the world from another's vantage point.

While the burden of this serial autobiography is essentially a recapturing of her own subjective experiences, Angelou's effort throughout her work is to describe the influences—personal as well as cultural, historical and social—that have shaped her life. Dominant in Angelou's autobiography is the exploration of the self—the self in relationship with intimate others: the family, the community, the world. Angelou does not recount these experiences simply because they occurred, but because they represent stages of her spiritual growth and awareness—what one writer calls "stages of self." ⟨. . .⟩

A study of Maya Angelou's autobiography is significant not only because the autobiography offers insights into personal and group experience in America, but because it creates a unique place within Black autobiographical tradition, not because it is better than its formidable autobiographical predecessors, but because Angelou, throughout her autobiographical writing, adopts a special stance in relation to the self, the community and the world. Angelou's concerns with family and community, as well as with work and her conceptions of herself as a human being, are echoed throughout her autobiography. The ways in which she faces these concerns offer instruction into the range of survival strategies available to women in America and reveal, as well, important insights into Black traditions and culture.

Dolly A. McPherson, *Order out of Chaos: The Autobiographical Works of Maya Angelou* (New York: Peter Lang, 1990), pp. 5–6

CAROL E. NEUBAUER   From time to time, Angelou sees marriage as the answer to her own sense of dislocation and fully envisions a perfect future with various prospective husbands. While in New York, she meets Vusumzi Make, a black South African freedom fighter, and imagines that he will provide her with the same domestic security she had hoped would develop from other relationships: "I was getting a husband, and a part of that gift was having someone to share responsibility and guilt." Yet her hopes are even more idealistic than usual, inasmuch as she imagines herself participating in the liberation of South Africa as Vus Make's wife: "With my courage added to his own, he would succeed in bringing the ignominious white rule in South Africa to an end. If I didn't already have the qualities he needed, then I would develop them. Infatuation made me believe in my ability to create myself into my lover's desire." In reality, Angelou is only willing to go so far in re-creating herself to meet her husband's desires and is all too soon frustrated with her role as Make's wife. He does not want her to work but is unable on his own to support his expensive tastes as well as his family. They are evicted from their New York apartment just before they leave for Egypt and soon face similar problems in Cairo. Their marriage dissolves after some months, despite Angelou's efforts to contribute to their financial assets by working as editor of the *Arab Observer*. In *Heart of a Woman*, she underscores the illusory nature of her fantasy about marriage to show how her perspective has shifted over the years and how much understanding she has gained about life in general. Re-creating these fantasies in her autobiography is a subtle form of truth telling and a way to present hard-earned insights about her life to her readers.

Carol E. Neubauer, "Maya Angelou: Self and a Song of Freedom in the Southern Tradition," *Southern Women Writers: The New Generation*, ed. Tonette Bond Inge (Tuscaloosa: University of Alabama Press, 1990), pp. 127–28

ROBERT FULGHUM   After five volumes of autobiography and five volumes of poetry, Maya Angelou offers us this very small volume of 24 poetically entitled essays so carefully crafted they cover only 54 actual pages of writing. Her publisher, Random House, has assigned the book to the publishing category "Inspiration/Self-Help." But *Wouldn't Take Nothing for My Journey Now* really belongs in an even more prestigious location in a bookstore, labeled "Wisdom Literature." ⟨. . .⟩

Angelou has dedicated this book to Oprah Winfrey. Not a casual gesture, it is a salute to the speaker at the head table of the banquet of sisterhood.

Maya Angelou has, of course, become one of these wise women herself, as her new book so clearly demonstrates. At the end of the first essay, she writes: "Women should be tough, tender, laugh as much as possible, and live long lives. The struggle for equality continues unabated, and the woman warrior who is armed with wit and courage will be among the first to celebrate victory." As of this past January, millions of Americans realize how certainly this celebration is underway. ⟨. . .⟩

To read these essays carefully, slowly, even one a day over a month, is to feel you are there with Maya Angelou on her day away, leaning back in the shade of an old tree on a hot afternoon; after an arduous journey you have come home. The companion who has waited for you is older than you are. She knows where you've been. Like the prodigal son, she too has wandered in foreign lands and returned again and again to the place where she began. She has known pain and sorrow, sinfulness and saintliness. Yet she can sing and dance, recite poems, speak with words of silence and make you laugh or cry. There is no finer company than hers. She has something to tell you now. Listen. She is wise.

Robert Fulghum, "Home Truths and Homilies," *Washington Post Book World*, 19 September 1993, p. 4

Bibliography

I Know Why the Caged Bird Sings. 1969.
Just Give Me a Cool Drink of Water 'Fore I Diiie: The Poetry of Maya Angelou.
        1971, 1988 (with *Oh Pray My Wings Are Gonna Fit Me Well*).
Gather Together in My Name. 1974, 1985.
Oh Pray My Wings Are Gonna Fit Me Well. 1975.
Singin' and Swingin' and Gettin' Merry Like Christmas. 1976.
And Still I Rise. 1978.
Weekend Glory. 198-.
The Heart of a Woman. 1981.
Poems. 1981, 1986.
Shaker, Why Don't You Sing? 1983.
All God's Children Need Traveling Shoes. 1986.
Now Sheba Sings the Songs. 1986.
Conversations with Maya Angelou. Ed. Jeffrey M. Elliot. 1989.
I Shall Not Be Moved. 1990.
Maya Angelou Omnibus. 1991.
On the Pulse of Morning. 1993.
Soul Looks Back in Wonder. 1993.
Lessons in Living. 1993.
Life Doesn't Frighten Me. 1993.
Wouldn't Take Nothing for My Journey Now. 1993.
I Love the Look of Words. 1993.
And My Best Friend Is Chicken. 1994.

Toni Cade Bambara
b. 1939

TONI CADE BAMBARA was born Toni Cade on March 25, 1939, in New York City. She and her brother Walter were raised by their mother, Helen Brent Henderson Cade; her father seems to have abandoned the family shortly after her birth. Bambara attended various schools in New York and New Jersey before attending Queens College, receiving a B.A. in theatre arts and English in 1959. In that same year she won the John Golden Award for fiction from Queens College and the Pauper Press Award for nonfiction from the *Long Island Star*; she also published a short story, "Sweet Town," in *Vendome* magazine.

After graduation Bambara studied briefly at the University of Florence and the Ecole de Mime Etienne Decroux in Paris before enrolling in an American fiction program at the City College of New York, from which she received a M.A. in 1964. Both in and out of school Bambara held a wide array of positions with various organizations, such as the Colony House in Brooklyn, the Metropolitan Hospital, the Equivalency Program, the Veteran Reentry Program, the 8th Street Play Program, and the Tutorial Program at the Houston Street Public Library. These positions reflected her desire to improve social and educational conditions for the black community. In later years she has been an instructor or artist in residence at various universities, including Rutgers, Stephens College, and Spelman College.

During the 1960s Bambara continued to write short stories, which appeared in such publications as the *Massachusetts Review*, *Prairie Schooner*, and *Redbook*. She also pursued an interest in dance, studying at various schools (including the Katherine Dunham Dance Studio) throughout the decade.

In 1970 Bambara edited an anthology of black American writing entitled *The Black Woman*. This volume, which contained writings by Nikki Giovanni, Alice Walker, Paule Marshall, and others, was an outgrowth of her work with the SEEK program at the City College of New York. A second anthology followed in 1971, *Tales and Stories for Black Folks*. This anthology,

16

like its predecessor, cut across lines of age and class and showed Bambara's increasing interest in personal and communal history. From an early age she was fascinated with her own family history, and in 1970 she adopted the family name Bambara when she found it scrawled on a sketchbook belonging to her great-grandmother.

In 1972 Bambara's first collection of short stories, *Gorilla, My Love*, appeared. This volume gathered most of her stories published between 1959 and 1970. The settings and characters were greatly influenced by her childhood wanderings, and a major concern of the collection is the role of black women in the family and the community. Reviewers received the collection with enthusiasm.

In 1973 Bambara went to Cuba, where she studied living and working conditions of Cuban women. She was much impressed by the power Cuban women had claimed through organization and solidarity. Bambara next visited Vietnam and finally landed in Atlanta, where she settled with her daughter Karma. Once again she became active in local affairs, as a founding member of the Southern Collective of African-American Writers and the Neighborhood Cultural Arts Center.

The Sea Birds Are Still Alive (1977), Bambara's second collection of stories, is marked by her interest in community affairs. The settings also move at times to the rural South and also overseas. Bambara was somewhat disappointed with the collection, and she promptly began work on a novel; *The Salt Eaters* appeared in 1980. Set in Georgia, the novel examines the workings of the black community and its relationship to other minority groups.

Most recently, Bambara has written for film and television, writing a number of screenplays for documentaries on black issues as well as a film adaptation of Toni Morrison's novel *Tar Baby* (1984). Three of her own short stories have been adapted as films.

Critical Extracts

JUNE JORDAN   In *Gorilla, My Love*, Toni Cade Bambara sure have made it wonderfully clear where her affections truthsay/lie and signify, and how she have the altogether craft, the, well, the mastery, in fact, to snatch us happy and believing right into the heart of things: Black heart of Black things ordinary, strange, amazing, crazy, typical, peculiar, everyday on streets on city roof or countrified in fields and flower gardens by the wood porch of her dynamic, Granddaddy Cain. ⟨. . .⟩

For me, *Gorilla, My Love* standing up right next to Richard Wright's *Uncle Tom's Children*. No lie; except my copy moving around so much so fast among my friends who pass it on that, see, it be hard to hold things up and draw what you might call comparisons.

But let me try one minute; do you/can you remember how *Uncle Tom's Children* made you know and grieve and understand a new way? (Blew my mind, entirely.) Well, here is *Gorilla, My Love*, ranging through the tall tale, kitchen skinny, photographic/phonographic real, and also through the mythopoeic, dreamer, facts-be-facts, material of our experience and it is beautiful, this ranging, this embrace by Sister Toni Cade Bambara: she is teaching beautiful plus make you laugh out loud. Or hurt. As hard as hurt can be to handle when that's what it's about ⟨. . .⟩

⟨. . .⟩ And when she does that special thing she does, that thing of speaking as a Black child probably talk and think and turn and jump, distinct from grown-up people, then I can't think of no one near to how she does that; she be doing it so persuasive you rejuvenated down to nine-years-old and digging it, the world, from there. But check it out; go get *Gorilla, My Love*: it's some natural sugar, overdue.

June Jordan, [Review of Gorilla, My Love], Black World 22, No. 9 (July 1973): 80

JOHN WIDEMAN   The novel's ⟨*The Salt Eaters*⟩ strengths are related to its weaknesses. Velma's trouble is obviously more than an individual neurosis, but how well do we get to know *her*, her plight, its resolution? Luminous moments imprint Velma's reality on the reader's consciousness, but do the scattered moments ultimately fuse, coalesce, so that we know and care who Velma is? Yes, we're all on this contaminated, exploited earth together and will have to learn to eat a lot of salt together before things get better, if they ever do, but does this truth justify the novelist's tendency to include all the woes besetting us? Digressions may be a way to achieve a panoramic, comprehensive overview, but they stretch the fabric of the narrative dangerously thin. The baroque convolutions of individual sentences, the proliferations of character and incident sometimes seem forced, detracting from the forward flow of the book.

Yet this demanding, haunting, funny, scary novel is persuasive. The words that open the book, the words Minnie Ransom addresses to Velma Henry as the two women perch on stools in the Southwestern Community Infirmary— "Are you sure, sweetheart, that you want to be well?"—ask a question of all of us. Getting well entails risk, honesty, a commitment to struggle, a collective effort that Toni Cade Bambara documents with the voices and lives of the Southwest Community's people. She makes us understand that what is at stake in Velma Henry's journey back to health is not only one woman's life but the survival of the planet: "tap the brain for any knowledge of initiation rites lying dormant there, recognizing that life depended on it, that initiation was the beginning of transformation and that the ecology of the self, the tribe, the species, the earth depended on just that."

John Wideman, "The Healing of Velma Henry," *New York Times Book Review*, 1 June 1980, p. 28

TONI MORRISON   Toni Cade Bambara has written two collections of short stories and one novel. She is a New Yorker, born and educated in that city with an intimate and fearless knowledge of it, and although the tone of most of her stories is celebratory, full of bravura, joyfully survivalist, the principal fear and grief of her characters is the betrayal of an adult who has abandoned not the role of providing for, but the role of advisor, competent protector. Of the sixteen stories in *Gorilla, My Love*, only two stories cannot fit that description. And one of the two, "The Survivor," describes a girl going to the country for help, succor, and regeneration at the hands of an elderly aunt who lives up to the demands of an ancestor exactly. ⟨. . .⟩

In "The Survivor," a rural story, Jewel, pregnant and reeling from an unfortunate marriage, has traveled from New York to her grandmother in a small town. When they first meet they stand in a field: "Miss Candy dainty but sinewy and solid, never hid from weather of any kind." And when she stoops to touch some roots, remarking on the need for rain, she "traced the travels of the tree roots barely bulging beneath the bristly grass. 'A good woman does not rot,' she said on her haunches like some ancient sage.'" Jewel has gone there because

> family ties [are] no longer knitted close and there was no one to
> say let's get our wagons in a circle when someone was in a crisis.

So she'd come to M'Dear, Miss Candy, the last of that generation
who believed in sustaining.

In her novel, *The Salt Eaters*, the theme is totally explicated. A would-
be suicide is literally and metaphorically healed by the ancestor: the witch
woman, the spiritual sage, the one who asks of this oh so contemporary
and oh so urban daughter of the sixties, "Are you sure you want to be well?"
Here is the village, its values, its resources, its determination not to live,
as Stevie Wonder has put it, "just enough for the city," and its requisites
for survival only. The village is determined to flourish as well, and it is that
factor that makes it possible for Velma to rise from the ancestor's shawl
and drop it to the floor "like a cocoon."

> Toni Morrison, "City Limits, Village Values: Concepts of the Neighborhood in Black
> Fiction," *Literature and the Urban Experience: Essays on the City and Literature*, ed.
> Michael C. Jaye and Ann Chalmers Watts (New Brunswick, NJ: Rutgers University
> Press, 1981), pp. 40–41

CLAUDIA TATE   C.T.: What determines your responsibility to
yourself and to your audience?

BAMBARA: I start with the recognition that we are at war, and that
war is not simply a hot debate between the capitalist camp and the socialist
camp over which economic/political/social arrangement will have hegemony
in the world. It's not just the battle over turf and who has the right to
utilize resources for whomsoever's benefit. The war is also being fought over
the truth: what is the truth about human nature, about the human potential?
My responsibility to myself, my neighbors, my family and the human family
is to try to tell the truth. That ain't easy. There are so few truth-speaking
traditions in this society in which the myth of "Western civilization" has
claimed the allegiance of so many. We have rarely been encouraged and
equipped to appreciate the fact that the truth works, that it releases the
Spirit and that it is a joyous thing. We live in a part of the world, for
example, that equates criticism with assault, that equates social responsibility
with naive idealism, that defines the unrelenting pursuit of knowledge and
wisdom as fanaticism.

I do not think that literature is *the* primary instrument for social transformation, but I do think it has potency. So I work to tell the truth about
people's lives; I work to celebrate struggle, to applaud the tradition of struggle

in our community, to bring to center stage all those characters, just ordinary folks on the block, who've been waiting in the wings, characters we thought we had to ignore because they weren't pimp-flashy or hustler-slick or because they didn't fit easily into previously acceptable modes or stock types. I want to lift up some usable truths—like the fact that the simple act of cornrowing one's hair is radical in a society that defines beauty as blonde tresses blowing in the wind; that staying centered in the best of one's own cultural tradition is hip, is sane, is perfectly fine despite all claims to universality-through-Anglo-Saxonizing and other madnesses.

It would be dishonest, though, to end my comments there. First and foremost I write for myself. Writing has been for a long time my major tool for self-instruction and self-development. I try to stay honest through pencil and paper. I run off at the mouth a lot. I've a penchant for flamboyant performance. I exaggerate to the point of hysteria. I cannot always be trusted with my mouth open. But when I sit down with the notebooks, I am absolutely serious about what I see, sense, know. I write for the same reason I keep track of my dreams, for the same reason I meditate and practice being still—to stay in touch with me and not let too much slip by me. We're about building a nation; the inner nation needs some building, too. I would be writing whether there were a publishing industry or not, whether there were presses or not, whether there were markets or not.

Claudia Tate, "Toni Cade Bambara," *Black Women Writers at Work* (New York: Continuum, 1983), pp. 17–18

RUTH ELIZABETH BURKS ⟨. . .⟩ while Bambara uses language to capture the speech patterns of the characters she idiomatically places in their time and space, Bambara eschews language, words, rhetoric, as the modus operandi for the people to attain their freedom. For Bambara, an innate spirituality, almost mystical in nature, must be endemic to the people if they are to have success. Her works juxtapose the inadequacy of language and the powers of the spirit, which needs no words to spread its light among the masses.

Words are only barriers to communication, here, in Bambara's first collection of short stories, *Gorilla, My Love*; a smile, a howl, a touch, a look, a hum, are the instruments with which her characters play in an attempt to communicate their joy, frustration, pain, confusion, and alienation.

These stories are all female ones, almost sung by Bambara in a first-person narrative voice reminiscent of the Negro spirituals with their strongly marked rhythms and highly graphic descriptions. Standard English is not so much put aside as displaced by constant repetition, a repetition bringing to mind the speech habits of a child who in just learning language constantly repeats himself, not fully convinced that language alone can communicate those needs and feelings so recently and so effectively expressed in tears and smiles.

And the childlike voices seem right here, and belong here, for each story is a vernal one—even those told by women who have long ceased to be girls—because each story is of initiation, of baptism, where the narrator is schooled in the ways of a world often cruel, more often disinterested, and rarely fair. ⟨. . .⟩

The paradoxical nature of Bambara's fictions manifests itself again when one realizes that, although each of these stories is narrated by a female, the pivotal character is male. Even in "The Lesson," where an individual male's action does not provoke the narration of the tale, "the man" as entity strikes the discordant note in the soul of a young Black girl, when a community worker forces her to visit F. A. O. Schwarz and to see with her own eyes what words cannot communicate—the needless oppression of her people by the white man.

Ruth Elizabeth Burks, "From Baptism to Resurrection: Toni Cade Bambara and the Incongruity of Language," *Black Women Writers (1950–1980): A Critical Evaluation*, ed. Mari Evans (New York: Anchor Books/Doubleday, 1984), pp. 49–51

KEITH E. BYERMAN   Toni Cade Bambara's stories focus on the ways gender roles, ideology, family, and community condition the experiences of black women. She portrays initiation as a painful but frequently rewarding ritual. Like ⟨James Alan⟩ McPherson, she seeks to take her characters from a state of certainty to a state of doubt, but unlike him, she does not so clearly define the conventions of that certainty. She implies that the realm of woman is more organic and less overtly confrontational than that of man. Nonetheless, a dialectic is clearly at work, one that is in some ways more complex since it adds to generational, racial, and cultural oppositions the polarity of male-female. While Bambara says that she is "much more concerned with the caring that lies beneath the antagonisms between black men and black women," she does repeatedly examine the nature of those antagonisms. Moreover, like ⟨Ernest J.⟩ Gaines and McPherson, she finds in folk material the means for her characters to resist fixed, dehumanizing identities, whether sexual, racial, or cultural. And also like these male writers, she tends to leave her characters at the edge of some new experience rather than with a sense of the completion of action and thus the resolution of oppositions.

"My Man Bovanne," the initial story in *Gorilla, My Love* (1972), links sexual and ideological conflicts. It tells the story of Hazel, a middle-aged black woman whose behavior scandalizes her ideologically correct children:

> "And you going to be standing there with your boobs out and that wig on your head and that hem up to your ass. And people'll say, 'Ain't that the horny bitch that was grindin with the blind dude?'
>
> "And then there's the drinkin. Mama, you know you can't drink cause next thing you know you be laughin loud and carryin on," and he grab another finger for the loudness. "And then there's the dancin. You been tattooed on the man for four records straight and slow draggin even on the fast numbers. How you think that look for a woman your age?"

The children, in their ideological purity, seek to eliminate the individuality and freedom of the mother. They implicitly fix the definitions of *mother* and *black* so as to satisfy the necessities of their political efforts. They justify those efforts in the name of "the people," and thus public recognition of the "grass roots," as Hazel calls herself, is mandatory. But the reality of those grass roots must be suppressed if the ideological system is to function efficiently. They rationalize such suppression as necessary to the struggle against the oppressor, the white social structure. Paradoxically, the children must control the mother because they see her as fitting the white society's stereotype of the licentious, irresponsible black woman. In the place of that image they would impose the image of the serious, puritanical mother. As Hazel understands, either imposition is a form of repression: "Felt just like the police got hold to me."

Keith E. Byerman, "Women's Blues: The Fiction of Toni Cade Bambara and Alice Walker," *Fingering the Jagged Grain: Tradition and Form in Recent Black Fiction* (Athens: University of Georgia Press, 1985), pp. 105–6

GLORIA T. HULL   ⟨In *The Salt Eaters*⟩ Bambara struggles with the
problem of finding words and ways to communicate these forms of knowledge
for which we, as yet, have no adequate vocabulary. Readers most versed in
these spiritual arts (and in this new age, that number is growing) understand
the work most deeply. The fact that The Master's Mind wears yellow and
white works on a generally symbolic level, but resonates on other frequencies
if one considers that yellow is the hue of intellect and a saint's nimbus and
that white is the harmonious blending of all colors. The basic meaning of
the number twelve will be easily grasped; but everyone will not know to
reduce the year 1871 (when the Infirmary was built) and the 107 years it
has been standing to their root "8," which signifies worldly involvement
and regeneration. Then, there is Cleotus Brown, "The Hermit." Porter is
planning to study with him when he is killed; Doc Serge directs Butch to
him for answers to his impertinent questions; he himself appears incognito/
in disguise to Jan (with Ruby), eerily reminding her of something she should/
does know but cannot quite remember. He is the arcane figure from the
Tarot (which Jan reads), who symbolizes the right, initiatory path to real
knowledge and truth. These three slight examples suggest how the entire
novel can be annotated in this manner. Integrally related here, too, are the
recurring symbols of mud, blood, salt, circles, mirrors, sight, water (rain),
fire, snakes, and serpents.

Devising a vocabulary and symbology for communicating spiritual matters
is only one aspect of Bambara's general quest for an adequate language and
structure. She says: "I'm just trying to tell the truth and I think in order
to do that we will have to invent, in addition to new forms, new modes
and new idioms." The process is an arduous one, beginning with the word,
the first unit of meaning:

> I'm trying to break words and get at the bones, deal with symbols
> as though they were atoms. I'm trying to find out not only how a
> word gains its meaning, but how a word gains its power.

It is further manifested in the overall composition of the book, Bambara's
"avoidance of a linear thing in favor of a kind of jazz suite." Predictably,
this approach results in a novel of extraordinary brilliance and density that
swirls the reader through multiple layers of sound and sense.

The literal plot, which takes place in less than two hours, is almost
negligible. However, while Velma and Minnie rock on their stools, other
characters are proceeding with their lives. We follow first one and then

another of them through the twelve chapters of the book. The effect is to recreate the discretely random, yet touching, simultaneity of everyday existence. A unifying focus—something shared in common by everyone—is the annual spring festival of celebration and rebirth. This basic structure, though, is complicated further by the near-seamless weaving in of flashbacks, flashwords, dreams, and visions.

> Gloria T. Hull, " 'What It Is I Think She's Doing Anyhow': A Reading of Toni Cade Bambara's *The Salt Eaters*," *Conjuring: Black Women, Fiction, and Literary Tradition*, ed. Marjorie Pryse and Hortense J. Spillers (Bloomington: Indiana University Press, 1985), pp. 220–21

ELLIOTT BUTLER-EVANS   The nationalist-feminist ideology in *Seabirds* is not solely generated by depictions of characters. It is reinforced by narrative texture and form. As a body of race- and gender-specific narratives, these stories draw on various Afro-American cultural practices—the oral storytelling tradition, the use of folklore, and the reinscription of Afro-American music forms. The incorporation of these practices is evident in the narrative structure, point of view, and semiotic texture of the stories.

Bambara has spoken and written extensively on the influence of Afro-American music on her work. What is most striking about her appropriation of jazz in *Seabirds*, however, is its role in emphasizing and reinforcing the ideology of the text. Jazz performances generally begin with a statement of theme, are followed by improvisations or extreme variations, and conclude with reiteration and resolution. An analogous pattern structures each of the stories in this collection. In "The Apprentice," for example, the narrative begins with the narrator's anxiety about her mission, moves to an encounter between a young Black man and a white policeman, then moves to a senior citizen's complex, and finally to a Black restaurant. It then refocuses on the narrator's concerns and reveals her resolution to remain committed to political engagement. In "Witchbird," each fleeting reflection of Honey's extended blues solo constitutes a comment on some aspect of her life—her career, her past relationships with men, and her overall perception of herself. And in "Christmas Eve at Johnson's Drugs N Goods," Candy begins by reflecting on Christmas and a possible visit from her father, moves on to individual episodes largely focused on characterizations of the store's customers, and concludes with accepting Obatale's invitation to a Kwanza celebration.

This mode of narration serves a significant ideological function. In its highlighting and summarizing, as well as its glossing over certain episodes, the text produces its ideological content largely through clusters of events. Hence, in "Broken Field Running," the renaming process by which Black children discard their "slave names" and appropriate African names to define themselves with the context of Black culture, the police harassment symbolized by the police car cruising in the Black community, and the destructive effect of ghetto life depicted in the criminal activities of Black males form a montage, a cluster of images each one of which might be said to encode a particular aspect of ideology. ⟨. . .⟩

Narrative structure and perspective are further complemented by the semiotic texture, or strategies of sign production, that inform the ideological context of the work. Since the major thrust of the collection is the awakening of cultural nationalist and feminist consciousness, clusters of signs keep the text grounded in those ideologies. The linguistic subcode itself, a reified construction of "Black English," becomes the sign of difference from the dominant culture and unity with the alternative Black community.

Elliott Butler-Evans, *Race, Gender, and Desire: Narrative Strategies in the Fiction of Toni Cade Bambara, Toni Morrison, and Alice Walker* (Philadelphia: Temple University Press, 1989), pp. 119–21

MARTHA M. VERTREACE   Bambara's stories present a decided emphasis on the centrality of community. Many writers concentrate so specifically on character development or plot line that community seems merely a foil against which the characters react. For Bambara the community becomes essential as a locus for growth, not simply as a source of narrative tension. Thus, her characters and community do a circle dance around and within each other as learning and growth occur.

Bambara's women learn how to handle themselves within the divergent, often conflicting, strata that compose their communities. Such learning does not come easily; hard lessons result from hard knocks. Nevertheless, the women do not merely endure; they prevail, emerging from these situations more aware of their personal identities and of their potential for further self-actualization. More important, they guide others to achieve such awareness.

Bambara posits learning as purposeful, geared toward personal and societal change. Consequently, the identities into which her characters grow envision change as both necessary and possible, understanding that they themselves play a major part in bringing about that change. This idea approximates the nature of learning described in Paulo Freire's *Pedagogy of the Oppressed,* in which he decries the "banking concept," wherein education becomes "an act of depositing, in which the students are the depositories and the teacher is the depositor." Oppressive situations define the learner as profoundly ignorant, not possessing valuable insights for communal sharing.

Although many of Bambara's stories converge on the school setting as the place of learning in formal patterns, she liberates such settings to admit and encourage community involvement and ownership. Learning then influences societal liberation and self-determination. These stories describe learning as the process of problem solving, which induces a deepening sense of self, Freire's "intentionality."

> Martha M. Vertreace, "Toni Cade Bambara: The Dance of Character and Community," *American Women Writing Fiction: Memory, Identity, Family, Space,* ed. Mickey Pearlman (Lexington: University Press of Kentucky, 1989), pp. 155–56

JACQUELINE DE WEEVER   The "psychic set," the psychological territory of both protagonists and antagonists, becomes very important for understanding the metaphors used, and determines, in the majority of cases, the outcomes of the plots ⟨in black women's fiction⟩. The images that build the metaphors are culled from nature, from creatures of the earth in most cases, with creatures of the air—the bird for example— used occasionally. The capacity of metaphor to illuminate "untranslatable experiences" is startlingly borne out in the metaphors of insects and animals. ⟨. . .⟩

Toni Cade Bambara uses the spider metaphor for describing Minnie Ransom, the healer who presides over the birth of Velma's sanity at the Southwest Community Infirmary in a ritual of healing:

> Minnie Ransom, the legendary spinster of Claybourne, Georgia, spinning out a song, drawing her of all people up. . . . Velma caught, caught up, in the weave of the song Minnie was

humming, of the shawl, of the threads, of the silvery tendrils that extended from the healer's neck and hands disappeared into the sheen of the sunlight.

As the embodiment of the power that transforms Velma, Minnie is a "spinster," one who spins. Thus the first sentence of the passage establishes her function in the novel. The sustained metaphor of the spider represents Minnie's wisdom, derived from her spirit guide, an old conjure woman named Karen Wilder. Minnie is a kind of shaman, meditating between the visible and invisible forces that have created the tensions in Velma's soul. In close touch with her spirit-guide, Minnie is a medial woman; she calls forth or evokes the inner spirit. The feminist theologian Mary Daly sees the work of woman as spinster thus: "Spinsters spin and weave, mending and creating unity of consciousness. In doing so we spin through and beyond the realm of multiple split unconsciousness. In concealed workshops, Spinsters unsnarl, unknot, untie, unweave. We knit, knot, interlace, entwine, whirl, and twirl."

Minnie is such a spinster. It is her job to unravel the snakes in Velma's head, to bring her back to lucidity. Nor Hall writes that "it is the medial woman's function to be of assistance in time of difficult passage. As midwife to the psyche she is constellated in 'emergency' situations where a spirit, a song, an alternative, a new being is emerging. . . . She has not only the power to inspire but also the power to intoxicate or induce stupor and sleep." Velma sinks into a kind of sleep as her state begins to change. Minnie says:

> "You'll have to choose, sweetheart. Choose you own cure."
> "Choose?" Sleepriding and sleeptalking, not sure where she
> was, Velma felt herself sinking.

The depiction of Minnie as a spider not only delineates her function and relationship to Velma in her madness but also the possibility of Velma's cure. And where the spider hangs, the snake waits. As Velma slowly becomes aware of the Minnie the spinster, she who spins, she also sees the bandages "unraveled and curled at the foot of the stool like a sleeping snake." By linking spider and snake at the beginning of the work, Bambara establishes a therapeutic connection, maintained throughout, between Minnie and the patient who has snakes in her head. The diverse meanings elicited by the emblem of the spider and snake show the complexity of the symbol. ⟨Toni⟩ Morrison uses it to depict the differences in the essences of the two friends in the life paths they choose, while Bambara shows the interdependence of Minnie and Velma as they face each other as healer and patient. Minnie's spirit-guide says to her: "You and that gal on the stool cut from the same cloth."

Jacqueline de Weever, *Mythmaking and Metaphor in Black Women's Fiction* (New York: St. Martin's Press, 1992), pp. 62, 82–83

Bibliography

The Black Woman: An Anthology (editor). 1970.

Tales and Stories for Black Folks (editor). 1971.

Gorilla, My Love. 1972.

The Sea Birds Are Still Alive: Collected Stories. 1977.

The Salt Eaters. 1980.

Raymond's Run. 1990.

Daughters of the Dust: The Making of an African American Woman's Film (with Julie Dash and bell hooks). 1992.

⊠ ⊠ ⊠

Jessie Redmon Fauset
1882–1961

JESSIE REDMON FAUSET was born on April 26, 1882, in Fredericksville, New Jersey, the seventh child of the Reverend Redmond Fauset and Anna Seamon Fauset. Fauset's mother died when she was very young, and her father married Belle Huff shortly thereafter. Fauset graduated from the Philadelphia Girls' School in 1900 but was then denied admission to a local teacher's college; she applied to Bryn Mawr, but the school put off a decision about accepting her and urged her to accept a scholarship that she received from Cornell University. In 1905 Fauset became the first black woman to graduate from Cornell.

Wishing to become a teacher, Fauset was denied a position in the Philadelphia school system. She went to Baltimore, where she taught for a year before going to Washington, D.C., where she taught French for fourteen years at the M. Street High School (later named Dunbar High). In 1912 she began contributing articles to the *Crisis*, and in 1919 was urged by its editor, W. E. B. Du Bois, to move to New York to become the literary editor of the journal. In that same year she received a master's degree in French from the University of Pennsylvania.

All four of Fauset's novels deal with racial prejudice. In *There Is Confusion* (1924), the protagonist, Joanna Marshall, battles against discrimination against her and her lover. In *Plum Bun* (1929), a black woman attempts to "pass" as white but in doing so becomes ostracized from her darker-skinned sister. *The Chinaberry Tree* (1931) tells of a love affair between a freed slave woman and her white master. *Comedy, American Style* (1933) is a bitter novel in which the alienating effects of "passing" are again emphasized.

Fauset's later life was uneventful. In 1927 she began teaching at the De Witt Clinton High School in New York City. Having married Herbert E. Harris in 1929, she moved with him to Montclair, New Jersey, in 1939. Fauset retired from teaching in 1944, by which time she had abandoned writing and ceased to be involved in black intellectual circles. She died on May 2, 1961.

Although her novels received mixed reviews upon publication and were dismissed after her death, Fauset is now gaining praise for her "novels of manners," which attempt to depict the role of the black middle class in white society. She is also attaining recognition as an early black feminist for her sharp portrayals of black women.

Critical Extracts

MONTGOMERY GREGORY   ⟨*There Is Confusion*⟩ is a sincere effort to view the life of the race artistically—objectively. Heretofore we have either imbibed the depreciatory estimates of our enemies or gulped down the uncritical praise of our friends. We have not dared to see ourselves as we really are nor have our artists treated our life as material to be objectively moulded into creations of beauty. Our writers of the younger school have been the first to catch this sound point of view and upon their strict adherence to it in the future depends the successful development of Negro art and literature. Even Miss Fauset occasionally errs in this respect and diverts the reader's interest from her story into bypaths of special pleading against race prejudice.

Technically *There Is Confusion* more than reaches the level of the better class of contemporary American fiction. The romance of Peter Bye and Joanna Marshall, etched on the interesting background of the family life of the cultured Negroes of Philadelphia and New York, is well conceived and skillfully executed. The plot holds the interest of the reader unflaggingly to the end. There are fewer faults of construction than might be expected in a "first" novel. It may be said, however, that the latter part of the story is the least convincing. ⟨. . .⟩ The characters are cleverly drawn, especially that of Maggie Ellersley who, like Brutus, although not intended to be the leading figure in the story, certainly appeals to the reviewer as the finest achievement of the author. On the other hand, the white Byes, young Meriweather Bye and his grandfather seem to make their entrance on the stage as supernumeraries and to add little to the value of the novel.

Montgomery Gregory, "The Spirit of Phyllis Wheatley," *Opportunity* 2, No. 6 (June 1924): 181–82

GWENDOLYN BENNETT   Many there will be who will quibble over Miss Fauset's fortunate choice of incident by which all her characters and happenings are brought together ⟨in *Plum Bun*⟩. This will not be altogether fair since "Truth is stranger than Fiction." I'll wager that Miss Fauset could match every incident in her book with one from real life. I imagine this book will be even less convincing to members of the white race. They still conjecture over the possibility of a Negro's completely submerging himself in their group without a shadow of detection. But here again Miss Fauset can smile benignly up her writing sleeve and know whereof she speaks.

The author of this story does not seem concerned to a great extent with the inner workings of her characters. In this day of over-emphasis on the mental musings of people and things this may be called a fault but I feel that the author was wise in not delving into the mental recesses of people to whom so much was happening. This is a task for a master psychologist. Who can tell how the minds of white Negroes work? Is it not a problem to stump the best of us that they who are so obviously white should feel a "something" that eventually draws them from the luxury and ease of a life as a white person back to the burden of being a Negro? Miss Fauset tells her story, packed as it is with the drama and happenings of a life of passing for white. It is better for the story that Miss Fauset avoided too much of a metaphysical turn.

> Gwendolyn Bennett, [Review of *Plum Bun*], *Opportunity* 7, No. 9 (September 1929): 287

RUDOLPH FISHER   In *The Chinaberry Tree* it is the author's stated intention to "depict something of the home life of the colored American who is not being pressed too hard by the Furies of Prejudice, Ignorance and Economic Injustice." What are Negroes like, she asks, when they are not thinking of the race problem? ⟨. . .⟩

The pace of the book is leisurely, the writing simple and unaffected, the descriptions clear-cut with occasional touches of poetry, and the depictions of home life unexciting enough to be entirely credible. Characterizations are lightly drawn. The primary interest is situational. It is plain that anybody, whatever his degree of pigmentation, would have done just about what these people did in this situation. It is plain, as Miss Fauset intended it to be, that these Americans are not essentially different from other Americans.

The inclusion of the restaurant scene, in which Laurentine and Denleigh are embarrassed by a white waiter, is unfortunate, because it is so much more dramatic than most of the other episodes, yet has no place in either the story or the author's voluntary exclusion of the race problem. Otherwise the chronicle travels smoothly toward its climax.

Rudolph Fisher, "Where Negroes Are People," *New York Herald Tribune Books*, 17 January 1932, p. 6

GERALD SYKES   The greater portion of *The Chinaberry Tree* is devoted to the love affair of two colored high-school students who do not know that they are brother and sister. This dramatic theme, singularly enough, is the least exciting part of the story. We learn most about Miss Fauset's book as a whole not through Melissa and Malory, or their narrowly averted incestuous marriage; but through Laurentine, the beautiful apricot-colored dressmaker who is the book's real heroine and symbol of the world it depicts; Laurentine, who sat as a child under the Chinaberry Tree and wondered why other children, either white or black, wouldn't play with her. ⟨. . .⟩

⟨Laurentine⟩ is brought up in comparative luxury, but is a double outcast. And the passion which animates her is closely allied to the passion which animates the book. What does the illegitimate mulatto grow up to want? Respectability. Once she cries: "Oh God, you know all I want is a chance to show them how decent I am." This might serve as the motto for *The Chinaberry Tree*. It is so much the book's real theme that once recognized it helps to explain the striking gentility of certain passages, as well as the exceptional importance attached to small material comforts that most white people would take for granted. ⟨. . .⟩ The book attempts to idealize this polite colored world in terms of the white standards that it has adopted. And here lies the root of Miss Fauset's artistic errors. When she parades the possessions of her upper classes and when she puts her lovers through their Fauntleroy courtesies, she is not only stressing the white standards that they have adopted; she is definitely minimizing the colored blood in them. This is a decided weakness, for it steals truth and life from the book.

Is not the most precious part of a Negro work of art that which is specifically Negroid, which none but a Negro could contribute?

We need not look far for the reason for Miss Fauset's idealization. It is pride, the pride of a genuine aristocrat. And it is pride also that makes her such a remarkable psychologist. However many her artistic errors, Miss Fauset has a rare understanding of people and their motives. ⟨. . .⟩ Every great psychologist has been a thin-skinned aristocrat. Considering the position of a sensitive, educated Negro in America, it is no wonder then that an aristocrat like Miss Fauset has idealized her little world, has made it over-elegant! Inspired by the religious motive which so many Negro writers seem to feel, she has simply been trying to justify her world to the world at large. Her mistake has consisted in trying to do this in terms of the white standard.

Gerald Sykes, "Amber-Tinted Elegance," *Nation*, 27 July 1932, p. 88

MARY ROSS   As in her earlier stories, Miss Fauset writes ⟨in *Comedy: American Style*⟩ with dignity and force about a group of Americans whose lives are little known because they are lived quietly in their own comfortable homes and by preference within intellectual and cultivated circles of their own kind. The tragedy of the book—the title is ironic—is not primarily the limitations imposed by white people but the consequences of those restrictions and prejudices in the interrelationships of these people of mixed blood. ⟨. . .⟩

The lights and shades of the story are harsh, occasionally so violent as to lessen their effectiveness. So strong is the conflict that moves in and about these people that at times situation rather than character becomes the fulcrum of the narrative, and type rather than individuality crops up even in details. The flowers at Theresa's party were "of the aster variety." Her partner was "the type that holds his partner lightly but firmly." . . . If Miss Fauset, however, does at times insist on the situation of her characters so strongly as a little to overwhelm their personalities, that defect is one aspect of the book's virtues: its vigor, honesty and warmth.

Mary Ross, "The Tragedy of Mixed Blood," *New York Herald Tribune Books*, 10 December 1933, p. 6

WILLIAM STANLEY BRAITHWAITE   I daresay, as a novelist Miss Fauset would be credited with many a virtue by certain eminent critics, if she were but obliging enough to ignore the *conventional* ideals and triumphs of the emerged group of the Race. She has been infinitely more honest with her characters than her critics have cared to acknowledge, indeed, to have even suspected. After all, her purpose, whether conscious or unconscious, has been to create in the pages of fiction a society which outside the Race simply did not and preferably, in accordance with granted assumption, could not be allowed to exist. The spirit, the consciousness of pride, dignity, a new quality of moral idealism, was breathed into this darker body of human nature by her passionate sympathy and understanding of its ironic position in the flimsy web of American civilization. Only recently a review of Miss Fauset's latest novel, *Comedy: American Style*, in one of the leading Negro papers, resented what the reviewer charged was a lack of climax and philosophy in the recital of Olivia Cary's color obsession and the pain it brought her family. The philosophy in this latest novel, as in the three earlier ones, is not, and never was intended to be, an imposed thesis upon the surface of the story. Miss Fauset is too good an artist to argue the point; to engrave a doctrine upon so intangible an element as Truth, or to array with a misfitting apparel of rhetoric the logic which like a pagan grace or a Christian virtue should run naked as the wind through the implications that color and shape the lives of her characters and their destinies. I am afraid that Negro critical eyes as well as white critical eyes have quite often failed to discern these implications in which are contained the philosophy of a tremendous conflict; the magnificent Shakespearean conflict of *will* and *passion* in the great tragedies from *Titus Andronicus* to *Coriolanus;* for in this Negro society which Miss Fauset has created imaginatively from the realities, there is the *will*, the confused but burning *will*, to master the *passion* of the organized body of lusty American prejudice.

William Stanley Braithwaite, "The Novels of Jessie Fauset," *Opportunity* 12, No. 1 (January 1934): 26–27

ABBY ARTHUR JOHNSON   In all ⟨Fauset's⟩ stories, she portrayed black professionals, as she would in her novels. Her main characters were industrious physicians, teachers, engineers and business men and women. With the fiction published in *Crisis* and with the novels which followed, Fauset seemed preoccupied with matters far different from the concerns of her essays. She wrote of people who lived on the borderline of two races and who flirted with the idea of passing. She pictured structured and elite black communities, modeled after old Philadelphia. At times, she showed distinctions among Negro socialites living in Philadelphia, Washington and Baltimore. With such interests, she wrote to a small segment of the black population. Her essays, however, appealed to a wider audience. She discussed issues and events germane to the black community, such as Pan-Africanism. She applauded novels and poems written about ghetto life and Afro-Americans who were not formally educated. She used a rhetoric which modulated from enthusiasm to anger and which attracted the more militant young Negroes.

Robert Bone thought Fauset a "paradox" because he could not see a connecting link between her work as editor and as novelist. Fauset's work does, nevertheless, mesh into a comprehensible unit. As an educated woman, open to many interests, she could appreciate the changes and new expressions in the Negro community. She tried, while on the staff of *Crisis*, to encourage diversified interests and to attract a large number of readers. When composing fiction, however, she could only write from herself, of the life she knew best.

Abby Arthur Johnson, "Literary Midwife: Jessie Redmon Fauset and the Harlem Renaissance," *Phylon* 39, No. 2 (June 1978): 149

CAROLYN SYLVANDER   If the promotion of the Black middle class, the displaying to whites the virtues of socially and economically select Blacks, is not Fauset's central concern in *There Is Confusion*, it is necessary to look at the book carefully, without preconceptions, to discover the themes which do emerge. There *is* exploration of the kind of racial discrimination and inheritance a Northern urban Black faces. Beyond this exposure, Fauset looks at a wide range of characters and actions possible given American slave history, racially mixed heredity, and various environments. In quiet, subtle ways, she tiptoes across "acceptable" topics and conclusion to explore alternatives to her society's sometimes limiting norms. ⟨. . .⟩ Black folk material as the basis for possible uniqueness in Black artistry is a nicely underplayed but repeated idea present in Joanna's use of a Black children's dance-game as her entree into the theatrical world. The entire book explores the limited alternatives available to women, especially Black women, and also show women breaking out of these limits without being excessively punished. If it is desirable to select "a" theme in *There Is Confusion* to include all the above thematic ideas, probably the best statement of it would be: Life is a corrective, individually and collectively, experientially and historically.

⟨. . .⟩ There is no one "best" way to be Black and to be Black American ⟨in *There Is Confusion*⟩. Such moralizing is foreign to Fauset's interest in individual psychology. There are, however, often "better" ways for each character to deal with his or her life, and the book's plot becomes the story of how each major character makes the discoveries and changes which lead him or her to the best individual perspective. This plot pattern is essentially the same as that of the traditional British *Bildungsroman* where growth of character is depicted in the movement from disordered and confused value distinctions to a revelation of true differences.

Carolyn Sylvander, *Jessie Redmon Fauset, Black American Writer* (Troy, NY: Whitson, 1981), pp. 152, 155

DEBORAH E. McDOWELL   To be sure, ⟨Fauset⟩ was traditional to some extent, both in form and content, but as Gary de Cordova Wintz rightly observes, "in spite of her conservative, almost Victorian literary habits," Fauset "introduced several subjects into her novels that were hardly typical drawing room conversation topics in the mid-1920s. Promiscuity, exploitative sexual affairs, miscegenation, even incest appear in her novels. In fact prim and proper Jessie Fauset included a far greater range of sexual activity than did most of Du Bois's debauched tenth."

When attention is given Fauset's introduction of these challenging themes, it becomes possible to regard her "novels of manners" less as an indication of her literary "backwardness" and more as a self-conscious artistic stratagem pressed to the service of her central fictional preoccupations. Since many of Fauset's concerns were unpalatable to the average reader of her day and hence unmarketable in the publishing area, the convention of the novel of manners can be seen as protective mimicry, a kind of deflecting mask for her more challenging concerns. ⟨. . .⟩

In addition to the protective coloration which the conventional medium afforded, the novel of manners suited Fauset's works in that the tradition

"is primarily concerned with social conventions as they impinge upon character." Both social convention and character—particularly the black female
character—jointly form the nucleus of Fauset's literary concerns. The protagonists of all of her novels are black women, and she makes clear in each
novel that social conventions have not sided well with them but, rather,
have been antagonistic.

Without polemicizing, Fauset examines that antagonism, criticizing the
American society which has institutionalized prejudice, safeguarded it by
law and public attitude, and in general, denied the freedom of development,
the right to well-being, and the pursuit of happiness to the black woman.
In short, Fauset explores the black woman's struggle for democratic ideals
in a society whose sexist conventions assiduously work to thwart that struggle.
Critics have usually ignored this important theme which even a cursory
reading of her novels reveals. This concern with exploring female consciousness is, in a loose sense, feminist in impulse, placing Fauset squarely among
the early black feminists in Afro-American literary history. ⟨. . .⟩ A curious
problem in Fauset's treatment of feminist issues, however, is her patent
ambivalence. She is alternately forthright and cagey, alternately "radical"
and conservative on the "woman question." On the one hand, she appeals
for women's right to challenge socially sanctioned modes of feminine behavior, but on the other, she frequently retreats to the safety of traditional
attitudes about women in traditional roles. At best, then, we can grant that
Fauset was a quiet rebel, a pioneer black literary feminist, and that her
characters were harbingers of the movement for women's liberation from
the constrictions of cultural conditioning.

Deborah E. McDowell, "The Neglected Dimension of Jessie Redmon Fauset," <i>Conjur-
ing: Black Women, Fiction, and Literary Tradition</i>, ed. Marjorie Pryse and Hortense J.
Spillers (Bloomington: Indiana University Press, 1985), pp. 87–88

MARY JANE LUPTON   As a woman writer writing *as* a woman,
if not *for* women, Fauset was likely to notice the aesthetic relationship
between skin and clothing. This kind of thing is important in the daily
lives of most middle-class women and, I would guess, of many middle-class
men. By including chestnut hair and puff sleeves in her fictional world ⟨of
Comedy: American Style⟩, Fauset is only being true to the tradition of American realism. But these concerns are not merely gratuitous. ⟨. . .⟩ Fauset uses

clothing as a way to articulate not only the racial differences between mother and daughter but also the hierarchy of class/race which she then addresses throughout the novel: the desperate, white-identified mother; the middle-class daughter caught between her mother's notion of "a cruder race" and her own desire to be like her peers; the Black-identified Marise in her "glowing, gay colors"; the naturally gifted, light-skinned Phebe, who is already accumulating capital.

Fauset also captures 〈. . .〉 the excitement of adolescent anticipation, the thrill of choosing for oneself what one is to wear and not to wear. Thus Teresa is transformed, through clothing, from "mouse" to warm, young Black woman. As she puts her "nice narrow feet" into "bronze slippers," she becomes reminiscent of Cinderella on her way to the ball—in this case a neighborhood party. It is in fact Teresa's crowning moment. For later she meets a young Black man, falls in love, and is humiliated by her mother, who forces her into a disastrous marriage. The Cinderella Line has reversed itself irrevocably.

Near the end of the novel Olivia visits her daughter: "She found Teresa silent, pale, subdued, the ghost of her former self, still wearing dresses taken from the wardrobe which her mother had chosen and bought for her during her last year of college. The dresses had been turned, darned, cleaned, and made over, combined in new and bizarre fashions. Their only merit was that they were quite large enough. Certainly Teresa had put on no weight." 〈. . .〉 Teresa's "former self" has become a "ghost." She is colorless, as are the dresses of unnamed hue. Literally, Teresa has lost her color, her racial identity. As Phebe had once made Teresa the beautiful party dress, so now Teresa makes over and mends the dress of her past. This recreation of identity, however, operates within the closed system of passing or death.

In dismantling the Cinderella Line, Fauset leaves as an alternative a more feminist bourgeois hope in the person of Phebe the dressmaker. Through hard work and through affirmation of her Blackness, Phebe manages to rise from shopgirl to highly paid fashion designer. Her marriage to Teresa's brother, Christopher, is part of the bargain.

Mary Jane Lupton, "Clothes and Closure in Three Novels by Black Women," *Black American Literature Forum* 20, No. 4 (Winter 1986): 412–13

HAZEL V. CARBY   Deborah McDowell, in her introduction to the new edition of Fauset's *Plum Bun*, pleads for a sympathetic consideration

for the progressive aspects of Fauset's novels, especially in relation to her
implicit critique of the structures of women's romance. However, I would
argue that ultimately the conservatism of Fauset's ideology dominates her
texts. In *The Chinaberry Tree*, for example, which focused on two women,
the movement of the text is away from the figures of isolated unmarried
mothers and daughters supporting themselves through their own labor,
toward the articulation of a new morality and community in which black
women were lifted from the abyss of scandal and gossip, which threatened
to overwhelm them, by professional black men who reinserted them into
a newly formed and respectable community as dependent wives. The individual and collective pasts of the female characters led them to flounder in
the waters of misdirected desires; their history was anarchic and self-destructive. The future, within which the women could survive, was secured when
they were grounded, protected, and wrapped around by decent men. In
order to represent a new, emergent social group, Fauset by necessity had to
sever ties with the past; the characteristics of the new class were those of
individual success and triumph over ties to and previous interpretations of
history. ⟨. . .⟩ in *The Chinaberry Tree*, Fauset constructed a chaotic and
irrelevant history to which the heroes, not the heroines, brought a new
order and meaning. The new middle class both emerged from and changed
previous history and its interpretations; the forces of previous history alone
could not provide a basis for its future. Fauset adapted but did not transcend
the form of the romance. It is important that her work did reveal many of
the contradictory aspects of romantic conventions of womanhood, but her
imaginary resolutions to what were social contradictions confirmed that
women ultimately had to be saved from the consequences of their independence and become wives.

  Hazel V. Carby, *Reconstructing Womanhood: The Emergence of the Afro-American
  Woman Novelist* (New York: Oxford University Press, 1987), pp. 167–68

ELIZABETH AMMONS The dilemma that Fauset struggles with
in *There Is Confusion*, and then throughout her career as a novelist, is basic.
In order to survive at all in the art world, an environment both racist and
sexist, Joanna must be ruthless and utterly self-centered. In order to be part
of the black community, she must think of the group, must be willing to
put other people's needs before her own. She must be able to give and to
receive love, which involves compromise, sacrifice, and often self-denial.

This choice—between making art or being a loving, embraced member of the black community—is unbearable. It translates most directly into having her art or having a relationship with a man. ⟨. . .⟩ The latter choice, which Fauset backs, *is* conservative and *is* disappointing. But given the alternative that she says America constructs, what is the choice? Joanna can center herself in the white world—as a second-class performer, bear in mind—and remain a hard, driven, selfish person who arrogantly sets herself up above Maggie Ellersley and Peter Bye and whose plot spins off individualistically on its own self-absorbed trajectory. Or she can make a choice in favor of staying within the black community, a choice that encourages rather than discourages the giving, feeling parts of her personality and, significantly, keeps her plot line tangled with Maggie's and Peter's.

This theme of art dehumanizing the black woman artist and cutting her off from the black community, especially from sisters and mothers, is so strong and persistent in Fauset's fiction that it very likely articulates her own deepest fears as an African American woman trying both to stay connected to her heritage and community and to succeed as a publishing artist in a commercial and intellectual world dominated and controlled by whites. The protagonist or strongest central character of each of Fauset's four novels is a black woman who physically or emotionally (or both) cuts herself off from her mother—a rupture which, according to Fauset, constitutes becoming "white." ⟨. . .⟩

For Fauset ⟨. . .⟩ this issue of mother-daughter separation was virtually insoluble. The problem was largely political. As an artist, Fauset had to live in the white world, had no choice but to separate herself from her mother's life. The white world ⟨. . .⟩ was where the publishers, editors, and reviewers were. To create—to express herself as an artist—Jessie Fauset had to pass over into that territory, learn its rules, play its games, adopt its values. Her preoccupation with "passing" in her fiction, like that of other turn-of-the-century black women writers, was not simply deference to a conventional theme in African American literature. It was one way of talking about her own impossible situation as a black woman writer in a publishing world controlled by whites. As an artist, the black woman writer constantly had to "pass," to cross over into and negotiate the white world, whether she wanted to or not. She had to leave her mother. What did that mean? What would that do to her as a woman? As a human being?

Elizabeth Ammons, "Plots: Jessie Fauset and Edith Wharton," *Conflicting Stories: American Women Writers at the Turn into the Twentieth Century* (New York: Oxford University Press, 1991), pp. 151, 154

VASHTI CRUTCHER LEWIS   Fauset does not give Laurentine much racial consciousness ⟨in *The Chinaberry Tree*⟩; however, she is the vehicle through which the reader experiences culture of the Harlem Renaissance. Fauset, a 1920s resident of Harlem, allows Laurentine and the reader to become acquainted with the famed Lafayette Theatre, notable restaurants, and nightclubs of the era. Laurentine's uneasiness with an animated black folk culture in Harlem cabarets indicates Fauset's own rejection of it, as well as that of Du Bois, her mentor. Fauset provides Laurentine with thoughts that mirror some of the reasons why Du Bois was critical of Harlem Renaissance writers who depicted what he considered the exotic in African-American culture. Laurentine is puzzled over reasons why anyone would frequent clubs where a "drunken black woman . . . slapped a handsome yellow girl," and "where a dark, sinuous dancer, singing . . . making movements . . . postured . . ." ⟨. . .⟩

Fauset's portrayals of African-American women who are overly class- and color-conscious must be assessed against the stereotypical images that bordered on the caricature that white writers were using to depict men and women of African descent at the turn of the twentieth century and later. It is not difficult to understand her desire to reverse those images and to write with sympathy and understanding about an educated African-American middle/upper class to which she belonged. The real paradox of so much interest in class-conscious mulattoes is, as suggested earlier, that they depict a select group who have never been representative in number or lifestyle of African-American women. And just as important, the highly class-conscious mulatto has served to perpetuate a divisiveness within African-American culture since the genesis of a mulatto caste in the era of American slavery. Certainly the very images of black female arrogance so often depicted in Fauset's novels are ones that have caused "other Blacks to look at mulattoes as Greeks whose gifts should always bear watching."

Vashti Crutcher Lewis, "Mulatto Hegemony in the Novels of Jessie Redmon Fauset," *CLA Journal* 35, No. 4 (June 1992): 382–83, 385–86

Bibliography

There Is Confusion. 1924.
Plum Bun: A Novel without a Moral. 1929.
The Chinaberry Tree: A Novel of American Life. 1931.
Comedy: American Style. 1933.

Pauline E. Hopkins
1859–1930

PAULINE ELIZABETH HOPKINS was born in 1859 in Portland, Maine, the daughter of Northrup and Sarah Allen Hopkins. Shortly after her birth her parents moved to Boston, where she attended the public schools. At fifteen she won a writing contest sponsored by William Wells Brown and the Congregational Publishing Society on the theme of temperance.

Hopkins's first literary work was a play, *Slaves' Escape; or, The Underground Railroad*, written in 1879 and produced the next year by a touring group organized by her family, the Hopkins' Colored Troubadours, in which her mother, her stepfather, and Hopkins herself acted. The play was later published as *Peculiar Sam; or, The Underground Railroad*, although the date of publication is not known. Hopkins earned considerable renown as an actress and singer, acquiring the nickname "Boston's Favorite Soprano." She also wrote at least one further play, *One Scene from the Drama of Early Days*, but it was apparently never performed and the manuscript is now lost.

Around 1892 Hopkins enrolled in a stenography course and earned her livelihood in this profession for several years, working for four years at the Bureau of Statistics. In 1900 the founding of the *Colored American* magazine changed the course of her career and her writing. She began writing voluminously for the magazine, and by the second issue had joined its staff. Her earliest work for it was a short story, "The Mystery within Us," published in the magazine's first issue (May 1900).

Hopkins's one separately published novel, *Contending Forces: A Romance Illustrative of Negro Life North and South*, was issued in 1900 by the Colored Co-operative Publishing Company, the publisher of *Colored American*. This historical romance of a love affair between a mulatto, Will Smith, and an octoroon, Sappho Clark, is a powerful examination of the life of black women within white society, and touches upon many fundamental issues of black social life. Although it employs many of the conventions of the popular sentimental romance of the period, it probes such concerns as the sexual exploitation of black women, the searing effects of slavery, the need for strong family ties, and other matters.

The *Colored American* also serialized three novels by Hopkins: *Hagar's Daughter: A Story of Southern Caste Prejudice* (March 1901–March 1902); *Winona: A Tale of Negro Life in the South and Southwest* (May–October 1902); and *Of One Blood; or, The Hidden Self* (November 1902–November 1903). *Hagar's Daughter*, published under the pseudonym Sarah A. Allen, is the story of a woman, Hagar, who is married to a Southern white planter and discovers that she has black ancestry; the novel treats of her and her daughter's attempts to come to terms with their blackness. *Winona* deals with a woman born of a white man who becomes the chief of an Indian tribe and a fugitive slave woman. Winona goes to England with her British lover in the hope of escaping prejudice. In *Of One Blood* Reuel Briggs, about to commit suicide because he is black, is rescued by a light-skinned black singer, Dianthe Lusk; Reuel himself then resuscitates Dianthe after a train accident and marries her, but she is stolen from him by his white friend Aubrey Livingston, who rapes and kills her. In the end it is revealed that Reuel, Dianthe, and Aubrey all have a common mother and are therefore "of one blood." These three novels have been collected in *The Magazine Novels of Pauline E. Hopkins* (1988).

In addition to fiction, Hopkins wrote a considerable amount of nonfiction and journalism for the *Colored American*. A series of articles entitled "Famous Men of the Negro Race" (February 1901–September 1902) dealt with such figures as Frederick Douglass and William Wells Brown, while "Famous Women of the Negro Race" (November 1901–October 1902) discussed Sojourner Truth, Harriet Tubman, Frances E. W. Harper, and others.

By 1904 Hopkins had become too ill to work on the magazine. She continued writing, however, and published a series, "The Dark Races of the Twentieth Century," in *Voice of the Negro* (February–July 1905). She herself published a treatise, *A Primer of Facts Pertaining to the Greatness of Africa* (1905). This was, however, the last of her major writings, aside from a novelette, "Topsy Templeton," published in 1916 in *New Era*.

Hopkins resumed her stenographic work, being employed by the Massachusetts Institute of Technology. She died as a result of a freak accident on August 13, 1930. Her work suffered critical neglect until the 1970s, when *Contending Forces* was hailed as a pioneering work of black American fiction. Her short stories and journalism, however, remain uncollected.

☒ *Critical Extracts*

ANN ALLEN SHOCKLEY   By November, 1903, ⟨Hopkins⟩ had become Literary Editor of the *Colored American*. Much of her personal time and effort was now spent in promoting the magazine. For example, in January, 1904, she was one of the founders of the Colored American League in Boston (fictionalized in a chapter of her *Contending Forces* as "The American Colored League")—an organization comprised of "some twenty or more representative ladies and gentlemen of the colored citizens of Boston" ⟨*Colored American*, March 1904⟩ which helped sustain the *Colored American* during the summer months in a series of public meetings over the country to gain interest and support for the magazine.

Miss Hopkins's spirit and love for the magazine were demonstrated as well by her prolific contributions to it. Six of her short stories appeared in the publication, among these "Talma Gordon," "George Washington: A Christmas Story," and "Bro'r Abr'm Jimson's Wedding. A Christmas Story." Two short novels which dealt with interracial love were also serialized in the *Colored American*. The first one, *Winona: A Tale of Negro Life in the South and Southwest in the 1840's*, was serialized in twenty-four chapters. Winona was the daughter of a white man in Buffalo, New York, who joined an Indian tribe and became its chief. The chief married a fugitive slave girl who died while giving birth to Winona. The plot was sensational and complicated, filled with adventurous escapades, murder, and romance. In the conclusion, Winona and her white English lover go to England where the "American caste prejudice could not touch them beyond the sea." Her second short novel, *Of One Blood or The Hidden Self*, began serializing in the October, 1902 issue immediately following the conclusion of *Winona*. It was a similarly complicated tale of interracial romance, and filled with the mysticism of the mind and spirit.

The recurring theme of interracial love in Miss Hopkins's serials was noted by a white reader, Cornelia A. Condict, who wrote a letter to the editor saying: "Without exception, they have been of love between the colored and white. Does that mean that your novelists can imagine no love beautiful and sublime within the range of the colored race, for each other?" Miss Hopkins replied to this with candor while stating the basic philosophy of her fiction:

> . . . My stories are definitely planned to show the obstacles persistently placed in our paths by a dominant race to subjugate

us spiritually. Marriage is made illegal between the races and the mulattoes increase. Thus the shadow of corruption falls on the blacks and on the whites, without whose aid the mulattoes would not exist.

Ann Allen Shockley, "Pauline Elizabeth Hopkins: A Biographical Excursion into Obscurity," *Phylon* 33, No. 1 (Spring 1972): 24–25

CLAUDIA TATE   The structure of ⟨*Winona*⟩ conforms to basic conventions. But *Winona* is even more sensational than *Contending Forces* in that there are more incredible coincidences, swashbuckling adventures, and exaggerated heroic descriptions, all held together with a very sentimental love story. Winona's appearance, as we might expect, conforms to the tragic mulatto mold: "Her wide brow, about which the hair clustered in dark rings, the beautifully chiselled features, the olive complexion with a hint of pink." And her hero, Maxwell, is equally as handsome, though fair: ". . . a slender, well-knit figure with a bright, handsome face, blue eyes and a mobile mouth slightly touched with down on his upper lip." The virtuous pair are rewarded with prosperity and happiness, while the villain suffers a painful death.

Hopkins placed this novel into the genre of the fugitive slave story and identified her protest as that against the arbitrary segregation and subjection of black Americans:

> Many strange tales of romantic happenings in this mixed community of Anglo-Saxons, Indians and Negroes might be told similar to the one I am about to relate, and the world stand aghast and may try to find the dividing line supposed to be a natural barrier between the whites and the dark-skinned race.

Thus, as is the case with *Contending Forces*, the central issue of *Winona* is its protest against racial injustice, but unlike *Contending Forces*, *Winona* outlines no program of social reform other than that offered by escape. Whereas escape offered a possible resolution to the slave's dilemma prior to 1864, Hopkins's contemporary scene of 1901 afforded virtually no ostensible reason for her to write an abolitionist novel. Perhaps she wrote the novel as an exercise in nostalgia, intended to arouse sympathy for oppressed black Americans. There was, however, more than sufficient reason to condemn the practices of employment and housing discrimination, separate public accommodations, mob violence, and lynching, as she had done in *Contending Forces*. Whereas her first novel was very sensitive to the racial issues of 1900 and consequently addressed each of them, *Winona* seems to be essentially an escapist, melodramatic romance in which Hopkins used sentimental love as a means for supporting an appeal for racial justice. Though, granted, Hopkins does dramatize the fact that being black in America means being subjected to racial abuse, she offers little hope to those who cannot escape like Winona and Jude.

Women's issues, which were central to the argument of *Contending Forces*, have been abandoned entirely in *Winona*. Although marriage is depicted as woman's ambition in both *Contending Forces* and *Winona*, in the latter novel a woman's role is seen exclusively as finding a suitable husband and tending to his needs. Love is translated singularly into duty, and duty finds expression only on the domestic front. We do not see women, like Mrs. Willis of *Contending Forces*, who are their husbands' helpmates in the struggle for racial advancement. On the contrary, marriage offers women its own blissful escape in *Winona*, and marital love is portrayed as the balm which soothes their worldly wounds. When we turn our attention to the subject of the advancement of black women, we find no discussion of this topic at all. Although Hopkins was, nevertheless, a product of the nineteenth century's rising consciousness of women's concerns, it is surprising to find that this issue appears so inconsistently in her work.

> Claudia Tate, "Pauline Hopkins: Our Literary Foremother," *Conjuring: Black Women, Fiction, and Literary Tradition*, ed. Marjorie Pryse and Hortense J. Spillers (Bloomington: Indiana University Press, 1985), pp. 60–61

JANE CAMPBELL   *Contending Forces* fictionalizes women's collective efforts to create a countermythology. In the chapter entitled "The Sewing Circle," a large group of women gather to make garments for a church fair. Mrs. Willis, who plays a significant role in this chapter, serves as the embodiment of the black women's club movement. Although women's organizations existed before the Civil War, during the 1890s these clubs, led by such esteemed members as Frances Harper, Mary Church Terrell, and Fannie Barrier Williams, achieved greater prominence than they had earlier, in part because of the formation of the National Association of

Colored Women in 1896. Gerda Lerner notes that it is unclear whether this association spawned new clubs or whether existing clubs began to attain recognition; nevertheless, the club movement as a whole deserves credit for uniting black women in the crusades against lynching and Jim Crow and for integration. When characters in the sewing circle discuss woman's role in racial upbuilding, they turn to Mrs. Willis for direction. Mrs. Willis echoes Harper's injunction that mothers, as culture bearers, constitute black America's future, and she applauds African women's native virtue, suggesting that black American women, by extension, are innately virtuous. She goes on to caution her listeners that black women must not assume responsibility for the sexual exploitation of their ancestors and themselves. With this chapter, Harper charts black woman's role in changing history through her solidarity with other women, who help her to forge a new vision that runs counter to the one white culture promulgates. At the same time, the cult of domesticity, a motif pervading *Contending Forces*, enshrines the possibilities inherent in the home, where a sewing circle can become a political forum.

Hopkins's concept of history, exhibited in the aforementioned chapter and elsewhere, presupposes an educated, "cultured" class of leaders who will foster the rest of Afro-America so that it may evolve into ideal humanity. Patronizing as her mythmaking seems, it mirrors the attitudes of other post-Reconstruction black writers in its evolutionary concept of history. Unlike Harper, however, Hopkins conveys no notion that blacks are inherently more moral than whites or that black leaders will enhance white evolution. If anything, Hopkins hazards the idea that racial intermixture with Anglo-Saxons, however much it exploits women, has improved Afro-Americans, infusing blacks with characteristics of "the higher race." This blatant endorsement of racial supremacy has been responsible, in part, for the critical neglect of Hopkins's fiction; whether she was collapsing under the weight of the dominant cultural ideology or merely appealing to a white audience fails to excuse her. Yet paradoxically, Hopkins insists that, regardless of skin color, African descent people must identify with Afro-American. In addition, she avows in her epigraph from Emerson that whites have debased themselves by racial oppression. Finally, *Contending Forces* challenges "the best" of both races to consolidate in order to bring about historical change. Denouncing violence for agitation, Hopkins seeks to arouse moral urgency in black and white readers alike.

Jane Campbell, "Female Paradigms in Frances Harper's *Iola Leroy* and Pauline Hopkins's *Contending Forces*," *Mythic Black Fiction: The Transformation of History* (Knoxville: University of Tennessee Press, 1986), pp. 39–40

HAZEL V. CARBY   What Hopkins concentrated on ⟨in *Contending Forces*⟩ was a representation of the black female body as colonized by white male power and practices; if oppositional control was exerted by a black male, as in the story of Mabelle's father, the black male was destroyed. The link between economic/political power and economic/sexual power was firmly established in the battle for the control over women's bodies. Hopkins repeatedly asserted the importance of the relation between histories: the contemporary rape of black women was linked to the oppression of the female slave. Children were destined to follow the condition of their mothers into a black, segregated realm of existence from where they were unable to challenge the white-controlled structure of property and power. Any economic, political, or social advance made by black men resulted in accusations of a threat to the white female body, the source of heirs to power and property, and subsequent death at the hands of a lynch mob. A desire for a pure black womanhood, an uncolonized black female body, was the false hope of Sappho's pretense. The only possible future for her black womanhood was through a confrontation with, not denial of, her history. The struggle to establish and assert her womanhood was a struggle of redemption: a retrieval and reclaiming of the previously colonized. The reunited Mabelle/Sappho was a representation of a womanhood in which motherhood was not contingent upon wifehood, and Will was a representation of a black manhood that did not demand that women be a medium of economic exchange between men. The figure of Mabelle/Sappho lost her father when he refused to accept that his daughter was a medium of cash exchange with his white stepbrother. Beaubean had his fatherhood denied at the moment when he attempted to assert such patriarchal control and was slaughtered by a white mob. Instead of representing a black manhood that was an equivalent to white patriarchy, Hopkins grasped for the utopian possibility that Will could be a husband/partner to Mabelle/Sappho, when he accepted her sexual history, without having to occupy the space of father to her child.

Contending Forces was the most detailed exploration of the parameters of black womanhood and of the patriarchal limitations of black manhood in Hopkins's fiction. In her following three novels, Hopkins would adopt the more popular conventions of womanhood and manhood that defined heroes and heroines as she produced a magazine fiction that sought a wide audience. Hopkins continued to write popular fiction at the same time as she adopted popular fictional formulas and was the first Afro-American author to produce a black popular fiction that drew on the archetypes of dime novels and story papers.

Hazel V. Carby, " 'Of What Use Is Fiction?': Pauline Elizabeth Hopkins," *Recon-structing Womanhood: The Emergence of the Afro-American Woman Novelist* (New York: Oxford University Press, 1987), pp. 143–44

DICKSON D. BRUCE, JR.   ⟨*Hagar's Daughter*⟩ begins with a version of the tragic mulatto story, as Hagar, the beautiful young wife of a southern planter named Ellis Enson, is discovered to have black ancestry. In her grief and despair, she jumps with her child from a high bridge crossing the Potomac, apparently to her death. The scene is virtually identical to a similar episode at the conclusion of William Wells Brown's *Clotel*. But Hopkins departed from the usual treatment of the tragic mulatto. Commonly, in such stories, the heroine's tragedy is a result of the sexual hypocrisy of the white man. In Hopkins' story, the element of sexual hypocrisy does not appear. Hagar decides upon suicide because Ellis has apparently died while trying to arrange for their removal to Europe, where they can continue to live openly as husband and wife, away from the prejudices of white America. Like ⟨George Marion⟩ McClellan's "Old Greenbottom Inn," Hopkins' *Hagar's Daughter* held out the possibility of a real interracial love that triumphed over prejudice.

But Hopkins also went a step further than McClellan in her treatment of interracial love. As the word *apparently* in the synopsis indicates, neither Hagar nor Ellis actually dies in the early going of the novel. After spinning a complex tale of Washington intrigue, set twenty years beyond the apparent deaths of husband and wife, Hopkins reunited them through a series of coincidences. Again, Ellis, knowing full well Hagar's background, wants her to be his wife, creating a marriage that makes race irrelevant. The only tragic sidelight is that a young white man in love with Hagar's daughter spurns the girl because of her ancestry. In the end, he sees the error of his ways; but he cannot do anything about it. She has died, the victim of a fever. Here, of course, is the tragic mulatto, but presented in a way—balanced by her parents' unhappiness—that displays the alternative to, rather than the inevitability of, the young girl's tragic end, an alternative that even her misguided young man has come to see.

Hagar's Daughter was a frank espousal of the possibility and rightness of interracial romance. It was like "Talma Gordon" ⟨*Colored American*, October 1900⟩ in this regard, portraying a perspective consistent with but still more fully assimilationist than that of *Contending Forces*. Hopkins recognized that if racial barriers were to be represented as truly possible to overcome, then even the barrier to intermarriage had to be seen as artificial. Critic Claudia Tate has pointed out that marriage as a source of identity and stability was important in all of Hopkins' novels. In *Hagar's Daughter*, Hopkins used interracial marriage to encapsulate a vision of the irrelevance of racial identity in a decent world.

> Dickson D. Bruce, Jr., *Black American Writing from the Nadir: The Evolution of a Literary Tradition 1877–1915* (Baton Rouge: Louisiana State University Press, 1989), pp. 150–51

CLAUDIA TATE   Mrs. Willis ⟨in *Contending Forces*⟩ is the principal proponent for the law of the mother. In the chapter entitled "The Sewing Circle," she advises Sappho, on hearing her fictitious version of her personal history. Sappho recalls: "I once knew a woman who had sinned. . . . She married a man who would have despised her had he known her story; but as it is, she is looked upon as a pattern of virtue for all women. . . . Ought she not to have told her husband before marriage? Was it not her duty to have thrown herself upon his clemency?" Mrs. Willis replies: "I am a practical woman of the world and I think your young woman builded wiser than she knew. I am of the opinion that most men are like the lower animals in many things—they don't always know what is for their best good." Mrs. Willis's advice does not sanction the father's law; instead, she insists that man's view is finite, while God's judgment is infinite. She interprets God's infinity as "[Sappho's] duty . . . to be happy and bright for the good of those about [her]." The preeminence of the mother's law also directs the lives of Will Smith and his sister, Dora. For them their father is a sacred memory, connecting them to a history of racial strength as well as oppression. However, his absence also mitigates the strength of patriarchal values on their immediate lives and permits their mother to become the authority figure who not only nurtures them but manages the household affairs. Although the text makes no explicit mention of her managerial skills, it informs us that she runs a comfortable rooming house, and has a son enrolled at Harvard and a daughter who does not work outside the home. These details represent Mrs. Smith's proficiency in financial management and encourages the characters (and us) to regard women not as masculine complements but as individuals in their own right, deserving respect. Equally important to the evolving plot, the absence of the father and his law permits Will to follow his own desire in selecting his wife, rather than institutionalized patriarchal desire for premarital virginity. As a result he is free to marry the so-called ruined woman and to father her child as if it were his own.

The fact that Mrs. Willis is also a widow is important because she and Mrs. Smith are the principal means for inscribing the absence of the black patriarch. Mrs. Smith is the ideal maternal figure, which the text underscores by repeatedly referring to her as Ma Smith. Her widowhood is idealized, while Mrs. Willis's widowhood is problematic. The text describes Mrs. Willis's deceased husband as "a bright Negro politician" who had secured "a seat in the Legislature." In addition, she had "loved [him] with a love ambitious for his advancement." Despite "the always expected addition to [their] family," she was the woman behind the man. However, at his death there was no trust fund to meet her financial needs, and she has to work. For her the question becomes what line of work can fulfill both her financial needs and ambition. No longer able to represent her ambition as desire for her husband's advancement, Mrs. Willis has to find a cause. "The best opening, she decided after looking carefully about her, was in the great cause of the evolution of true womanhood in the work of the 'Woman Question' as embodied in marriage and suffrage." Thus, Mrs. Willis comes to the Woman Question not out of a burning passion for women's rights but out of a desire to advance herself as well as black women and the race. In short, she is a professional, or, in her own words, "a practical woman of the world" who has "succeeded well in her plans," which the text continues to describe as "conceived in selfishness, they yet bore glorious fruit in the formation of clubs of colored women banded together . . . [to] better the condition of mankind." To her audience she is a "brilliant widow" who "could talk dashingly on many themes." However, Mrs. Willis incites "a wave of repulsion" in Sappho; yet "Sappho [is] impressed in spite of herself, by the woman's words." Mrs. Willis is a model for the successful professional woman of that epoch who has stepped far into the public realm of political ambition. Sappho detects Mrs. Willis's conscious desire for power as well as the will to grasp it, and this detection excites her contradictory feelings about women's ambitions for power and conventional gender prescriptives designating it as inappropriate, which Hopkins's contemporaries no doubt also experienced.

Claudia Tate, "Allegories of Black Female Desire; or, Rereading Nineteenth-Century Sentimental Narratives of Black Female Authority," *Changing Our Own Words: Essays on Criticism, Theory, and Writing by Black Women*, ed. Cheryl A. Wall (New Brunswick, NJ: Rutgers University Press, 1989), pp. 122–23

ELIZABETH AMMONS   Very far removed from the social-documentary style of *Contending Forces*, *Of One Blood* mixes in unstable and therefore highly productive and unsettling combinations the ingredients of narrative realism, travelog, allegory, and dream prophecy. Unlike ⟨Frances E. W.⟩ Harper's work, in which much the same mixing of forms suggests generic searching, Hopkins's fusion, confusion, and irresolution of genre—the strange complexity of *Of One Blood*'s "fantastical plot," to recall Watson's characterization—suggests brilliant, even if not totally realized, purpose. Hopkins is not entering herself in the American romance tradition. She does not, like Hawthorne, use the supernatural as symbol. Rather, like Toni Morrison after her, she asserts the supernatural as reality. She breaks boundaries—enters the secret, long lost kingdom of black power in Africa—not in a mind trip but in a *real* trip, as *Of One Blood*'s literal volatility of form expresses. She moves with complete logic and ease between material and supernatural reality, past and present. In Charlotte Perkins Gilman's work about a woman artist, spirits and the supernatural are products of mind—and of deranged mind at that (the wobbling heads in the wallpaper, the creeping female forms). In Hopkins's narrative, experience from the other side (of life/of the world) is not the product of mind, much less of insanity. It is part of what is here. To "say" this in fiction—to say the opposite of what a Poe or Gilman might imply in their contextualizing of the supernatural in madness, or what Hawthorne might suggest in using the supernatural as moral or psychological symbol—Hopkins *does* create, by "realistic" high-culture western standards, a most strange and fantastical narrative: elaborate, dense, utterly decentered in its instability as realism. Clearly her last published long fiction, *Of One Blood*, suggests her desire to break out of the inherited high western narrative tradition, her desire to craft new form by drawing on antidominant realities of multiconsciousness and pan-African wholeness.

As an allegory about art, Hopkins's elaborate, bitter story shows the black woman artist, whose roots go deep into African history, half-dead and then completely dead in the United States. Dianthe, Candace's spiritual double and daughter, should be strong like her African forbear: regal, powerful, constantly renewed by the society in which she lives, and ready to unite with the black man to redeem the past and create the future. In Hopkins's myth, however, this tremendous possibility for creativity, including union with her black brother, meets total destruction at the hands of the white man, whose policy it is to deceive, silence, exploit sexually, and finally kill the black woman if she attempts to free herself from him. Whatever guarded optimism Hopkins might have felt about the future of the African American woman artist at the time she wrote *Contending Forces* was gone by the time she wrote *Of One Blood*. Grounding the black woman artist's story in unrequited heterosexual desire, violent sexual violation by white America, and erasure of her empowering African heritage, Hopkins tells in her "fairy tale," her wildly unbelievable fiction (if looked at in conventional western realistic terms), the awful truth about the African American woman artist's reality at the beginning of the twentieth century. In *Of One Blood* the black American woman artist *has* a past. It is ancient, potent, brilliant—full of voice. What she does not have is ownership of that past, or a future. ⟨. . .⟩

With *Of One Blood* Pauline Hopkins changed history. She pushed narrative form fully over into the mode of allegorical vision, prophecy, and dream projection that African American fiction, and particularly fiction by women—Toni Morrison, Rosa Guy, Gloria Naylor—would brilliantly mine later in the twentieth century. Without the *Colored American Magazine*, however, Pauline Hopkins, whose last major fiction in that magazine dramatized the violent silencing and death of the black American woman artist, disappeared as a productive artist.

Elizabeth Ammons, "The Limits of Freedom: The Fiction of Alice Dunbar-Nelson, Kate Chopin, and Pauline Hopkins," *Conflicting Stories: American Women Writers at the Turn into the Twentieth Century* (New York: Oxford University Press, 1991), pp. 83–85

Bibliography

Contending Forces: A Romance Illustrative of Negro Life North and South. 1900.

A Primer of Facts Pertaining to the Greatness of the African Race and the Possibility of Restoration by Its Descendants. 1905.

Magazine Novels: Hagar's Daughter; Winona; Of One Blood. Ed. Hazel V. Carby. 1988.

Peculiar Sam; or, The Underground Railroad. n.d.

▨ ▨ ▨

Zora Neale Hurston
c. 1891–1960

ZORA NEALE HURSTON was born probably on January 7, 1891, although she frequently gave her birth date as 1901 or 1903. She was born and raised in America's first all-black incorporated town, Eatonville, Florida. Her father, John Hurston, was a former sharecropper who became a carpenter, preacher, and three-term mayor in Eatonville. Her mother, Lucy Hurston, died in 1904; two weeks after her death, Hurston was sent to Jacksonville, Florida, to school, but wound up neglected by her remarried father and worked a variety of menial jobs. A five-year gap in her personal history at this time has led some biographers to conjecture that she was married; however, no evidence exists to support or disprove this speculation. In 1917 she began studies at Morgan Academy in Baltimore and in 1918 attended Howard University, where her first short story appeared in the college literary magazine. She later won a scholarship to Barnard College to study with the eminent anthropologist Franz Boas.

While living in New York Hurston worked as a secretary to the popular novelist Fannie Hurst. Though she only lived in New York for a short time, Hurston is considered a major force in the Harlem Renaissance of the 1920s and 1930s. She was an associate editor for the one-issue avant-garde journal *Fire!!* and she collaborated on several plays with various writers, including *Mule Bone: A Comedy of Negro Life,* written with Langston Hughes. Boas arranged a fellowship for Hurston that allowed her to travel throughout the South and collect folklore. The result of these travels was the publication of Hurston's first collection of black folk tales, *Mules and Men* (1935). Hurston is thought to be the first black American to have collected and published Afro-American folklore, and both of her collections have become much used sources for myths and legends of black culture. Her interest in anthropology took her to several Latin American countries, including Jamaica, Haiti, and Honduras. Her experiences in Jamaica and Haiti appear in her second collection of folk tales, *Tell My Horse* (1938).

Hurston's first novel, *Jonah's Gourd Vine* (1934), is loosely based on the lives of her parents in Eatonville. It was written shortly after *Mules and Men* (although it was published first) and has been criticized as being more of an anthropological study than a novel. Her best-known work, the novel *Their Eyes Were Watching God*, was published in 1937. Written after a failed love affair, *Their Eyes Were Watching God* focuses on a middle-aged woman's quest for fulfillment in an oppressive society. Hurston also wrote *Moses, Man of the Mountain* (1939), an attempt to fuse biblical narrative and folk myth. In addition to her life as a writer, Hurston worked temporarily as a teacher, a librarian at an Air Force base, a staff writer at Paramount Studios, and as a reporter for the *Fort Pierce* (Florida) *Chronicle*.

Her autobiography, *Dust Tracks on a Road*, won the 1943 Annisfield Award. Her final novel, *Seraph on the Suwanee*, appeared in 1948. An attempt to universalize the issues addressed in *Their Eyes Were Watching God*, *Seraph* is Hurston's only novel to feature white protagonists. Hurston's other honors include Guggenheim Fellowships in 1936 and 1938. She wrote for various magazines in the 1950s, but her increasingly conservative views concerning race relations effectively alienated her from black intellectual culture. She died on January 28, 1960, in Fort Pierce, Florida.

Critical Extracts

H. I. BROCK   The writer has gone back to her native Florida village—a Negro settlement—with her native racial quality entirely unspoiled by her Northern college education. She has plunged into the social pleasures of the black community and made a record ⟨*Mules and Men*⟩ of what is said and done when Negroes are having a good gregarious time, dancing, singing, fishing, and above all, and incessantly, talking. ⟨. . .⟩

The book is packed with tall tales rich with flavor and alive with characteristic turns of speech. Those of us who have known the Southern Negro from our youth find him here speaking the language of his tribe as familiarly as if it came straight out of his own mouth and had not been translated into type and transmitted through the eye to the ear. Which is to say that a very tricky dialect has been rendered with rare simplicity and fidelity into symbols so little adequate to convey its true values that the achievement is remarkable.

H. I. Brock, "The Full, True Flavor of Life in a Negro Community," *New York Times Book Review*, 18 November 1935, p. 4

STERLING A. BROWN   Janie's grandmother ⟨in *Their Eyes Were Watching God*⟩, remembering how in slavery she was used "for a work-ox and a brood sow," and remembering her daughter's shame, seeks Janie's security above all else. But to Janie, her husband, for all his sixty acres, looks like "some old skull-head in de graveyard," and she goes off down the road with slack-talking Jody Sparks. In Eatonville, an all-colored town, Jody becomes the "big voice," but Janie is first neglected and then browbeaten. When Jody dies, Tea-Cake, with his contagious high spirits, whirls Janie into a marriage, idyllic until Tea-Cake's tragic end. Janie returns home, grief-stricken but fulfilled. Better than her grandmother's security, she had found out about living for herself.

Filling out Janie's story are sketches of Eatonville and farming down "on the muck" in the Everglades. On the porch of the mayor's store "big old lies" and comic-serious debates, with the tallest of metaphors, while away the evenings. The dedication of the town's first lamp and the community burial of an old mule are rich in humor but they are not cartoons. Many incidents are unusual, and there are narrative gaps in need of building up. Miss Hurston's forte is the recording and the creation of folk-speech. Her devotion to these people has rewarded her; *Their Eyes Were Watching God* is chock-full of earthy and touching poetry. ⟨. . .⟩

But this is not *the* story of Miss Hurston's own people, as the foreword states, for *the* Negro novel is as unachievable as the Great American Novel. Living in an all-colored town, these people escape the worst pressures of class and caste. There is little harshness; there is enough money and work to go around. The author does not dwell upon the "people ugly from ignorance and broken from being poor" who swarm upon the "muck" for short-time jobs. But there is bitterness, sometimes oblique, in the enforced folk manner, and sometimes forthright. The slave, Nanny, for bearing too light a child with gray eyes, is ordered a terrible beating by her mistress, who in her jealousy is perfectly willing to "stand the loss" if the beating is fatal. And after the hurricane there is a great to-do lest white and black victims be buried together. To detect the race of the long-unburied corpses, the conscripted grave-diggers must examine the hair. The whites get pine coffins; the Negroes get quick-lime. "They's mighty particular how dese dead folks goes tuh judgment. Look lak they think God don't know nothin' 'bout de Jim Crow law."

Sterling A. Brown, " 'Luck Is a Fortune,' " Nation, 16 October 1937, pp. 409–10

RICHARD WRIGHT   *Their Eyes Were Watching God* is the story of Zora Neale Hurston's Janie who, at sixteen, married a grubbing farmer at the anxious instigation of her slave-born grandmother. The romantic Janie, in the highly charged language of Miss Hurston, longed to be a pear in blossom and have a "dust-bearing bee sink into the sanctum of a bloom; the thousand sister-calyxes arch to meet the love embrace." Restless, she fled from her farmer husband and married Jody, an up-and-coming Negro business man who, in the end, proved to be no better than her first husband. After twenty years of clerking for her self-made Jody, Janie found herself a frustrated widow of forty with a small fortune on her hands. Tea Cake, "from in and through Georgia," drifted along and, despite his youth, Janie took him. For more than two years they lived happily; but Tea Cake was bitten by a mad dog and was infected with rabies. One night in a canine rage Tea Cake tried to murder Janie, thereby forcing her to shoot the only man she had ever loved.

Miss Hurston can write; but her prose is cloaked in that facile sensuality that has dogged Negro expression since the days of Phillis Wheatley. Her dialogue manages to catch the psychological movements of the Negro folk-mind in their pure simplicity, but that's as far as it goes.

Miss Hurston *voluntarily* continues in her novel the tradition which was *forced* upon the Negro in the theater, that is, the minstrel technique that makes the "white folks" laugh. Her characters eat and laugh and cry and work and kill; they swing like a pendulum eternally in that safe and narrow orbit in which America likes to see the Negro live: between laughter and tears.

⟨. . .⟩ The sensory sweep of her novel carries no theme, no message, no thought. In the main, her novel is not addressed to the Negro, but to a white audience whose chauvinistic tastes she knows how to satisfy. She

exploits the phase of Negro life which is "quaint," the phase which evokes
a piteous smile on the lips of the "superior" race.

> Richard Wright, "Between Laughter and Tears," *New Masses*, 5 October 1937, p.
> 25

ZORA NEALE HURSTON   〈. . .〉 I see nothing but futility in
looking back over my shoulder in rebuke at the grave of some white man
who has been dead too long to talk about. That is just what I would
be doing in trying to fix the blame for the dark days of slavery and the
Reconstruction. From what I can learn, it was sad. Certainly. But my ancestors who lived and died in it are dead. The white men who profited by
their labor and lives are dead also. I have no personal memory of those
times, and no responsibility for them. Neither has the grandson of the man
who held my folks. I see no need in Button-holing that grandson like the
Ancient Mariner did the wedding guest and calling for the High Sheriff to
put him under arrest.

I am not so stupid as to think that I would be bringing this descendant
of a slave-owner any news. He has heard just as much about the thing as
I have. I am not so humorless as to visualize the grandson falling out on
the sidewalk before me, and throwing an acre of fits in remorse because his
old folks held slaves. No, indeed! If it happened to be a fine day and he
had had a nice breakfast, he might stop and answer me like this:

"In the first place, I was not able to get any better view of social conditions
from my grandmother's womb than you could from your grandmother's. Let
us say for the sake of argument that I detest the institution of slavery and
all that it implied, just as much as you do. You must admit that I had no
more power to do anything about it in my unborn state than you had in
yours. Why fix your eyes on me? I respectfully refer you to my ancestors,
and bid you a good day."

If I still lingered before him, he might answer me further by asking
questions like this:

> "Are you so simple as to assume that the Big Surrender
> (Southerners, both black and white speak of Lee's surrender to
> Grant as the Big Surrender) banished the concept of human
> slavery from the earth? What is the principle of slavery? Only the
> literal buying and selling of human flesh on the block? That was

only an outside symbol. Real slavery is couched in the desire to
and the efforts of any man or community to live and advance
their interests at the expense of the lives and interests of others.
All of the outward signs come out of that. Do you not realize that
the power, prestige and prosperity of the greatest nations on earth
rests on colonies and sources of raw materials? Why else are great
wars waged? If you have not thought, then why waste time with
your vapid accusations? If you have, then why single *me* out?"
And like Pilate, he will light a cigar, and stroll on off without
waiting for an answer.

Anticipating such an answer, I have no intention of wasting my time
beating on old graves with a club. I know that I cannot pry aloose the
clutching hand of Time, so I will turn all my thoughts and energies on the
present. I will settle for from now on.

And why not? For me to pretend that I am Old Black Joe and waste my
time on his problems, would be just as ridiculous as for the government of
Winston Churchill to bill the Duke of Normandy the first of every month,
or for the Jews to hang around the pyramids trying to picket Old Pharaoh.
While I have a handkerchief over my eyes crying over the landing of the
first slaves in 1619, I might miss something swell that is going on in 1942.
Furthermore, if somebody were to consider my grandmother's ungranted
wishes, and give *me* what *she* wanted, I would be too put out for words.

Zora Neale Hurston, *Dust Tracks on a Road: An Autobiography* (1942; rpt. New York:
HarperPerennial, 1991), pp. 206–8

WORTH TUTTLE HEDDEN   Though *Seraph on the Suwanee* is
the love story of a daughter of Florida Crackers and of a scion of plantation
owners, it is no peasant-marries-the-prince tale. Arvay Henson, true Cracker
in breeding, is above her caste in temperament; James Kenneth Meserve is
plain Jim who speaks the dialect and who has turned his back on family,
with its static living in the past, to become foreman in a west Florida
turpentine camp. Neither is it a romance of the boy-meets-girl school.
Beginning conventionally enough with a seduction (a last minute one when
Arvay is in her wedding dress), it ends twenty-odd years later when the
protagonists are about to be grandparents. In this denouement the divergent
lines of Miss Hurston's astonishing, bewildering talent meet to give us a
reconciliation scene between a middle-aged man and a middle-aged woman

that is erotically exciting and a description of the technique of shrimping that
is meticulously exact. Emotional, expository; meandering, unified; naive,
sophisticated; sympathetic, caustic; comic, tragic; lewd, chaste—one could
go on indefinitely reiterating this novel's contradictions and still end helplessly with the adjective unique. ⟨. . .⟩

Reading this astonishing novel, you wish that Miss Hurston had used
the scissors and smoothed the seams. Having read it, you would like to be
able to remember every extraneous incident and every picturesque metaphor.

Worth Tuttle Hedden, "Turpentine and Moonshine: Love Conquers Caste Between
Florida Crackers and Aristocrats," *New York Herald Tribune Books*, 10 October 1948,
p. 2

ROBERT BONE   The genesis of a work of art may be of no moment
to literary criticism but it is sometimes crucial in literary history. It may,
for example, account for the rare occasion when an author outclasses himself.
Their Eyes Were Watching God (1937) is a case in point. The novel was
written in Haiti in just seven weeks, under the emotional pressure of a
recent love affair. "The plot was far from the circumstances," Miss Hurston
writes in her autobiography, "but I tried to embalm all the tenderness of
my passion for him in *Their Eyes Were Watching God*." Ordinarily the
prognosis for such a novel would be dismal enough. One might expect
immediacy and intensity, but not distance, or control, or universality. Yet
oddly, or perhaps not so oddly, it is Miss Hurston's best novel, and possibly
the best novel of the period, excepting *Native Son*.

The opening paragraph of *Their Eyes Were Watching God* encompasses
the whole of the novel's meaning: "Ships at a distance have every man's
wish on board. For some they come in with the tide. For others they sail
forever on the horizon, never out of sight, never landing, until the Watcher
turns his eyes away in resignation, his dreams mocked to death by Time.
That is the life of man" (p. 9). For women, the author continues, the dream
is the sole reality. "So the beginning of this was a woman, and she had
come back from burying the dead."

Janie has been gone for almost two years as the action of the novel
commences. The townspeople know only that she left home in the company
of a lover much younger than herself, and that she departed in fine clothes
but has returned in overalls. Heads nod; tongues wag; and the consensus is

that she has played the fool. Toward the gossiping women who, from the safety of a small-town porch "pass notions through their mouths," Janie feels only contempt and irritation: "If God don't think no mo' 'bout 'em than Ah do, they's a lost ball in de high grass." To Phoeby, her kissing-friend, she tells the story of her love for Tea-Cake, which together with its antecedents comprises the main body of the novel.

Robert Bone, *The Negro Novel in America* (New Haven: Yale University Press, 1958), pp. 127–28

ROBERT HEMENWAY   What I should like to conclude with is the hypothesis that one reason Zora Neale Hurston was attracted to the scientific conceptualization of her racial experience during the late twenties and early thirties was its *prima facie* offering of a structure for black folklore. That is, it offered a pattern of meaning for material that white racism consistently distorted into "Negro" stereotypes. A folk singer was a cultural object of considerable scientific importance to the collecting anthropologist precisely because his folk experience affirms his humanity, a fact that Hurston could know subjectively as she proved it scientifically. The scientific attraction became so strong that she was led into seriously planning a career as a professional anthropologist, and it continued to affect her writing even after she had rejected such a possibility. When she used Eatonville as fiction in *Jonah's Gourd Vine* (1934), and folklore as personal narrative in her collection, *Mules and Men* (1935), she was in the process of rejecting the scientific conceptualization, but had not yet reached the aesthetic resolution in fiction that characterized her two masterpieces of the late thirties, *Their Eyes Were Watching God* (1937), and *Moses, Man of the Mountain* (1939). Hurston never denied the usefulness of the Barnard training, but she made it clear that something more was needed for the creation of art. As she once told a reporter: "I needed my Barnard education to help me see my people as they really are. But I found that it did not do to be too detached as I stepped aside to study them. I had to go back, dress as they did, talk as they did, live their life, so that I could get into my stories the world I knew as a child."

In sum, then, Zora Neale Hurston was shaped by the Harlem Renaissance, but by Boas as well as by Thurman and Hughes, by Barnard as well as by Harlem. This should not necessarily suggest that the Boas experience was of a superior quality; in many ways it seriously hindered her development as an artist. Nor should it suggest that the aesthetic excitement among the Harlem literati failed to influence her thought. It does mean that the attraction of scientific objectivity was something Hurston had to work through to arrive at the subjective triumphs of her later books. But the ferment of the Harlem Renaissance should also not be underestimated. Hughes, in particular, showed Hurston the poetic possibilities of the folk idiom and she was continually impressed when a reading from Hughes's poems would break the ice with dock loaders, turpentine workers, and jook singers. The mutual effort involved in the creation of *Fire*, the nights at Charles S. and James Weldon Johnson's, the *Opportunity* dinners, even the teas at Jessie Fauset's helped make Zora Hurston aware of the rich block of material which was hers by chance of birth, and they stimulated her thinking about the techniques of collecting and presenting it.

Robert Hemenway, "Zora Neale Hurston and the Eatonville Anthropology," *The Harlem Renaissance Remembered*, ed. Arna Bontemps (New York: Dodd, Mead, 1972), pp. 212–13

S. JAY WALKER   It comes as something of a shock to discover that Zora Neale Hurston's neglected 1937 masterpiece, *Their Eyes Were Watching God*, deals far more extensively with sexism, the struggle of a woman to be regarded as a person in a male-dominated society, than racism, the struggle of blacks to be regarded as persons in a white-dominated society. It is a treatment virtually unique in the annals of black fiction, and in her handling of it, Ms. Hurston not only shows an aching awareness of the stifling effects of sexism, but also indicates why the feminist movement has failed, by and large, to grasp the imaginations of black womanhood.

Janie Killicks Starks Woods, the heroine of the novel, is followed through three marriages, the first of which brings her safety, the second wealth and prestige, and the third love. On the surface, it sounds indistinguishable from the woman's-magazine fiction which has been denounced as the most insidious form of sexism. Yet a great deal goes on beneath the surface of Hurston's novel, leading to a final interpretation of love that denies not sexuality but sex-role stereotypes. The love that completes the novel is one that the previous marriages had lacked because it is a relationship between acknowledged equals. Janie and "Tea Cake," her husband, share resources, work, decisions, dangers, and not merely the marriage bed.

It is something less than a primer of romanticized love. At one point, Tea Cake, jealous of a suspected rival, beats Janie; at another, Janie, having the same suspicion, beats Tea Cake. Each has weaknesses, fears; but in the final analysis each respects the other as a person, and it is that respect that allows them to challenge the world's conventions and to find each other, and themselves.

> S. Jay Walker, "Zora Neale Hurston's *Their Eyes Were Watching God*: Black Novel of Sexism," *Modern Fiction Studies* 20, No. 4 (Winter 1974–75): 520–21

ALICE WALKER   It has been pointed out that one of the reasons Zora Neale Hurston's work has suffered neglect is that her critics never considered her "sincere." Only after she died penniless, still laboring at her craft, still immersed in her work, still following *her* vision and *her* road, did it begin to seem to some that yes, perhaps this woman *was* a serious artist after all, since artists are known to live poor and die broke. But you're up against a hard game if you have to die to win it, and we must insist that dying in poverty is an unacceptable extreme.

We live in a society, as blacks, women, and artists, whose contests we do not design and with whose insistence on ranking us we are permanently at war. To know that second place, in such a society, has often required more work and innate genius than first, a longer, grimier struggle over greater odds than first—and to be able to fling your scarf about dramatically while you demonstrate that you know—is to trust your own self-evaluation in the face of the Great White Western Commercial of white and male supremacy, which is virtually everything we see, outside and often inside our own homes. That Hurston held her own, literally, against the flood of whiteness and maleness that diluted so much other black art of the period in which she worked is a testimony to her genius and her faith.

As black women and as artists, we are prepared, I think, to keep that faith. There are other choices, but they are despicable.

Zora Neale Hurston, who went forth into the world with one dress to her name, and who was permitted, at other times in her life, only a single pair of shoes, rescued and recreated a world which she labored to hand us whole, never underestimating the value of her gift, if at times doubting the good sense of its recipients. She appreciated us, in any case, *as we fashioned ourselves*. That is something. And of all the people in the world to be, she chose to be herself, *and more and more of herself*. That, too, is something.

> Alice Walker, "On Refusing to Be Humbled by Second Place in a Contest You Did Not Design: A Tradition by Now," *I Love Myself When I Am Laughing . . . and Then Again When I Am Looking Mean and Impressive: A Zora Neale Hurston Reader*, ed. Alice Walker (New York: The Feminist Press, 1979), p. 4

HENRY LOUIS GATES, JR.   Hurston's achievement in *Dust Tracks* is twofold. First, she gives us a *writer's* life—rather than an account of "the Negro problem"—in a language as "dazzling" as Mr. Hemenway says it is. So many events in the book were shaped by the author's growing mastery of books and language, but she employs both the linguistic rituals of the dominant culture and those of the black vernacular tradition. These two speech communities are the sources of inspiration for Hurston's novels and autobiography. This double voice unreconciled—a verbal analogue of her double experiences as a woman in a male-dominated world and as a black person in a non-black world—strikes me as her second great achievement.

Many writers act as if no other author influenced them, but Hurston freely describes her encounter with books, from Xenophon in the Greek through Milton to Kipling. Chapter titles and the organization of the chapters themselves reflect this urge to testify to the marvelous process by which the writer's life has been shaped by words. "The Inside Search" and "Figure and Fancy" reveal the workings of the youthful Hurston's mind as she invented fictional worlds, struggled to find the words for her developing emotions and learned to love reading. "School Again," "Research" and "My People! My People!"—printed in the original form for the first time—unveils social and verbal race rituals and customs with candor that shocks even today. Hurston clearly saw herself as a black woman writer and thinker first and as a specimen of Negro progress last. What's more, she structured her autobiography to make such a reading inevitable.

> Henry Louis Gates, Jr., " 'A Negro Way of Saying,' " *New York Times Book Review*, 21 April 1985, pp. 43, 45

JOHN LOWE   Humor is a basic, continuing component in Hurston; to her, laughter was a way to show one's love for life, and a way to bridge the distance between author and reader. But more than this, she was deter-mined to create a new art form based on the Afro-American cultural tradi-tion, something she helped recover and define, as an anthropologist. ⟨. . .⟩ It now seems clear that humor played a crucial role in her initial reception by, and later relations with, the other members of the Harlem Renaissance; in her sense of folklore and its functions; in the anthropological aspect of Hurston's humor, which grew out of her training as a professional folklorist; and in the ever changing and increasing role humor played in her fiction, including her masterworks, *Their Eyes Were Watching God* and *Moses, Man of the Mountain.* ⟨. . .⟩

Dust Tracks never bores the reader, largely because the book, in celebrating Zora Neale Hurston, also salutes the culture that made her. The text is larded with humor, both as structure and adornment. Hurston uses comic expressions, jokes, and entire collections of humorous effects, to amplify, underline, and sharpen the points she makes. These deceptively delightful words often contain a serious meaning, just as the slave folktales did. Hurston skillfully trims and fits folk saying into integral parts of her narrative; on the first page, for instance, she describes her hometown by saying "Eatonville is what you might call hitting a straight lick with a crooked stick. The town . . . is a by-product of something else." This type of description becomes more pungent when she combines these materials with her own imaginative coinages, as in the following description of her father's family: "Regular hand-to-mouth folks. Didn't own pots to pee in, nor beds to push 'em under. . . . No more to 'em than the stuffings out of a zero." This utterance alone gives utterance to Hurston's assertion that the Negro's greatest contri-butions to the language were (1) the use of metaphor and simile ("hand-to-mouth folks"); (2) the use of the double descriptive ("pot . . . nor beds"); and (3) the use of verbal nouns ("stuffings"). It also reveals the way such tools can be used to revitalize language by working simultaneously in the comic mode.

John Lowe, "Hurston, Humor, and the Harlem Renaissance," *The Harlem Renaissance Re-examined*, ed. Victor A. Kramer (New York: AMS Press, 1987), pp. 284–85, 289

KARLA F. C. HOLLOWAY   Hurston develops her character Janie to the point that she is an assertive, self-fulfilled woman. Weaving her maturity through the natural imagery of the pear tree, through a fertile farmland with Logan Killicks where her spirit is spoiled, and into a town grown out of wilderness tamed, Hurston's word destroys sexual and natural fertility. Her word sweeps through with the force of a hurricane destroying all the structures so carefully framed from the opening pages of the novel. Hurston's text has warned the reader from the same early pages of its potential for destruction, teasing itself with the "ships at a distance" puzzle that sets the narrative tone. This often-quoted paragraph (perhaps so much so because its ambiguity invites a variety of critical comment) is a linguistic trope, a tease. It is language used to tell on, to signify upon, itself. It warns the reader through such signification that here is a text that talks its own structure into existence. I think it is less important to try to discover what Hurston's opening paragraphs mean than it is to point out that these paragraphs signal a text with an internal force that will gather strength through its manipulations of language. ⟨Henry Louis⟩ Gates's observation of the importance of this text's structure clarifies its importance:

> Hurston . . . has made *Their Eyes Were Watching God* into a
> paradigmatic signifying text, for this novel resolves that implicit
> tension between the literal and the figurative contained in
> standard English usages of the term "signifying." *Their Eyes*
> represents the black trope of signifying both as thematic matter
> and as a rhetorical strategy of the novel itself.

I would take Gates's point further and assert that *Eyes* represents a vocal structure that is something more basic than "strategy." He observes that Janie, the protagonist, "gains her voice, as it were, in her husband's store not only by engaging with the assembled men in the ritual of signifying . . . but also by openly signifying upon her husband's impotency." I support this statement with an emendation important to my thesis of voice: Janie gains her voice from the available voice of the text and subsequently learns to share it with the narrator ⟨. . .⟩ This is a vital extension of Gates's discussion of *Eyes*. I must credit the voice gained to the structure itself. Certainly the traditions of signifying belong to a black community, but Hurston has made them belong to a literary text in ways that empower them to take on their own life forms. This is a tradition of voice let loose in *Jonah* and re-merged to the literary text in *Eyes*. I think it is the same voice because Hurston uses it as character—investing it with active power. Sometimes her "word" is a teasing ambiguity; other times, it is an innocent bystander. But lest we fail to take it seriously, it returns in a whirlwind to exact its due on the very world it had created in the beginning. We know this is so because in the final pages of the novel, which are really the opening pages because the novel is a flashback (another show of power by the recursive word), Janie talks to her friend Phoeby, telling her what she must tell those who criticize what she has done with her life. "Then you must *tell* [emphasis added] them," Janie says, and if we have attended to that power of the word to speak itself into being, we know that Janie too has learned that through telling her spirit will rest fulfilled. "Love is lak de sea," she tells Phoeby, while the narrative voice finishes the image that opened the novel and speaks of Janie pulling "in her horizon like a great fish-net" and calling her soul "to come and see." The images of water and air collapse in these final pages; the wind turns peaceable and waits for its next embodiment.

Karla F. C. Holloway, *The Character of the Word: The Texts of Zora Neale Hurston* (Westport, CT: Greenwood Press, 1987), pp. 39–40

JENNIFER JORDAN   Despite her lack of veracity, critics like Alice Walker, Robert Hemenway, and Mary Helen Washington have managed to maintain both a certain objectivity about Hurston's weaknesses and a respectful fondness for her daring and talent. This same openmindedness and tolerance for ambivalence are not always reflected in the critical responses to her greatest work, *Their Eyes Were Watching God.* Hurston's independence, her refusal to allow her love interests and marriages to hamper her career, and her adventuresomeness in confronting the dangers of anthropological research in the violent turpentine camps of the South and in the voodoo temples of Haiti make her a grand candidate for feminist sainthood. Difficulties arise, however, when critics transfer their narrow conception of Hurston's personal attitudes and history to their readings of *Their Eyes Were Watching God,* a novel that reflects Hurston's ambiguity about race, sex, and class. The result is the unsupportable notion that the novel is an appropriate fictional representation of the concerns and attitudes of modern black feminism. ⟨. . .⟩

Their Eyes Were Watching God is a novel that examines with a great deal of artistry the struggle of a middle-class woman to escape the fetters of traditional marriage and the narrow social restrictions of her class and sex. But Janie Killicks Starks Woods never perceives herself as an independent, intrinsically fulfilled human being. Nor does she form the strong female and racial bonds that black feminists have deemed necessary in their definition of an ideologically correct literature. The novel fails to meet several of the criteria defined by black feminist criticism. Perhaps the acceptance and glorification of this novel as the bible of black women's liberation speak to the unconscious conflicts about emotional and financial dependence, sexual stereotyping, intraracial hostilities, and class interests inherent within the black feminist movement. In its very ambivalences Hurston's *Their Eyes Were Watching God* may serve as a Rorschach test by which these conflicts are revealed and thus is an appropriate manifesto for black feminism.

But the novel's success or failure as an ideological document does not diminish its aesthetic worth. It remains one of the great novels of black literature—a novel that is laughing out-loud funny, that allows black people to speak in their own wonderful voices, and that portrays them in all their human nobility and pettiness.

Jennifer Jordan, "Feminist Fantasies: Zora Neale Hurston's *Their Eyes Were Watching God*," *Tulsa Studies in Women's Literature* 7, No. 1 (Spring 1988): 106–7, 115

NELLIE McKAY   Unlike the solitary but representative hero of male autobiography, Janie Starks and Zora Neale Hurston join voices to produce a personal narrative that celebrates an individual and collective black female identity emerging out of the search for an autonomous self. Although the structure of this text is different, the tradition of black women celebrating themselves through other women like themselves began with their personal narratives of the nineteenth century. Female slave narratives, we know, generally had protagonists who shared their space with the women who instilled pride of self and love of freedom in them. The tradition continued into the twentieth century. For instance, much of the early portion of Hurston's autobiography, *Dust Tracks on a Road*, celebrates the relationship she had with her mother and the lessons she learned, directly and indirectly, from other women in the community. Thus, Hurston's structure for Janie's story expands that already existing tradition to concretize the symbolic rendering of voice to and out of the women's community by breaking away from the formalities of conventional autobiography to make Janie's text an autobiography about autobiographical storytelling, in the tradition of African and Afro-American storytelling. Hurston, struggling with the pains and ambivalences she felt toward the realities of a love she had to reject for the restraints it would have placed on her, found a safe place to embalm the tenderness and passion of her feelings in the autobiographical voice of Janie Crawford, whose life she made into a very fine crayon enlargement of life.

Nellie McKay, " 'Crayon Enlargements of Life': Zora Neale Hurston's *Their Eyes Were Watching God* as Autobiography," *New Essays on* Their Eyes Were Watching God, ed. Michael Awkward (New York: Cambridge University Press, 1990), pp. 68–69

MAYA ANGELOU   Zora Neale Hurston chose to write her own version of life in *Dust Tracks on a Road*. Through her imagery one soon learns that the author was born to roam, to listen and to tell a variety of stories. An active curiosity led her throughout the South, where she gathered up the feelings and the sayings of her people as a fastidious farmer might gather eggs. When she began to write, she used all the sights she had seen, all the people she encountered and the exploits she had survived. One reading of Hurston is enough to convince the reader that Hurston had dramatic adventures and was a quintessential survivor. According to her own account in *Dust Tracks on a Road*, a hog with a piglet and an interest in some food Hurston was eating taught the infant Hurston to walk. The sow came snorting toward her, and Zora, who had never taken a step, decided that the time had come to rectify her reluctance. She stood and not only walked but climbed into a chair beyond the sow's inquisitive reach.

That lively pragmatism which revealed itself so early was to remain with Hurston most of her life. It prompted her to write and rewrite history. Her books and folktales vibrate with tragedy, humor and the real music of Black American speech.

⟨. . .⟩ Is it possible that Hurston, who had been bold and bodacious all her life, was carrying on the tradition she had begun with the writing of *Spunk* in 1925? That is, did she mean to excoriate some of her own people, whom she felt had ignored or ridiculed her? The *New Yorker* critic declared the work a "warm, witty, imaginative, rich and winning book by one of our few genuine grade A folk writers."

There is, despite its success in certain quarters, a strange distance in this book. Certainly the language is true and the dialogue authentic, but the author stands between the content and the reader. It is difficult, if not impossible, to find and touch the real Zora Neale Hurston. The late Larry Neal in his introduction to the 1971 edition of *Dust Tracks on a Road* cited,

"At one moment she could sound highly nationalistic. Then at other times she might mouth statements which in terms of the ongoing struggle for Black liberation were ill conceived and were even reactionary."

There is a saying in the Black community that advises: "If a person asks you where you're going, you tell him where you've been. That way you neither lie nor reveal your secrets." Hurston called herself the "Queen of the Niggerati." She also said, "I like myself when I'm laughing." *Dust Tracks on a Road* is written with royal humor and an imperious creativity. But then all creativity is imperious, and Zora Neale Hurston was certainly creative.

Maya Angelou, "Foreword," *Dust Tracks on a Road* (New York: HarperPerennial, 1991), pp. viii–xii

🔷 Bibliography

Jonah's Gourd Vine. 1934.

Mules and Men. 1935.

Their Eyes Were Watching God. 1937.

Tell My Horse. 1938, 1939 (as *Voodoo Gods: An Inquiry into Native Myths and Magic in Jamaica and Haiti*).

Moses, Man of the Mountain. 1939.

Dust Tracks on a Road: An Autobiography. 1942.

Caribbean Melodies for Chorus of Mixed Voices and Soloists by William Grant Still (editor). 1947.

Seraph on the Suwanee. 1948.

I Love Myself When I Am Laughing . . . and Then Again When I Am Looking Mean and Impressive: A Zora Neale Hurston Reader. Ed. Alice Walker. 1979.

The Sanctified Church. 1981.

Spunk: Selected Stories. 1985.

Mule Bone: A Comedy of Negro Life (with Langston Hughes). Ed. George Houston Bass and Henry Louis Gates, Jr. 1991.

Gayl Jones
b. 1949

GAYL JONES was born on November 23, 1949, the daughter of Franklin and Lucile (Wilson) Jones. She grew up in a segregated neighborhood in Lexington, Kentucky, where she was influenced by extant oral traditions—mostly in the form of street chatter and storytelling (both her mother and grandmother wrote stories and plays, sometimes solely for Gayl's amusement). Jones began writing at an early age, and even her early stories are full of the colloquial language of her neighborhood. She received a B.A. in English from Connecticut College in 1971; she then received an M.A. (1973) and D.A. (1975) in creative writing from Brown University. In 1975 she joined the faculty of the University of Michigan, attaining the rank of professor of English by the time she left in 1983.

Jones's first book was a play, *Chile Woman*, produced at Brown in 1973 and published in 1974. She then wrote two novels in quick succession—*Corregidora* (1975) and *Eva's Man* (1976)—followed by a collection of short stories, *White Rat* (1977). These fictions are distinguished for their uncompromising subject matter and their faithful and lyrical replication of the language of the street and the ghetto. *Corregidora* examines a brutal world of sexual violence and incest caused, primarily, by the slave system. In *Eva's Man* the sexual violence becomes more explicit, culminating in an act of dismemberment that lands Eva in prison. The novel, an explicit attack on male dominance, was not as well received as its predecessor. *White Rat* contains stories written and published between 1970 and 1977. Here the focus shifts to an intense examination of character, usually from within (most of the stories are written in the first person), occasionally with Gothic effects reminiscent of Poe or Kafka. This volume too received only mixed reviews, some critics complaining of its unrelenting grimness.

In recent years Jones has turned to poetry, producing three volumes, *Song for Anninho* (1981), *The Hermit-Woman* (1983), and *Xarque and Other Poems* (1985). These works reveal many of the same concerns as her fiction. *Song for Anninho* is a long narrative poem with an historical setting in seventeenth-century Brazil and tells the story of the troubled love of two fugitive slaves, Anninho and Almeyda. The poem is considerably more optimistic than Jones's previous works. She is now at work on another novel as well as a nonfiction study of Brazilian history in the sixteenth and seventeenth centuries; both these works appear to focus on Brazilian settlements for escaped slaves. In 1991 she published a critical work, *Liberating Voices: Oral Tradition in African American Literature*.

◈ *Critical Extracts*

JOHN UPDIKE   *Corredigora* persuasively fuses black history, or the mythic consciousness that must do for black history, with the emotional nuances of contemporary black life. The novel is about, in a sense, frigidity, about Ursa's inability to love. ⟨. . .⟩ Her interior monologues, where they do not concern Corregidora, are addressed to her first husband, Mutt, whose attempted domination of her, climaxed by her fateful fall down the stairs, nevertheless quickened a response she cannot give her second, gentle husband, Tadpole. Throughout the span of her life that is related—in the end she is forty-seven—Ursa rejects the advances made to her by her husbands, by amorous night-club clients, by lesbian sisters. Similarly, her mother, having rejected Martin, lives alone, spurning the courtship of a friendly neighbor. The interweave of past shame and present shyness gives the dialogue depth ⟨. . .⟩ The book's innermost action ⟨. . .⟩ is Ursa's attempt to "get her ass together," to transcend a nightmare black consciousness and waken to her own female, maimed humanity. She does it, in the end, with a sexual act that she imagines was what "Great Gram did to Corregidora"— an act combining pain and pleasure, submission and possession, hate and love, an act that says, in love, "I could kill you." This resolution is surprising but not shocking; one of the book's merits is the ease with which it assumes the writer's right to sexual specifics, and its willingness to explore exactly how our sexual and emotional behavior is warped within the matrix of family and race.

> John Updike, "Selda, Lilia, Ursa, Great Gram, and Other Ladies in Distress," *New Yorker*, 18 August 1975, pp. 81–82.

DARRYL PINCKNEY   The men in this second novel ⟨*Eva's Man*⟩ complain of Eva's isolation, of her impenetrability. She constantly refuses to explain herself to the men she encounters. She is utterly unwilling to talk. Initially we see this as a defense against ruthlessness, but what is offered the reader is somewhat insufficient: the torment she suffers as a woman is not unusual, unfortunately, due to its frequency. No, this is not meant to depreciate the daily nature of a woman's pain; but not all women become schizophrenic, destructive. Both novels are relentlessly about fornication and sex, as an act, as a burden, central to the plot of existence, a dialogue between the deprived. The most private and reduced relations between the characters is all that is needed to indicate their social oppression. There is a continual sense of suffocation in these novels, as if their lives took place in a closet. The stasis and isolation are haunting. Locations are ignored: bus stops, taverns and cut-rate hotels all melted to a bleak, bare, unpaved texture. There does not even seem to be a white side of town. No doubt this is a source of the novels' power, as well as the distant and withheld quality of the heroines. The wife, a woman, is a matter of possession and property is always defined by the necessity for protection. Jealousy is a kind of aggression and Gayl Jones' novels are, finally, indictments against black men. The women are denied by convention what Angela Davis has called "the deformed equality of equal oppression."

The imbalances in *Eva's Man* are discomforting. Fixations with menstruation, erections, even the treatment of the characters' diets—scrambled eggs, onions, cooked sausage, cucumbers, cabbage, mustard, grease—create an aversion, repulsion, as if the sensual were not a relief from existences miserable and difficult, but a destiny bearing down without mercy. The skin of her neighbor in jail is covered with scabs. A man is missing a thumb. Women wear unnecessary amounts of perfume, cosmetics, jewelry. "You just sitting right on the pot and scared to shit." Odors leap up from every page. *Eva's Man*, then, is a tale of madness; one exacerbated if not caused by frustration, accumulated grievances. Girlhood is reduced to incidents of assault: little boys experiment on her with "a dirty popsicle stick," and demand she fondle their genitals; old men accost and intimidate. Poverty is not as evident in Eva's remembrance of New York slums as is another kind of scarcity—women and men in doorways, under stairs; lurid remarks; rape. ⟨. . .⟩

Gayl Jones places her heroines between victory and defeat where deprivation is a narcotic. Though they are women of intense and complicated feelings, their severity suggests an impasse. How does one sustain or add to the pitch of these books? There are hints of fragmentation and strain in the conception of *Eva's Man*. And there are risks in offering the novel as a forum for poetic and violent tirades of the solitary self: the limitations of tradition are exchanged for the narrowness of inaccessibility. Opaque, flat, peculiar, in her fiction Gayl Jones has presented problems that are living, historical and important additions to the current American—not just black—scene. These novels are genuinely imaginative creations.

Darryl Pinckney, [Review of *Eva's Man*], *New Republic*, 19 June 1976, pp. 27–28

JOHN WIDEMAN   Gayl Jones ⟨. . .⟩ exhibits debt to a literary tradition, but it is a tradition including Wheatley and Pope, Faulkner and Ellison, a tradition richer in models and less foreign to American speech. The salient issue here is not the throng of influences on *Corregidora* which may be mustered from other works of literature, but rather the relationship between literature and oral traditions in Jones' novel. Gayl Jones is a member of a black speech community and this membership implicates a significant dimension of her literary style. In contrast to Wheatley for whom oral traditions black or white are negligible, the fluency of Jones in two language cultures permits her to create a considerable dramatic tension between them, a tension responsible for much of the novel's impact and uniqueness. One critic's comment that "The book is written with almost embarrassing power" is evidence of how difficult this tension is to resolve. In ⟨. . .⟩ *Corregidora* there is no hierarchical relationship between black speech and a separate literary language, no implicit dependency. The norms of black oral tradition exist full bodied in the verbal style of the novel: lexicon, syntax, grammar, attitudes towards speech, moral and aesthetic judgments are rendered in the terms of the universe they reflect and reinforce. Through the filter of the narrator's sensibility the entire novel flows, and Corregidora's sensibility is constructed of blocks of black speech, her own, her men's, the speech of the people who patronize Happy's bar, the voices of her mother and the dead black women keeping alive the memories of slavery. Black speech is allowed to do (the author insists that it can) everything any other variety of literary language can do. The message comes through loud and clear to the reader: there is no privileged position from which to view this fictional world, no terms into which it asks to be translated, its rawness is not incidental, not local color or exoticism from which other, more familiar voices will relieve you. A black woman's voice creates the only valid terms for Corregidora's world; the authority of her language is not subordinated to other codes; the frame has disappeared.

> John Wideman, "Frame and Dialect: The Evolution of the Black Voice in American Literature," *American Poetry Review* 5, No. 5 (September/October 1976): 35–36

MICHAEL S. HARPER   [HARPER]: Do you have any models for artistic conception, literary, historical, or autobiographical?

[JONES]: I used to say that I learned to write by listening to people talk. I still feel that the best of my writing comes from having *heard* rather than having read. This isn't to say that reading doesn't enrich or that reading isn't important, but I'm talking about foundations. I think my language/ word foundations were oral rather than written. But I was also learning how to read and write at the same time I was listening to people talk. In the beginning, *all* of the richness came from people rather than books because in those days you were reading some really unfortunate kinds of books in school. I'm talking about the books children learned to read out when I was coming up. But my first stories were heard stories—from grown-up people talking. I think it's important that we—my brother and I—were never sent out of the room when grown-up people were talking. So we heard their stories. So I've always heard stories of people generations older than me. I think that's important. I think that's the important thing.

Also, my mother would write stories for us and read them to us. She would read other stories too, but my favorite ones were the ones she wrote herself and read to us. My favorite one of those was a story called "Esapher and the Wizard." So I first knew stories as things that were heard. That you listened to. That someone spoke. The stories we had to read in school— I didn't really make connections with them as stories. I just remember us sitting around in the circle and different people being called on to read a sentence. But my mother's reading the stories—I connected with that. And I connected with the stories people were telling about things that happened back before I was born.

When I was in the fifth grade, I had a teacher who would have us listen to music and then write stories. We had to write the stories that came to us while we were listening and then we would have to read the stories aloud to the whole class. I had started writing stories when I was in the second or third grade, when I was seven or eight, but didn't show them to anybody until her. Of course, my mother knew I was writing. Of course, I showed things to her. But my fifth-grade teacher was the first teacher I showed any work to. Her name was Mrs. Hodges. I remember I used to make stories and put the names of people in the class in them so that everybody would laugh. So then there was the music and the heard stories. It was an all-black school. I went to an all-black school until the tenth grade when there was integration. I say that because I think it's important. I think it's important about the music and the words, too.

A lot of connections I made with tradition—with historical and literary things—I started making later. I was writing stories in first-person before I made connections with the slave narrative tradition or the tradition of black autobiography, before "oral storytelling" became something you talked about. At first, I just felt that the first-person narrative was the most authentic way of telling a story, and I felt that I was using my own voice—telling a story the way I would talk it. I liked the way the words came out better than the way they came out in third-person. And I liked writing dialogue in stories, because I was "hearing" people talk. But I hadn't made any of the kinds of connections you make with your traditions other than the connections you make in living them and being a part of them. I didn't really begin to make the other kinds of connections till graduate school. I still don't like to stand away from the traditions, talking about them. You ought to be able to talk about them standing right inside them.

Michael S. Harper, "Gayl Jones: An Interview" (1977), *Chant of Saints: A Gathering of Afro-Amrican Literature, Art, and Scholarship*, ed. Michael S. Harper and Robert B. Stepto (Urbana: University of Illinois Press, 1979), pp. 352–53

DIANE JOHNSON   In the work of Gayl Jones one sees other literary influences—of Hemingway, perhaps, or Jean Rhys, highly wrought and economical—but also of those bus station thrillers in which a female narrator describes her loss of innocence, her sexual exploitation by a relentless string of single-minded lechers. The ancestress of Ursa Corregidora, the abused heroine of Jones's first novel, is the lusty, busty high-yellow beauty so beloved on paperback covers. The difference is that Jones's women, brutalized and dull, seem all too real. It is skillful expoitation of the stereotype.

The stories in her collection *White Rat* were written in some cases earlier than her novels, so they confirm one's sense of her direction and preoccupations: sex is violation, and violation is the principal dynamic of human relationships. In the sexual relation lies the struggle for power, the means of survival, the symbol of adulthood, the cause of suffering. Where ⟨Toni⟩ Morrison is an art novelist, who can invoke black speech for striking effect, Jones is a vernacular novelist with a marvelous ear, for whom black speech is the only medium. A boy says to the narrator of "The Women,"

> "You got a nice house," . . .
> "If you don't got to live in it."
> "Your mama keep things around."
> "What nots."
> "Yeah, my mama got those around too. She paint pictures and put them on the wall. Daddy tell her take 'em down. She say she don't like look at the bare wall."
> "Aw."

The monosyllables with which the characters conduct their lives suggest their defended isolation. It is as if there were only so much information to go around, and each person, jealous of the advantage it confers, is reluctant to share his. The jazzy banter that Morrison and ⟨James Alan⟩ McPherson both portray so well has the same back-to-the-wall quality. Though ignorance these days has lost much of its traditional status as a routinely stigmatized enemy of human happiness—indeed it is often admired—the plight of these characters renews one's sense of its virulence.

The women characters in Morrison are all eccentric, brave, and resolute. Gayl Jones presents women who are stunned and withdrawn. But both writers arrange their narratives in such a way as to avoid preachiness and, perhaps, to avert accusations of disloyalty. Morrison often lets a character have a say, like Lena, in *Song of Solomon,* who asks her brother "Where do you get the *right* to decide our lives? . . . I'll tell you where. From that hog's gut that hangs down between your legs. Well, let me tell you something, baby brother, you will need more than that."

Moral comment in Jones is more oblique. Ursa Corregidora, asleep, dreams resentfully of her possessive lover, "talking about *his* pussy. Asking me to let him see his pussy. Let me feel my pussy. The center of a woman's being. Is it?" When she wakes up she denies her resentment. "The shit you can dream." (His beatings have required her to lose her womb.) Because she writes entirely in the first person, Jones seems to record what people say and think as if it were no fault of hers, and Morrison seems to assert no more control over the exotic events of her narratives than the teller of a tall tale does. Perhaps art is always subversive in this way.

Diane Johnson, "The Oppressor in the Next Room," *New York Review of Books*, 10 November 1977, pp. 6–7

VALERIE GRAY LEE   Gayl Jones' *Corregidora* is another work by a black woman in which the womenfolk spend their time discussing the menfolk. Whereas the folktalk that Janie ⟨in Zora Neale Hurston's *Their Eyes Were Watching God*⟩ uses in discussing the men is romantic and Sula's ⟨in Toni Morrison's *Sula*⟩ is earthy, Ursa Corregidora's is downright bawdy. The four-letter sexual street language is in keeping with the trials and pathos of Ursa's story. Old Man Corregidora, the Portuguese slavemaster, mated with Ursa's grandmother and great grandmother. All of the flashbacks of the novel, all of Ursa's thoughts, revolve around Corregidora and what he did with his "womens." Ursa's great grandmother passed the story down from generation to generation so that there would always be evidence of what had gone on. According to Great Gran, Old Man Corregidora first "broke his womens hisself." She explained to Ursa over and over again the situation:

> "He liked his womens black, but he didn't wont us with no black mens. It wasn't color cause he didn't even wont us with no light black mens, cause there was a man down there as light as he was, but he didn't wont us with him . . . cause when he send them white mens in there to me he didn't look like that, cause he be nodding and saying what a fine piece I was, said I was a fine speciment of a woman, finest speciment of a woman he ever seed in his life."

There is nothing in the novel that does not connect to this sexual theme. Ursa has to come to grips with the story passed down by her ancestors before she can produce her own life story. Because of Ursa's hysterotomy, she is not able to make generations in the literal way that grandmothers and mother did. Instead she turns to folk music—the blues. The blues help her to explain what she cannot explain. They are the evidence that she leaves behind.

Just as Janie and Sula have best friends with whom they discuss "the menfolks," so does Ursa. Ursa tries to explain to Catherine ("Cat") some of her present problems with men. Ursa has an ex-husband and a lover who both claim to love her. Her husband, Mutt, unfortunately, does not view her as a whole person, but refers to her in a derogatory folk language as his "piece of ass." Ursa does not want to be a piece of anything. She dreams of telling Mutt off in a dirty-dozens duel. Mutt needs to realize that there will have to be some changes before Ursa takes him back.

The recurring question in *Corregidora* is, "What's a husband for?" Is he someone who literally knocks the womb out of his woman? Is he someone who owns her? Is he someone only to take care of her sexual needs? What's a husband for? The bawdy folk language captures, in a way that "conventional English" cannot, the answers to these questions. It does indeed make the work read like an extended blues lyric.

Valerie Gray Lee, "The Use of Folktalk in Novels by Black Women Writers," *CLA Journal* 23, No. 3 (March 1980): 270–71

JERRY W. WARD, JR.   In the American penal system, female prisoners are often subjected to more psychosexual abuse than their male counterparts. The same condition obtains, according to our most perceptive writers, in American society outside the prison walls. The abuse of women and its psychological results fascinate Gayl Jones, who uses these recurring themes to magnify the absurdity and the obscenity of racism and sexism in everyday life. Her novels and short fictions invite readers to explore the interiors of caged personalities, men and women driven to extremes. Her intentions seem less analytic than synthetic, the strategies of her fictions themselves being indices of contemporary disorder as norm rather than deviation. Throughout Jones's fictions, prisons and asylums function as settings for problematic narratives and as clues for the interpretation of outsideness. In the very act of concretizing these fictions as aesthetic objects, readers find themselves caught. The pleasure of experiencing such irony, and of gradually coming to know how accurately it confirms our habitation of an invisible penal colony, is justification for attending to Gayl Jones's achievement.

The unpredictable structures of *Corregidora* and *Eva's Man* and of the short fiction of *White Rat* provoke questions about how we construct meaning from allowing our minds to play through the texts. The author invites us into semantic realms for which we may have no guides other than cultivated literary competence, previous knowledge of other texts. We cannot begin to speak of the value of the experience until we understand how we have been seduced. Indeed, we may find ourselves posing unusual questions. What does it mean to think in fiction? Does thinking in a fiction lead us to experience states of mind ostensibly *represented* in the fiction? And how does one distinguish thinking in fiction from its mimesis? Where does such inquiry lead us? Does it offer any insights about qualitative differences between fictions by male and female writers?

Definitive, universal answers to such questions are unlikely. Yet raising them encourages us to think seriously about the verbal entrapment that is so pervasive a quality of modern fiction. Like the magic of Circe and Faust, modern fictions can transfom us—while we permit their influence—into the beings that our humanity disguises. As readers we begin to grasp that neither man nor woman is immune to the siren song of Jones's fictions.

Jerry W. Ward, Jr., "Escape from Trublem: The Fiction of Gayl Jones" (1982), *Black Women Writers (1950–1980): A Critical Evaluation,* ed. Mari Evans (New York: Anchor Books/Doubleday, 1984), pp. 249–50

KEITH E. BYERMAN   Gayl Jones, of all the writers discussed thus far, creates the most radiant worlds. Not only are the societies depicted the most thoroughly and correctly oppressive, but she also denies readers a "sane" narrative center through which to judge world and narrator. Most frequently, her narrators have already been judged insane by the society; and this assessment, given the teller's actions and obsessions, seems reasonable. But we cannot therefore assume that we have entered a Poesque world of confessors of personal guilt or madness, for it is equally apparent that society has its own obsessions and that its labeling of the narrators as mad facilitates evasion of the implications of those obsessions. ⟨. . .⟩

"Asylum" is an extreme case of Jones's attitude. The narrator, a young woman committed to an asylum because of her irrational behavior, refuses to allow the doctor to examine her genital area, yet she was admitted after deliberately urinating in the living room when her nephew's teacher visited their home. She explains to the reader (though not to the psychiatrist) her motive for the latter action: "She [the teacher] just sit on her ass and fuck all day and it ain't with herself."

Obsessed with acts of violation, whether sexual, intellectual, or psychological, she reveals her madness in rendering this sense of violation in graphic terms. Thus, her feeling that the teacher functions as an exploiter of children and thus provides a humanly worthless education is effectively expressed by presenting and using the family slop jar. Significantly, when the psychiatrist explains the means by which she is to be made "normal," she sees those means as schoolwork.

She considers the whole process of physical and mental examination to be rape. Whenever she has been examined, she sees a "big black rubbery thing look like a snake" emerging from either her vagina or her anus. Those examining her define her resistance and sensibility as narcissistic sexual obsession, needing correction by experts. What Jones accomplishes through selection of narrator is a rebuttal of such a reductive notion. Even if the narrator is insane, our access to her thoughts informs us that the probing and objectification of her by the doctors is woefully inadequate. The pain and disorder she experiences are unrelieved and even aggravated by such clinical clichés as: "libido concentrated on herself."

Moreover, she associates this reification and violence with whites. In a dream, the narrator sees the black nurse becoming "chalk white" when she assists in the examinations. More important, the narrator dreams that she herself takes on white characteristics and is thereafter unable to prevent the vaginal exploration.

The final conversation of the story suggests the dilemma facing the narrator:

> "What does this word make you feel?"
> "Nothing."
> "You should tell me what you are thinking?"
> "Is that the only way I can be freed?"

The asylum microcosm of the totalitarian state. Those in authority determine what constitutes sane behavior and thought. Not to speak is to condemn oneself to imprisonment as a mental incorrigible. But the act of speaking is collaboration in one's dehumanization since it leads to categorization and "treatment," which in effect is imposition of values and modes of behavior designed to make one a functioning cog in the social machine. In other words, there is no freedom, no escape from this "refuge."

Keith E. Byerman, "Beyond Realism: The Fictions of Gayl Jones and Toni Morrison," *Fingering the Jagged Grain: Tradition and Form in Recent Black Fiction* (Athens: University of Georgia Press, 1985), pp. 171–72, 176–77

RICHARD K. BARKSDALE   Two conclusions can be drawn from studying the patterns of sexual conflict in Jones's two novels. First, the roots of the black woman's sexual slavery are deeply buried in the physical violence and degradation of African chattel slavery. Here, too, are the roots of black concubinage, often incestuous and sadomasochistic. This lamentable side of black history in the diaspora has been widely documented. Dorothy Sterling, for instance, in a chapter entitled "Seduction, Rape, and Concubinage" in *We Are Your Sisters* (New York: Norton, 1984), shows how black women, entrapped and exploited in a violent system, resorted to desperate stratagems to survive and retain their sanity and their womanly self-esteem. As Sterling reports, sometimes, in their travail, black women in slavery sang:

> Rains come wet me
> Sun come dry me
> Stay back, white man
> Don't come nigh me.

Obviously a little song like this could not stop the savage whippings and the physical, mental and emotional indignities suffered by the black slave woman. For further documentation of her status, we have Frederick Douglass' tragic portrait of his mother (actually, his half-sister as well as his mother), who was driven to an early death by cruel and inhumane treatment.

The second conclusion to be drawn from the Jones novels is that, with slavery's end, black men like the Mutt Thomases of the world began to imitate the sexual behavior of their former masters. Stripped of political and economic power and harassed by a still-dominant white majority, they sought to enjoy their new freedom in whatever limited sense they could under the circumstances. Within this context they sought to hold sexual mastery over their women, and to some extent, unless a former master intervened, the black freedmen enjoyed and exploited this power. So over

the years there occurred a mirror-imaging exchange of power, and in his sexual relations with his women the black man replaced his former master.
Richard K. Barksdale, "Castration Symbolism in Recent Black American Fiction," *CLA Journal* 29, No. 4 (June 1986): 406–7

MELVIN DIXON   The action in *Eva's Man* (1976) begins where *Corregidora* left off and envelops us in the despair of one woman's self-inflicted failure to achieve refuge or redemption. The unrelenting violence, emotional silence, and passive disharmony in *Eva's Man* are the undersides of the blues reconciliation and active lovemaking in *Corregidora*. Eva Medina Canada poisons her lover Davis Carter and castrates him with her teeth once he is dead. Important to our brief study here is that Eva never gains control over her voice, her past, her place, or her identity. Instead of wielding language as useful evidence for justice and regeneration as Ursa has done, Eva is defeated by words and brandishes first a pocket knife against Moses Tripp, then arsenic and teeth against Davis. Eva never comes to terms with her past; she chooses to embrace received images of women as *femmes fatales*. Ursa and Eva are further separated by their vastly different ability to experience love.

In view of Jones's concern with opening avenues for reconciliation between the sexes, it is important to see *Eva's Man* and *Corregidora* as companion texts. Primarily through the protagonists' attitudes toward language and their fluency with idioms necessary for personal deliverance, we encounter one woman's fall and another's rise. The clear contrast between them makes Ursa appear as Eva's alter ego and reveals Jones to be a gifted ironist: Eva, surnamed Canada, the promised land and refuge for fugitive slaves, contrasts with Corregidora, Brazilian slave master in one of the larger regions of New World slavery. Yet it is Ursa who frees herself from bondage and Eva who succumbs to it. Eva has chained herself to the debilitating stereotypes of Queen Bee, Medusa, and Eve long before she is locked away in prison for her crime. And Eva is only partly aware of her own responsibility in getting there. ⟨. . .⟩

Eva fails to deliver herself from the wilderness. She remains "looking like [the] wild woman" she first appeared to be in newspaper photos of her arrest, and she erroneously believes in the surface meaning of the blues song she hears, "Wild Women Don't Get the Blues." Eva misreads the song's irony and Ursa's example. Although Ursa inhabits an interior space of the past in her memory of Corregidora, she succeeds in breaking free. The mountain tunnel releases the train in her song. Ursa travels to another height of self-possession. The geography of the journey for Gayl Jones is both sexual and musical.

Melvin Dixon, "Keep Me from Sinking Down: Zora Neale Hurston, Alice Walker, and Gayl Jones," *Ride Out the Wilderness: Geography and Identity in Afro-American Literature* (Urbana: University of Illinois Press, 1987), pp. 117, 120

FRANÇOISE LIONNET   ⟨. . .⟩ Eva's self-representation ⟨in *Eva's Man*⟩ as well as the way she feels about herself and her actions cannot be separated from the cultural images of women that are common currency around her. Consequently, when the psychiatrist who tries to "help" her asks her how she feels, she can only recall other instances of people asking her and other women how "it feels," for how is a woman supposed to feel about her own sexuality when its value is repeatedly denied, when she knows nothing about her own desires, and when male sexuality expresses itself in the form of sexual harassment? The doctor is an obvious composite of the male protagonists who have used her in the past: his name is David Smoot, recalling young Freddy Smoot as well as Davis Carter himself. In fact, just as Eva is made to represent a certain stereotype of fatal woman, all the men eventually merge into one single paradigm of male dominance, the voice of "all them Dr. Frauds" that, since Freud, keeps on interrogating femininity: "Why won't you talk about yourself?" "Why did you kill him?" "What did he do?" "What happened?" "Did you want to do anything you did?" This is the same voice that has always puzzled over "what a woman wants." ⟨. . .⟩ Eva refuses to explain herself: "I don't like to talk about myself," and this is the only way she has of resisting the dominant discourses that imprison her inside certain labels: "Her silences are . . . ways of maintaining . . . autonomy," Gayl Jones has said. Her seemingly passive compliance is a way of resisting the double bind, what ⟨Hélène⟩ Cixous has called the "phallocentric representationalism" that distorts and objectifies: "You keep all your secrets, don't you?" Davis says, when there are in fact no "secrets" to keep, only the impossibility for the woman to accede to the symbolic realm of language without simultaneously putting herself under erasure, risking misunderstanding, or confirming the patriarchal representations that preexist her speech: "A motive was never given. She never said anything. She just took the sentence." It is this apparent "serenity" that leads to the insanity plea: "When a woman done something like you done and serene like that, no wonder they think you crazy," as Elvira explains. Eva instinctively knows what the entire United States would be forced to watch during Anita Hill's testimony before the U.S. Senate in September 1991: that what a black woman might feel, and what she might want, are so inconceivable to the imagination of a patriarchal nation, so threatening, that she must be neutralized by stereotypical accusations of feminine instability and unreliability. ⟨. . .⟩

On a structural level, Jones makes no attempt to placate her readers; *Eva's Man* is a difficult book, a tale of great intensity that resists closure. ⟨. . .⟩ it is a story about men, about their obsessive sexuality and exploitative relationships. Eva's own personal story is not really told, since most of what we know of her is what the men in her life (Freddy, Mr. Logan, John Canada, Tyrone, Davis, Alfonso, Moses Tripp, James Hunn, and finally David Smoot) have done to the women she knows. The narrative shows how they have made Eva herself into a "little evil devil bitch," a "sweet [castrating] bitch." The narrative fragments do not add up to a coherent picture of the past, and the novel thematizes its structural discontinuities by stressing the gaps and the fissures in Eva's memory, by suggesting that it is thanks to those gaps that she can manage to slip out of the symbolic domain, and disrupt the culture's master narrative.

> Françoise Lionnet, "Geographies of Pain: Captive Bodies and Violent Acts in the Fictions of Myriam Warner-Vieyra, Gayl Jones, and Bessie Head," *Callaloo* 16, No. 1 (Winter 1993): 144–45

Bibliography

Chile Woman. 1974.
Corregidora. 1975.
Eva's Man. 1976.
White Rat. 1977.
Song for Anninho. 1981.
The Hermit-Woman. 1983.
Xarque and Other Poems. 1985.
Liberating Voices: Oral Tradition in African American Literature. 1991.

June Jordan
b. 1936

JUNE JORDAN was born in New York on July 9, 1936. Her parents, who were immigrants from Jamaica, wanted their daughter to be a doctor and sent her to the Northfield School, an exclusive girls' school in Massachusetts. One of the few black students in her class, Jordan graduated in 1953 and entered Barnard College in New York City that fall. Two years later she married a Columbia graduate student, Michael Meyer, and abandoned her own studies to take care of their son.

After moving with her husband to Chicago, Jordan returned to Harlem around 1960 and began working on Frederick Wiseman's film about life in the ghetto, *The Cool World*. Around this time she became interested in city planning and met R. Buckminster Fuller, with whom she devised plans for the revitalization of Harlem. In 1969 Fuller nominated Jordan for the Prix de Rome in Environmental Design, which she won. She spent the next year studying at the American University in Rome. Her marriage ended in 1965, and she continued to work as a freelance journalist, writing poetry in her spare time. A long poem titled *Who Look at Me* was published in 1969. It reflects the racial and political concerns that mark much of her poetry.

Since *Who Look at Me* appeared in 1969, Jordan has published seven more volumes of poetry, including *Some Changes* (1971), *New Days* (1974), and *Things That I Do in the Dark: Selected Poetry* (1977). *Passion* (1980) and *Living Room* (1985) gather the poems she wrote between 1977 and 1984, while *Lyrical Campaigns* (1989), *Naming Our Destiny* (1989), and *Haruko/ Love Poetry* (1993) present selections of her best poetic work. Jordan has also written several plays, including *The Issue* (1981) and *Bang Bang Uber Alles* (1986), which have been performed but not published.

In 1971 her first novel, *His Own Where*, was nominated for a National Book Award. This young adult book is written in dialect, referred to as Black English, which aroused much protest from parents who felt that their children should not be guided toward nonstandard English models of writing and dialogue. The case was decided in the Michigan courts, where a judge ruled that Black English was a viable alternative to standard English and could not be banned in public schools. Jordan continued writing fiction for children: the novels *Dry Victories* (1972), *New Life: New Room* (1975), and *Kimako's Story* (1981), and the biography *Fannie Lou Hamer* (1972). She has also published several collections of essays: *Civil Wars* (1981), *On Call* (1985), *Moving towards Home* (1989), and *Technical Difficulties* (1992). These essays, like much of her poetry, express Jordan's challenging and uncompromising views on political, literary, and social issues.

Jordan has held teaching positions at various colleges, including City College of the City University of New York, Connecticut College, Sarah Lawrence, and the State University of New York at Stony Brook. Since 1989 she has been a professor of Afro-American studies and women's studies at the University of California at Berkeley.

Critical Extracts

JAMES A. EMANUEL   Opposite the title page of *Who Look at Me* is a painting simply entitled "Portrait of a Gentleman." The gentleman is black. June Jordan's book suggests all black Americans are as unknown as the anonymous early 19th-centuury artist and his subject.

"We do not see those we do not know," she writes. "Love and all varieties of happy concern depend on the discovery of one's self in another. The question of every desiring heart is, thus, 'Who Look at Me?' In a nation suffering fierce hatred, the question—race to race, man to man, and child to child—remains: 'Who Look at Me?' We answer with our lives. Let the human eye begin unlimited embrace of human life."

By intermixing 27 paintings of black Americans from colonial times to the present with an original, understated but intense poem that comments indirectly on the paintings and enhances their meaning, she has given children a splendid opportunity to "begin unlimited embrace of human life."

James A. Emanuel, [Review of *Who Look at Me*], *New York Times Book Review*, 16 November 1969, p. 52

LOUIS L. MARTZ   June Jordan's book, *Some Changes*, inaugurates the new "Black Poets Series" edited by Julius Lester, who provides a brief introduction to the volume, where he says: "For some, her poetry may not qualify as 'black poetry' because she doesn't rage or scream. No, she's quiet, but the intensity is frightening. Her poetry is highly disciplined, highly controlled." It is indeed the skill of her control that is at a first reading most impressive about this volume ⟨. . .⟩ At the same time, the temper of the volume is tough-minded. There is a harsh poem in memory of Martin Luther King; there is a bitter rejoinder to L.B.J.:

> He lost the peace so
> he can keep the peril he
> knows war is nothing like please.

Louis L. Martz, "New Books in Review," *Yale Review* 59, No. 4 (June 1970): 561–62

SARAH WEBSTER FABIO   This book ⟨*His Own Where*⟩ begins: "*You be different from the dead. All them tombstones tearing up the ground, look like a little city, like a small Manhattan . . . Cemetery let them lie there belly close. . . .*"

Whose where? Why cemetery? How sex? At what early age? Between the first and last pages, for Buddy Rivers, 16-year-old protagonist, and his first love, Angela, the only progression is the short sleep in the cemetery, time for her young dream. The story of their trials, the immediacy of their physical attraction is told in flashback and dream flashes, filling the pages of the chapters from one to 17.

June Jordan, author and poet (*Who Look At Me* and *Some Changes*) knows the abandonment of this age. It is a limbo between childhood and young adult, where the void is so great as to be unbearable. It is true here that the mind often stammers for language and the heart only responds to song—to the radio, which you use like a compass on a music map. Angela, at 14, trying to understand Buddy, tells him, "Tune the dial to what you want." There must be bridges if we are to reach our young. *His Own Where* promises to be one. ⟨. . .⟩

Buddy's immediate problem is his father's hospitalization. This, when coupled with his mother's earlier desertion, creates alienation. Although his father has taught him how to fend for himself; how to clean, build, plant, draw plans, he still needs adult contact. At school, he agitates for free and healthy sex, contraceptives, a turned-on lunchroom, coeducational classes in anatomy; his principal suspends him from school and he is told not to return without a parent. Complications arise when he becomes involved with Angela, recognizing her imprisonment and seeing himself as the force of her liberation. Her cab-driving father, who drinks heavily, and her overworked mother, who is a nurse at the hospital, are united in their suspicion of her evilness. She is humiliated and beaten daily to keep her straight. This ends when she is beaten unmercifully; the parents are investigated for child abuse; the home is shattered. ⟨. . .⟩

Buddy sees himself as a man of action. In dream flashes, we see him attending to emergency room patients, liberating Angela from St. Margaret's, a Catholic Home for Girls, filling empty skyscrapers with children who need space to breathe. Finally, he moves with runaway Angela to the cemetery to create, even for a moment, "His own where, own place for loving made for making love."

Sarah Webster Fabio, [Review of *His Own Where*], *New York Times Book Review*, 7 November 1971, pp. 6, 28

JASCHA KESSLER   June Jordan assembles *Some Changes* out of the black experience, and she does so coherently. Her expression is developed out of, or through, a fine irony that manages to control her bitterness, even to dominate her rage against the intolerable, so that she can laugh and cry, be melancholic and scornful and so on, presenting always the familiar faces of human personality, integral personality. She adapts her poems to the occasions that they are properly, using different voices, and levels of thought and direction that are humanly germane and not disembodied rages or vengeful shadows; thus she can create her world, that is, people it for us, for she has the singer's sense of the dramatic and projects herself into a poem to express its special subject, its individuality. Of course it's always her voice, because she has the skill to use it so variously: but the imagination it needs to run through all her changes is her talent. Moreover she seems not to have rejected on principle what has been available to poets in the way of models; in other words, you can see all the white poets she has read, too. She has been assimilating their usages of phrase and stanza; she sees with her own eyes through them, speaks them with her own voice, which is another way of remarking that she is interested in poetry itself. No matter how she will use her poems, and most of them are political in thrust, she has the great good sense, or taste, not to politicize her poetry. There is a difference, even in love poetry, nature poetry, and she has some of that sort, between speaking as yourself and editorializing for others. She is both simple and strong; she is clear in the head, besides. Her compassion and suffering for others is put into lyrical statement, and not into poems which are weapons. I can't shield myself against her, and have no wish to do so, let alone feel myself forced to deliver counter-blows, forced to feel gratuitous pain, gratuitous outrage. It may be because Jordan is a woman, that even her anger and despair are kept within the bounds of the humane, where poetry is too. That is the circle I draw round myself, though it is often broken into, or broken out of, as the case may be. 〈. . .〉

When June Jordan goes through her changes, she does it; she doesn't talk about doing it. For us there is pleasure in that, because we can go through them with her. And that means she has poetry near her.

Jascha Kessler, "Trial and Error," *Poetry* 121, No. 5 (February 1973): 301–3

JUNE JORDAN   *The Black Poem . . . Distinctively Speaking.* What is it? Quite apart from individual volumes of Black poetry, I have learned that I hold decidedly different expectations of a Black Anthology, as compared to any other kind. If the single poem, or if the anthology qualifies as distinctively Black, then, as compared to a "white anthology" or a "white poem," I expect the following:

> *A striving for collective voice, or else its actual, happy accomplishment. Even if the person proceeds in the 1st person singular, I expect a distinctively Black poem to speak *for me*-as-part-of-an-*us*, a bounded group that the poem self-consciously assumes as an integral, guiding factor in her/his/their individual art.
>
> *From a reaching for collective voice, as a self-conscious value, it follows that a distinctively Black poem will be accessible to random readers, rather than "hard," or arrantly inaccessible. (This does not mean that prolonged/repeated study will not yield new compulsion. But it does mean that the first time around, which may be an only time, the poem has to "hit" and "stick," clearly, and openly, in a welcoming way.)
>
> *Collective voice necessarily refers to spoken language: Distinctively Black poems characteristically deal memories and possibilities of spoken language, as against literary, or written,

language. This partially accounts for the comparative *directness* and force of Black poetry; it is an intentionally collective, or *inclusive*, people's art meant to be shared, heard and, therefore, spoken—meant to be as real as bread.

*Sound patterns, rhythmic movement and change-ups often figure as importantly as specific words, or images, in distinctively Black poetry. (Even if the poet says nothing especially new, I can expect to take pleasure in the musical, textural aspects of the poem; they will be as intrinsic to the work, as the words.)

To conclude this second point: Distinctively Black poetry adheres to certain, identifiable values—political and aesthetic—that are open to adoption, enjoyment by anyone. Overriding everything else is the striving and respect for collective voice. These distinctive values also constitute the main sum of what I look for, and prize, in The Black Poem.

June Jordan, "The Black Poet Speaks of Poetry," *American Poetry Review* 3, No. 3 (May–June 1974): 50

DORIS GRUMBACH   In the *American Poetry Review* issue for May/June 1974 there are a number of interesting contributions, not the least of which, to my biased mind, is June Jordan's "The Black Poet Speaks of Poetry." Her thesis is that "white people/white editors, of major/nationwide magazines and publishing houses simply do not read and do not value and do not publish what I would call The Black Poem." There follow citations of who those major/nationwide magazines are and lo, *The New Republic* leads all the rest: "Although *TNR* regards itself as a political journal, when have you seen a political poem published there?"

You will note that the black poem, in the course of a few sentences, has transmuted itself to something called the *political* black poem. When I wrote to her to point out the notice *TNR* has taken of black poets and writers, she made this distinction: "The kind of poetry I am referring to is Distinctly Black/Political poetry." Disclaiming my citations of Alice Walker, Sterling Brown, Barbara Smith, Michael Harper, Ishmael Reed, Ivan Webster as examples of writers whom *TNR* either has published, is about to publish, or has dealt with critically, she said none of them qualified under her stringent definition, which by now had acquired a new word, "Distinctly." She accused *TNR* of "having been offered, and has steadily refused to publish Distinctly Black/Political Poetry many times in the last several years" (capital letters are all hers). My response was that I had no way of knowing for certain from the ms. that the DBP poetry *was* black, or was by a black. So it was entirely possible that, for reasons other than racist, I or my predecessor *had* returned the poetry offered to us by DBP poets. Our correspondence went on in this fashion, she accusing me of "patronizing response" that is "so apparently the nature of your immediate reaction to criticism by Black People."

This drove me not so much to anger as to June Jordan's own poetry, the only DBP poet she cited in her letter as having been rejected by us. (I am constrained to add that when I wrote telling her the names of other noted poets—*white*—whose poems I had rejected she suggested we discontinue our correspondence because she could not read my handwriting.) Her newest book is called *New Days*, published in September of this year by Emerson Hall publishers. It contains some very admirable poems, some very angry ones (clearly what she would call Political), but an even greater number that I would call love poems, or poems of exile and return in her words in which neither the color of the poet nor her politics are apparent. ⟨. . .⟩ There are other very good ones, some I like somewhat less, though they are not necessarily the Distinctly Black Political ones, and a few I liked not at all, convincing me that *TNR* or the other media she accuses—*NY Times*, *New Yorker*, *NY Review of Books*, *American Review*, *Harper's*, *Atlantic*, and a number of publishing houses—may have rejected poets for a number of reasons besides racism, among them, the private esthetic of the literary editor, the poetic value of the submitted poem, the state of things at the publishing house at the moment (some publications, like ours, are stocked for a year or more with accepted poetry) and, God help us, space limitations.

Doris Grumbach, "Fine Print," *New Republic*, 9 November 1974, p. 44

NTOZAKE SHANGE   To be in exile & be a poet is to be turned in on oneself / more than to be free of the trauma / there is a case that the whole nation of us who are African are in exile / here in this english-speakin place / but the collections of poems by june jordan ⟨*New Days*⟩ / & joseph jarman ⟨*Black Case*⟩ steer us away from a sense of dislocation / these are exiles returned / & more ourselves than many of us who stayed durin the holocausts & frenzy of sixties / illusions grow in newark & paris / whatever we have stepped outta cycle / outside ourselves / ⟨. . .⟩ aside from confrontin the vast disarray that is the contemporary world / circlin on itself / maybe swallowin us / loosin us in the momentum / less we do as jarman chants:

> can you look at your black skin
> your black self if you got one
> and then do itit is
> time
> say do it yes
> go sing
> the sound the music it is *fire*.

& jordan incants:

> YOUR BODY IS A LONG BLACK WING
> YOUR BODY IS A LONG BLACK WING

we shall twist in despair & distortion / in conceits & wrong information same as those jarman's ODAWALLA moved through 'the people of the Sun' teachin through 'the practice of the drum and silent gong' / or jordan's "Gettin Down to Get Over":

> momma momma
> teach me how to kiss
> the king within the kingdom
> teach how to t.c.b. / to make do
> an be
> like you
> teach me to survive my
> momma
> teach me how to hold a new life
> momma
> help me
> turn the face of history
> *to your face*

movin back in on ourselves / to discover all that is there / is not lovely worth holdin / but necessary to know / what is real / who we are / jordan & jarman examine mercilessly their own dilemmas / which become / all of ours

Ntozake Shange, [Review of *New Days: Poems of Exile and Return*], *Black Scholar* 8, No. 5 (March 1977): 53–55

DARRYL PINCKNEY   "Passion" is an appropriate title for this
gathering of 51 new poems. Miss Jordan, in the preface, calls for a "people's
poetry," hailing Walt Whitman and Pablo Neruda as notable examples. It
is impossible to accept her charge that there is a "vendetta" against Whitman
in America. Even before recent scholarly work that sympathetically discusses
the homoerotic in Whitman's sensibility, there was Randall Jarrell's
important essay. It is also difficult to understand why the quest for a "New
World" poetry must entail the rejection of T. S. Eliot, Robert Lowell,
Wallace Stevens or Elizabeth Bishop, four of the finest poets in the language.
There is no contradiction in admiring *The Waste Land* as well as lyrics from
the streets. One can learn from any tradition.

The poems in *Passion*, mostly in free verse, share many of the themes of
the essays. These poems are confidently within an oral tradition, and
although the oral can often mean the merely rhetorical, Miss Jordan serves
the tradition well, with a sensitive ear for the vernacular, for the ironic
tone. ⟨. . .⟩

The energy and seriousness of these poems are impressive and, like the
essays, they are the work of a writer of integrity and will.

> Darryl Pinckney, [Review of *Civil Wars* and *Passion*], *New York Times Book Review*,
> 9 August 1981, p. 26

PETER ERICKSON   Those who come to June Jordan's poetry
because of her reputation as a strictly political poet will be surprised at the
large number of love poems and of her constant recourse to this genre.
Setting aside political concerns, the poet indulges her erotic longing: "I can
use no historic no national no family bliss / I need an absolutely one to
one a seven-day kiss" ("Alla Tha's All right, but," *Passion*). What is here
a raucous assertion and celebration of sexual need has earlier—more often
than not—been an expression of intense vulnerability in love. Jordan's first
collection of poetry, *Some Changes* (1971), is divided into four untitled
sections, the implicit rationale for section two being love. This second
section, arguably the richest in the volume, has an important long-term
effect on Jordan's overall poetic development, thus providing a key to that
development.

An atmosphere of deep malaise—interrupted by occasional, though still
muted, bursts of erotic release of self-affirmation—dominate section two of

Some Changes. The last poem of section one, "I Live in Subtraction," makes the transition to the next section by firmly setting a dejected tone. Though "I" is the first word and subject of every line, the action of the poems is to reduce rather than enlarge this self, the continual subtracting effect culminating in the contemplation of suicidal gesture: "I can end a dream with death." We are not told how this psychological state came about, though we might guess the poet has been hurt by love when she says that she has forgotten or directs herself to "forget you name." Her demoralization is presented as a given, its origin and cause left a mystery.

Nor are we told the reason for the sadness in "My Sadness Sits Around Me." This title is reiterated in the poem's first and last lines, creating a literal enclosure which represents the emotional isolation that envelops the poet. We are forced simply to note and to accept this sadness which the poems gingerly explore without explaining more precisely. The same image of being cut and sealed off is reproduced in "Nobody Riding the Roads Today," where the last stanza can only repeat the first: "Nobody riding the roads today / But I hear the living rush / far away from my heart." The formal circularity mimics and heightens the poet's desolation.

The troubled mood of these poems can be usefully associated with the general background of Jordan's life during this period, so long as we do not insist on a one-to-one correspondence by which the life is supposed to explain the poetry. The two crucial events of which the reader needs to be aware are, in successive years, Jordan's divorce from her husband (1965) and her mother's suicide: first with a brief mention in *Civil Wars* (p. xvii), then at length in her second address at Barnard College. In the latter, Jordan presents her recollection of the suicide with such vivid immediacy that it is almost as if it were occurring in the present rather than fifteen years ago, as if Jordan must relive her confused feelings in order finally to attain expiation.

Peter Erickson, "The Love Poetry of June Jordan," *Callaloo* 9, No. 1 (Winter 1986): 223–24

SARAH BENTON   The threat of annihilation by white America is the pulse of June Jordan's writings. This makes hers a rare voice in the refined world of the political essay. From her account of a riot in Harlem in 1964 to her oration for the death of ⟨Jesse⟩ Jackson's Presidential bid in

1988 she measures all political movement against this irreducible standard: does it combat the likelihood of death by violence, by suffering or by suicide? With her fingers on this fear, she keeps herself in the bloodstream of the peoples to whom she feels herself thrice kin: blacks, women and the third world. For unlike them, June Jordan has earned an audience through her work as poet, public speaker and academic. ⟨. . .⟩

When she sees the world in simple black and white she jeopardises the fragile alliance for which she speaks, as in her attack on a group of Hassidic Jews. But she is again rare in her efforts to describe the conflicts between black, and women's and third world movements. Rarer still in seeing the solution in love, as in: "It is against such suicide, and is against such deliberate strangulation of the possible lives of . . . powerless peoples . . . everywhere that I work and live, now, as a feminist, trusting that I will learn to love myself well enough to love you . . ." The vulnerability of a form of writing that does not investigate, or write directly from, the lives of the oppressed, is that it can fall into a sententious moralism. Most of the time, the power of her words carries her argument through.

> Sarah Benton, "A Rare Voice" [Review of *Moving towards Home* and *Lyrical Campaigns*], *New Statesman and Nation*, 7 April 1989, p. 46

MARILYN HACKER   June Jordan's new book ⟨*Naming Our Destiny*⟩ is an anthology of causes won, lost, moot, private and public, forgotten and remembered. Anyone who doubts the relevance and timeliness of poetry ought to read Jordan, who has been among the front-line correspondents for almost thirty years and is still a young and vital writer. So should anyone who wants his or her curiosity and indignation aroused, or wants to read a voice that makes itself heard on the page. ⟨. . .⟩

What makes politically engaged poetry unique, and primarily poetry before it is politics? Jordan's political poetry is, at its best, the opposite of polemic. It is not written with a preconceived, predigested agenda of ideas and images. Rather, the process of composition is, or reproduces, the process of discovering how events are connected, how oppressions are analogous, how lives interpenetrate. Jordan's poems are strongest when they deal with interior issues, when she begins with a politics of the personal, with the articulate and colloquial voice of, if you will, "a woman speaking to women" (and to men) and ranges outward to illustrate how issues, lives and themes are inextricably interconnected. 〈. . .〉

How can a white critic say that a black poet has a spectacular sense of rhythm? Modestly, or courageously. Jordan writes (mostly) free verse. Many writers of free verse produce a kind of syntactically disjointed prose, expecting line breaks to provide a concentration and a syncopation not achieved by means of language. In Jordan's best poems there is a strong, audible, rhythmic counterpart to the line breaks, a rhythm as apparent to the reader as it is to the auditor who hears the poet deliver them. This is true of her poems that have been set to music by Bernice Reagon of the a cappella group Sweet Honey in the Rock ("Alla Tha's All Right, but" and "A Song of Sojourner Truth"), but it's equally true of dramatic monologues like "The Talking Back of Miss Valentine Jones" and "Unemployment Monologue," and of the interior monologues evolving into public declaration, like "Poem About My Rights."

The fluid speech-become-aria quality of Jordan's free verse poems also makes them difficult to quote, though never difficult to remember. They are not made of lapidary lines and epigrammatic stanzas. They gather momentum verbally, aurally. Most often, the effects of the voice and the statement are cumulative.

Why is this important? Because it fixes the poems in the reader's memory; because it makes these poems, even those on the most serious subjects, paradoxically fun to read. It is a reason for these texts to be written in verse, to be poetry. They are not fiction, journalism, essays or any other form of prose, even when they share qualities with these other genres. When Jordan's poems are unambiguous and straightforward, as well as when they are figurative, ironic or complex, her words create a music, create voices, which readers must hear the way they were written. Her poems read themselves to us.

Marilyn Hacker, "Provoking Engagement," *Nation*, 29 January 1990, pp. 135–36

DAVID BAKER   The issues of race and self-reliance (artistic and otherwise) are not the only political topics to which Jordan returns persistently. She speaks searingly in behalf of the hitherto silenced or subjugated: women, the poor and hungry, the imprisoned, the politically tyrannized in Nicaragua, the enslaved in Manhattan. I can think of very few contemporary

American poets who have been so willing to take on other people's troubles; decidedly, this is not the poetry of a sheltered, introspective confessional, not the work of a tidy scholar or a timid dormouse. Jordan's variety of poetic stances enacts her drive to connect and represent, for in addition to her principal mode of delivery—the poet talking directly to an audience—she also speaks through a number of other characters in persona poems, giving sympathetic articulation to lives, idioms, and concerns beyond her own. Like Carl Sandburg, she makes public art out of public occasion and the available word, and she does so with confidence and conviction.

David Baker, "Probable Reason, Possible Joy," Kenyon Review 14, No. 1 (Winter 1992): 154–55

ADELE LOGAN ALEXANDER   *Technical Difficulties* is a book about America—subtitled, as it is, "The State of the Union." This is America observed and found both noble and nurturing, brutal and malformed—often at the same time—by a brilliant and mature African American scholar who has looked at our country with her own unique clarity of vision and focus. Her subjects include affectionate tributes to her own Jamaican heritage ("For My American Family") and that of those other immigrants, not the Poles, Russians, Irish, or Germans but the too-often invisible and darker-skinned newcomers whose journeys through New York harbor, past the Statue of Literty and Ellis Island, have been largely overlooked in our romantic imaging of the American melting-pot. ⟨. . .⟩

Jordan tackles and dissects familiar themes: family, race, neighborhood ("two-and-a-half years ago," she writes, "I . . . returned to my beloved Brooklyn where, I knew, my eyes and ears would never be lonely for diversi-fied, loud craziness and surprise"), the love of men, women and children, the mutable American Constitution, education, creativity and politics (of nations and of sexuality, the "correct" and the "incorrect"). For many years she has been a teacher and writer, with several books of essays, including *Civil Wars, Moving towards Home* and *On Call,* to her credit, as well as collections of poetry, including the less well-known *Who Look at Me*—poems for children about African American artists and their work. These new essays, though they cover a variety of topics, come together into a unified and consistent whole. Adapting the Cubists' technique of viewing a subject from many different perspectives at once, Jordan sees all sides and then reassembles the fragments into a consistent, if multifaceted, whole. One should not say *Technical Difficulties* is "better" than what preceded it, but it is surely "more," and though a little of Jordan's well-muscled prose goes a long way, in this case it is also true that "more is better." ⟨. . .⟩

Jordan vigorously rants at our familiar "emperors," from George Washington to Ronald Reagan. She reminds us of the meaty, but non-mainstream, substance that has been deliberately omitted and obscured from our educational, cultural and political lives. I look to her not only to rail at the way things have been ("if you're not an American white man and you travel through the traditional twistings and distortions of the white Western canon, you stand an excellent chance of ending up *nuts*," she says) but to knock our white, male-centered world cockeyed from its moorings and provide more of the revised visions that we need.

> Adele Logan Alexander, "Stirring the Melting-Pot," *Women's Review of Books* 10, No. 7 (April 1993): 6–7

Bibliography

Who Look at Me. 1969.

The Voice of the Children (editor; with Terri Bush). 1970.

Soulscript: Afro-American Poetry (editor). 1970.

Some Changes. 1971.

His Own Where. 1971.

Dry Victories. 1972.

Fannie Lou Hamer. 1972.

Poem: On Moral Leadership as a Political Dilemma (Watergate, 1973). 1973.

New Days: Poems of Exile and Return 1970–1972. 1974.

New Life, New Room. 1975.

Niagara Falls. 1977.

Things That I Do in the Dark: Selected Poetry. 1977.

Unemployment: Monologue. 1978.

Passion: New Poems 1977–1980. 1980.

Kimako's Story. 1981.

Civil Wars. 1981.

Living Room: New Poems. 1985.

On Call: Political Essays. 1985.

Bobo Goetz a Gun. 1985.
Naming Our Destiny: New and Selected Poems. 1989.
Moving towards Home: Political Essays. 1989.
Lyrical Campaigns: Selected Poems. 1989.
Technical Difficulties: African-American Notes on the State of the Union. 1992.
Haruko/Love Poetry: New and Selected Poems. 1993.

◈ ◈ ◈

Nella Larsen
1891–1964

NELLA MARIE LARSEN was the daughter of an African–West Indian father and a Danish mother. Though the year of 1893 has been cited as the year of her birth, official working records reveal it to be April 13, 1891. Her father died when she was two; two years later her mother married a Danish man. Larsen was raised in an all-white household, in predominantly white surroundings, attending school in the primarily German and Scandinavian suburbs of Chicago. Larsen entered all-black Fisk University Normal School (high school) in 1907, attending for one year.

Larsen studied as a nurse in New York and later worked in that profession in Tuskegee, Alabama, and in New York. She quit nursing in 1921, but years later returned to the profession after abandoning all involvement in the literary world. In 1919 she married Dr. Elmer S. Imes, a physicist and a notorious womanizer. (Larsen always published either under her maiden name or a pseudonym.) Their rocky relationship finally ended in divorce in 1932 amidst great public scandal.

In 1922 Larsen became a librarian at the New York Public Library, in charge of children's books at the Countee Cullen branch. In 1926 the first of Larsen's two novels, *Quicksand*, was begun and, in 1928, published by Alfred A. Knopf. The book dealt with the then-unconventional theme of the mulatto in society. Although some critics cite fame and popularity as Larsen's guiding ambition, *Quicksand*'s treatment of bourgeois black Americans was a significant and financially risky departure from the most popular black American novels of the time, which dealt with lower-class nightlife in Harlem. Larsen was awarded the Harmon Foundation bronze medal for literature in 1928, and after the publication of her second novel, *Passing*, in 1929, she received the first Guggenheim Fellowship ever given to a black American woman.

In 1930 Larsen traveled to Mallorca to work on a new novel, but it was never published. She was accused of plagiarism in her short story "Sanctuary," which was published in *Forum* in 1930; although exonerated, she was profoundly disturbed by the incident. Owing to financial difficulties and her divorce, Larsen quit writing altogether and worked as a nurse in Brooklyn, New York, until her death on March 30, 1964. She is buried in Brooklyn's Cypress Hills Cemetery.

◈ *Critical Extracts*

ROARK BRADFORD   The real charm of ⟨*Quicksand*⟩ lies in Miss Larsen's delicate achievement in maintaining for a long time an indefinable, wistful feeling—that feeling of longing and at the same time a conscious realization of the impossibility of obtaining—that is contained in the idea of Helga Crane. (Helga is an idea more than she is a human being: drawing character does not seem to be one of Miss Larsen's major accomplishments.) ⟨. . .⟩

It leads directly to a splendid emotional climax. The brief scene is at a party in Harlem. Helga is alone for a moment with the man who first understood that strange emotions swelled within her bosom. (That was years before at Naxos. Now he is the husband of her best friend.) Her nerves are tuned to a high pitch; her soul is stirred; savagery tears at her heart; the black blood chokes the white, and Africa rumbles through her veins. And the man—suddenly the veneers of civilization crackle about him and—well, the reader is as tense as the two actors in the drama.

But alas! Without knowing just where it comes from, the reader suddenly catches a faint odor of talcum powder. And from that point on the book—in this reviewer's opinion—suffers from odors . . . Burnt cork, mostly.

In spite of its failure to hold up to the end, the book is good. No doubt it will be widely read and discussed. The reader, to get the maximum enjoyment, should begin with a mind as free as possible of racial prejudices and preconceived notions and conclusions. Miss Larsen seems to know much about the problems that confront the upper stratum of Negroes, and happily, she does not get oratorical about what she knows. She is quite sensitive to Negro life, but she isn't hysterical about it. There is a saneness about her

writing that, in these hysterical literary times, more than compensates for
her faults.

Roark Bradford, "Mixed Blood," *New York Herald Tribune Books,* 13 May 1928,
p. 22

W. E. B. DU BOIS   Nella Larsen's *Passing* is one of the finest novels
of the year. If it did not treat a forbidden subject—the inter-marriage of a
stodgy middle-class white man to a very beautiful and selfish octoroon—it
would have an excellent chance to be hailed, selected and recommended.
As it is, it will probably be given the "silence," with only the commendation
of word of mouth. But what of that? It is a good close-knit story, moving
along surely but with enough leisure to set out seven delicately limned
characters. Above all, the thing is done with studied and singularly successful
art. Nella Larsen is learning how to write and acquiring style, and she is
doing it very simply and clearly. ⟨. . .⟩

Nella Larsen ⟨. . .⟩ explains just what "passing" is: the psychology of the
thing; the reaction of it on friend and enemy. It is a difficult task, but she
attacks the problem fearlessly and with consummate art. The great problem
is under what circumstances would a person take a step like this and how
would they feel about it? And how would their fellows feel?

W. E. B. Du Bois, [Review of *Passing*], *Crisis* 36, No. 7 (July 1929): 234–35

ROBERT BONE   The key to the narrative structure of *Quicksand*
is contained in a passage toward the end of the novel in which Helga Crane
rebels against her lot as a brood mare: "For she had to admit it wasn't new,
this feeling of dissatisfaction, of asphyxiation. Something like it she had
experienced before. In Naxos. In New York. In Copenhagen. This differed
only in degree." Helga's quest for happiness has led her, floundering, through
a succession of minor bogs, until she is finally engulfed by a quagmire of
her own making. The basic metaphor of the novel, contained in its title,
is supported throughout by concrete images of suffocation, asphyxiation,
and claustrophobia. Associated always with Helga's restlessness and dissatisfaction, these symbols of a loathsome, hostile environment are at bottom
projections of Negro self-hatred: "It was as if she were shut up, boxed up

with hundreds of her race, closed up with that something in the racial character which had always been, to her, inexplicable, alien. Why, she demanded in fierce rebellion, should she be yoked to these despised black folk?"

On one level, *Quicksand* is an authentic case study which yields readily to psychoanalytic interpretation. Each of the major episodes in Helga's life is a recapitulation of the same psychological pattern: temporary enthusiasm; boredom, followed by disgust; and finally a stifling sense of entrapment. Then escape into a new situation, until escape is no longer possible. Race is functional in this pattern, for it has to do with Helga's initial rejection and therefore with her neurotic withdrawal pattern. Her tendency to with-draw from any situation which threatens to become permanent indicates that she is basically incapable of love or happiness. No matter how often she alters her situation, she carries her problems with her.

Deserted by her colored father and rejected by her white stepfather, Helga's quest may be viewed as the search for a father's love. The qualities of balance and security which she finds so appealing in Danish society; her attraction for Dr. Anderson, an older married man; her desire for "nice things" as a substitute for the security of parental love; and her belated return to religion can all be understood in these terms. Her degrading marriage to a jackleg preacher who "fathers" her in a helpless moment plainly has its basis in the Oedipal triangle. Her unconscious need to be debased is in reality the need to replace her mother by marrying a "no-account" colored man not unlike her gambler father. ⟨. . .⟩

The dramatic tension of the novel can be stated in terms of a conflict between Helga's sexuality and her love for "nice things." Her desire for material comfort is static; it is the value premise on which the novel is based: "Always she had wanted . . . the things which money could give, leisure, attention, beautiful surroundings. Things. Things. Things." Helga's sexuality, on the other hand, is dynamic; its strength increases until she is overwhelmed and deprived of the accouterments of gracious living forever. ⟨. . .⟩

⟨. . .⟩ Helga's tragedy, in Larsen's eyes, is that she allows herself to be declassed by her own sexuality. The tone of reproach is unmistakable. It is this underlying moralism which differentiates *Quicksand* from the novels of the Harlem School. It is manifested not in Helga's behavior, which is "naturalistic" and well motivated, even inevitable, but in the symbols of luxury which are counterposed to the bog, in the author's prudish attitude toward sex, and in her simple equation of "nice things" with the pursuit of beauty.

Robert Bone, *The Negro Novel in América* (New Haven: Yale University Press, 1958), pp. 103–6

CLAUDIA TATE   Race ⟨. . .⟩ is not ⟨*Passing's*⟩ foremost concern, but is merely a mechanism for setting the story in motion, sustaining the suspense, and bringing about the external circumstances for the story's conclusion. The real impetus for the story is Irene's emotional turbulence, which is entirely responsible for the course that the story takes and ultimately accountable for the narrative ambiguity. The problem of interpreting *Passing* can, therefore, be simplified by defining Irene's role in the story and determining the extent to which she is reliable as the sole reporter and interpreter of events. We must determine whether she accurately portrays Clare, or whether her portrait is subject to, and in fact affected by, her own growing jealousy and insecurity. In this regard, it is essential to ascertain precisely who is the tragic heroine—Irene who is on the verge of total mental disintegration or Clare whose desire for excitement brings about her sudden death.

Initially, *Passing* seems to be about Clare Kendry, inasmuch as most of the incidents plot out Clare's encounters with Irene and Black society. Furthermore, Irene sketches in detail Clare's physical appearance down to "[her] slim golden feet." Yet, she is unable to perceive the intangible aspects of Clare's character, and Larsen uses Irene's failure as a means of revealing disturbing aspects of her own psychological character. ⟨. . .⟩

Irene is literally obsessed with Clare's beauty, a beauty of such magnitude that she seems alien, impervious, indeed inscrutable. ⟨. . .⟩ Irene repeatedly describes Clare in hyperbole—"too vague," "too remote," "so dark and deep and unfathomable," "utterly strange," "incredibly beautiful," "utterly beyond any experience. . . ." These hyperbolic expressions are ambiguous. They create the impression that Clare is definitely, though indescribably, different from and superior to Irene and other ordinary people.

Irene's physical appearance, on the other hand, is drawn sketchily. We know that she has "warm olive skin" and curly black hair. Though Irene is not referred to as a beauty, given her confidence and social grace, we are inclined to believe that she is attractive. Despite the fact that little attention is given to Irene's physical portrayal, her encounter with Clare provides the occasion for the subtle revelation of her psychological character. Hence, the two portraits are polarized and mutually complementary—one is purely external, while the other is intensely internal.

> Claudia Tate, "Nella Larsen's *Passing:* A Problem of Interpretation," *Black American Literature Forum* 14, No. 4 (Winter 1980): 143–44

MARY HELEN WASHINGTON   Larsen's failure in dealing with ⟨. . .⟩ marginality is implicit in the very choice of "passing" as a symbol or metaphor of deliverance for her women. It is an obscene form of salvation. The woman who passes is required to deny everything about her past—her girlhood, her family, places with memories, folk customs, folk rhymes, her language, the entire long line of people who have gone before her. She lives in terror of discovery—what if she has a child with a dark complexion, what if she runs into an old school friend, how does she listen placidly to racial slurs? And more, where does the woman who passes find the equanimity to live by the privilege status that is based on the oppression of her own people?

Larsen's heroines are all finally destroyed somewhere down the paths they choose. Helga Crane loses herself in a loveless marriage to an old black preacher by whom she has five children in as many years. She finally retreats into illness and silence, eventually admitting to herself a suppressed hatred for her husband. *Passing's* Irene Redfield suspects an affair between her friend Clare (recently surfaced from the white world) and her black physician husband. This threatens her material and psychological security. In the novel's melodramatic ending, she pushes Clare off the balcony of a seventeenth-floor apartment and sinks into unconsciousness when she is questioned about Clare's death.

And Nella Larsen, who created Helga and Irene, chose oblivion for herself. From the little we know of the last 30 years of her life, she handled the problem of marginality by default, living entirely without any racial and cultural identity. Her exile was so complete that one of her biographers couldn't find an obituary for her: "I couldn't even bury Nella Larsen," she said.

But unlike the women in her novels, Larsen did not die from her marginality. She lived 70 years, was an active part of the high-stepping Harlem

Renaissance, traveled abroad, and worked as a nurse for 40 years. She was an unconventional woman by 1920s standards: she wore her dresses short, smoked cigarettes, rejected religion, and lived in defiance of the rules that most black women of her education and means were bound by. She lived through the conflicts of the marginal woman and felt them passionately. Why didn't she leave us the greater legacy of the mature model, the perceptions of a woman who confronts the pain, alienation, isolation, and grapples with these conundrums until new insight has been forged from the struggle? Why didn't she continue to write after 1929? ⟨. . .⟩

　　She did not solve her own problems, but Larsen made us understand as no one did before her that the image of the middle-class black woman as a coldly self-centered snob, chattering irrelevantly at bridge club and sorority meetings, was as much a mask as the grin on the face of Stepin Fetchit. The women in her novel, like Larsen, are driven to emotional and psychological extremes in their attempts to handle ambivalence, marginality, racism, and sexism. She has shown us that behind the carefully manicured exterior, behind the appearance of security is a woman who hears the beating of her wings against a walled prison.

　　　　Mary Helen Washington, "Nella Larsen: Mystery Woman of the Harlem Renais-
　　　　sance," Ms. 9, No. 6 (December 1980): 50

CHERYL A. WALL　　　The novels ⟨Larsen⟩ left behind prove that at least some of her promise was realized. Among the best written of the time, her books comment incisively on issues of marginality and cultural dualism that engaged Larsen's contemporaries, such as Jean Toomer and Claude McKay, but the bourgeois ethos of her novels has unfortunately obscured the similarities. However, Larsen's most striking insights are into psychic dilemmas confronting certain black women. To dramatize these, Larsen draws characters who are, by virtue of their appearance, education, and social class, atypical in the extreme. Swiftly viewed, they resemble the tragic mulattoes of literary convention. On closer examination, they become the means through which the author demonstrates the psychological costs of racism and sexism.

　　For Larsen, the tragic mulatto was the only formulation historically available to portray educated middle-class black women in fiction. But her protagonists subvert the convention consistently. They are neither noble nor long-suffering; their plights are not used to symbolize the oppression of blacks, the irrationality of prejudice, or the absurdity of concepts of race generally. Larsen's deviations from these traditional strategies signal that her concerns lie elsewhere, but only in the past decade have critics begun to decode her major themes. Both *Quicksand* and *Passing* contemplate the inextricability of the racism and sexism which confront the black woman in her quest for a wholly integrated identity. As they navigate between racial and cultural polarities, Larsen's protagonists attempt to fashion a sense of self free of both suffocating restrictions of ladyhood and fantasies of the exotic female Other. They fail. The tragedy for these mulattoes is the impossibility of self-definition. Larsen's protagonists assume false identities that ensure social survival but result in psychological suicide. In one way or another, they all "pass." Passing for white, Larsen's novels remind us, is only one way this game is played.

Cheryl A. Wall, "Passing for What? Aspects of Identity in Nella Larsen's Novels," Black American Literature Forum 20, Nos. 1–2 (Spring–Summer 1986): 97–98

DEBORAH E. McDOWELL   Although Irene is clearly deluded about her motives, her racial loyalty, her class, and her distinctness from Clare, the narrative suggests that her most glaring delusion concerns her feelings for Clare. ⟨. . .⟩ The narrative traces this developing eroticism in spatial terms. It begins on the roof of the Drayton hotel (with all the suggestions of the sexually illicit), intensifies at Clare's tea party, and, getting proverbially "close to home," explodes in Irene's own bedroom. Preoccupied with appearances, social respectability, and safety, however, Irene tries to force these emerging feelings underground. The narrative dramatizes that repression effectively in images of concealment and burial. Significantly, the novel's opening image is an envelope (a metaphoric vagina) which Irene hesitates to open, fearing its "contents would reveal" an "attitude toward danger." ⟨. . .⟩ Irene tries to preserve "a hardness from feeling" about the letter, though "brilliant red patches flamed" in her cheeks. Unable to explain her feelings for Clare, "for which she could find no name," Irene dismisses them as "Just somebody walking over [her] grave." The narrative suggests pointedly that Clare is the body walking over the grave of Irene's buried sexual feelings.

Lest the reader miss this eroticism, Larsen employs fire imagery—the conventional representation of sexual desire—introducing and instituting this imagery in the novel's opening pages. Irene begins her retrospective account of her reunion with Clare, remembering that the day was "hot," the sun "brutal" and "staring," its rays "like molten rain." Significantly, Irene, feeling "sticky and soiled from contact with so many sweating bodies," escapes to the roof of the Drayton Hotel where she is reunited with Clare, after a lapse of many years. (Irene is, ironically, "escaping" to the very thing she wants to avoid.) 〈. . .〉

Although the ending is ambiguous and the evidence circumstantial, I agree with Cheryl Wall that, "Larsen strongly implies that Irene pushes Clare through the window" 〈. . .〉 To suggest the extent to which Clare's death represents the death of Irene's sexual feelings for Clare, Larsen uses a clever objective correlative: Irene's pattern of lighting cigarettes and snuffing them out. Minutes before Clare falls from the window to her death, "Irene finished her cigarette and threw it out, watching the tiny spark drop slowly down to the white ground below." Clearly attempting a symbolic parallel, Clare is described as "a vital glowing thing, like a flame of red and gold" who falls from (or is thrown out of) the window as well. Because Clare is a reminder of that repressed and disowned part of Irene's self, Clare must be banished, for, more unacceptable than the feelings themselves is the fact that they find an object of expression in Clare. In other words, Clare is both the embodiment and the object of the sexual feelings that Irene banishes.

Larsen's becomes, in effect, a banishing act as well. Or put another way, the idea of bringing a sexual attraction between two women to full narrative expression is likewise, too dangerous a move 〈. . .〉 Larsen's clever narrative strategies almost conceal it. In *Passing* she uses a technique found commonly in narrative by Afro-American and women novelists with a "dangerous" story to tell: "safe" themes, plots, and conventions are used as the protective cover underneath which lie more dangerous subplots. Larsen envelops the subplot of Irene's developing if unnamed and unacknowledged desire for Clare in the safe and familiar plot of racial passing. Put another way, the novel's clever strategy derives from its surface theme and central metaphor— passing. It takes the form of the act it describes. Implying false, forged, and mistaken identities, the title functions on multiple levels: thematically, in terms of the racial and sexual plot; and strategically, in terms of the narrative's disguise.

Deborah E. McDowell, "Introduction," *Quicksand and Passing* (New Brunswick, NJ: Rutgers University Press, 1986), pp. xxvi–xxvii, xxix–xxx

HAZEL V. CARBY   Social relations which objectified the body permeate ⟨*Quicksand*⟩. Helga herself was represented as a consumer, a woman who defined a self through the acquisition of commercial products, consumer goods, and commodities. As a woman, she is at the center of a complex process of exchange. Money was crucial to Larsen's narrative, structuring power relations, controlling social movement, and defining the boundaries of Helga's environment. Money replaces kinship as the prime mediator of social relations: Helga's white uncle sent her money as he could not afford to acknowledge her relationship to him. This money allowed her social movement; she bought her way out of a Jim Crow car and eventually out of Harlem. In Chicago, Helga spent money, buying and consuming rather than facing her desperate conditions. While the possession of money disguises her real social predicament, the lack of money forced degradation and the recognition that in the job market her social position as a black woman was narrowly defined as domestic worker.

Although money permitted Helga's movement within the text, the direction of her journey reproduces the tensions of migration into a structure of oppositions between country and city. Helga's first movement in the text is from South to North, from the rural outskirts of Atlanta to industrial Chicago. Immediately upon arrival in Chicago, Helga became one of a crowd. Her initial identification was with the anonymity of the city, where she had the appearance of freedom but no actual home or friends. This anonymity brought brief satisfaction and contentment, while Helga could maintain her position as consumer, but she discovered her vulnerability as an object of exchange when her money ran out. Larsen represented the city as a conglomeration of strangers, where social relations were structured through the consumption of both objects and people. The imagery of commerce and this process of exchange dominated the text as it moved to New York and Copenhagen. This polarity between rural and urban experience frames the text; in the closing pages, all cities are finally abandoned and Helga is metaphorically and, the reader is led to assume, literally buried in the rural South. ⟨. . .⟩

⟨. . .⟩ Larsen's representation of both race and class are structured through a prism of black female sexuality. Larsen recognized that the repression of the sensual in Afro-American fiction in response to the long history of the exploitation of black sexuality led to the repression of passion and the repression or denial of female sexuality and desire. But, of course, the representation of black female sexuality meant risking its definition as primitive and exotic within a racist society. Larsen attempted to embody but could not hope to resolve these contradictions in her representation of Helga as a sexual being, making Helga the first truly sexual black female protagonist in Afro-American fiction. Racist sexual ideologies proclaimed the black woman to be a rampant sexual being, and in response black women writers either focused on defending their morality or displaced sexuality onto another terrain. Larsen confronted this denial directly in her fiction. Helga consistently attempted to deny her sensuality and repress her sexual desires, and the result is tragedy. Each of the crises of the text centered on sexual desire until the conclusion of the novel, where control over her body was denied Helga and her sexuality was reduced to its biological capacity to bear children. Helga's four children represented her entrapment as she was unable to desert them; her fifth child represented her certain death.

Hazel V. Carby, *Reconstructing Womanhood: The Emergence of the Afro-American Woman Novelist* (New York: Oxford University Press, 1987), pp. 173–74

ELIZABETH AMMONS   Clearly, Irene and Clare are doubles. Clare represents for Irene the dangerous side of herself—foreign, outlawed— that she as a respectable middle-class black woman has successfully denied. Clare is sexual, daring, creative. She has moved out of African American bourgeois culture; she roams free of its demands for conformity and social service and endless attention to familial and community uplift.

But where has this "freedom" taken Clare? Her life as a white woman is hollow and self-destructive; it represents a pact with self-loathing, a project in self-erasure. Her true self is so unknown to the white man she has married and with whom she has had a child that she lives daily with his racist and hideously ironic nickname for her, "Nig." To tell him why the appellation is particularly offensive would be to lose the position of "freedom" she has created for herself. To remain silent is to acquiesce in the system of self-degradation that she has bought into. ⟨. . .⟩

Complicating these conflicting possibilities even further, Larsen allows us to know Clare's story only through another woman no less conflicted, dishonest, or cowardly than Clare. Dutiful, repressed, correct, Irene clearly *needs* Clare dead. ⟨. . .⟩ She pushes Clare out the window.

Or does Clare jump? We cannot say. We can surmise either possibility— or, paradoxically, in this novel about split and conflicting identities and possibilities—both. If Clare and Irene, finally, are alienated parts of one potentially whole identity, to say that Clare jumped is the same as to say that Irene pushed her, and vice versa. In either case, Larsen's story about the black woman artist in *Passing* ends in permanent silence. The divisions between respectable middle-class feminine status and the woman artist, between heterosexual and lesbian desire, and between acceptance in white and black America are unbridgeable.

> Elizabeth Ammons, "Jumping out the Window: Nella Larsen's *Passing* and the End of an Era," *Conflicting Stories: American Women Writers at the Turn into the Twentieth Century* (New York: Oxford University Press, 1991), pp. 190–91

JONATHAN LITTLE   Larsen, obviously aware of the traditions before her, chooses not to depict such serene returns ⟨to the African-American community⟩ for her ⟨mulatto⟩ characters in *Passing*. Even after returning back across the color line into the Black community, Clare Kendry finds no peace, rest, loyalty—or any real security. Clare's racial origins are revealed to her white racist husband at a party held at the Freelands' apartment. The "freeland" is free in one respect. Clare is finally "let out" of her marriage by the discovery. Earlier she had told her friend, Irene Redfield, " 'But if Jack [her husband] finds out, if our marriage is broken, that lets me out. Doesn't it?' " The freeland Clare attains is finally ironic, however, since she promptly falls to her death, pushed by the same friend in whom she had so closely confided. In killing Clare off, Larsen does not depict any "freeland" or supportive community that will embrace Clare in her process of returning. Larsen undermines romantic convention, substituting ironic tragedy where there had been joy.

Even further, Larsen implies that there is no longer a Black community anywhere in the world to return to. Oddly enough, in *Passing*, Brazil, instead of Africa, is evoked as the quintessential text of racial equality and haven from North American white oppression. Irene Redfield, the narrative consciousness in *Passing*, reports that her husband Brian is enamored with Brazil and longs to escape there, away from racist Harlem, away from what he calls " 'this hellish place.' " Even this vision, however, is ironized, showing the extent of Brian's romantic delusions. By the end of the twenties, the hopes of a Brazilian paradise, the "Eldorado" of the South, were shattered. Thus Larsen chose Brazil instead of Africa for a reason: By the time she wrote *Passing* in 1929, Brazil symbolized a deflated and ironic hope for an alternative community that was more a romantic dream than a reality. Larsen's irony, then, extends beyond the confines of her text to show how the weave of disillusionment runs through the global environment, and not just through bourgeois Black Harlem.

Larsen's letters (1925–1932) to Carl Van Vechten (to whom, along with his wife, Fania Marinoff, Larsen dedicated *Passing*) affirm the view of Larsen as a skeptic. Consistent with her distance from the cause of racial uplift shown in her novels, she wrote to Van Vechten that she "wanted very much the pleasure of refusing" an invitation to the Women's Auxiliary of the NAACP tea held in her honor in 1928. At the same time, however, she also attacked misguided and perhaps unintentionally racist white liberal thinking ⟨. . .⟩

In her fiction and in her letters, Larsen does not offer any final messages or final Truth(s) that will clear away racial and social difficulties. This orientation prevents Larsen from portraying a triumphant character or social utopia. Every direction she offers is quickly undercut by a counter-dilemma— e.g., Brazil is no longer available as a social and racial utopia. Even the traditional passing for white plot is undermined. There is no supportive "birthright" to which her passers may serenely return.

Jonathan Little, "Nella Larsen's *Passing*: Irony and the Critics," *African American Review* 26, No. 1 (1992): 174–75

DAVID L. BLACKMORE   The implications of Larsen's "flirtation" ⟨in *Passing*⟩ with both female and male homosexuality are radical. For Irene, lesbianism offers an alternative to repressive middle-class marriages. As an African-American woman, Irene must inevitably confront the stereotype that women of her race are Jezebels. White American culture tells her that black female identity centers around desire, that in fact an African American woman is nothing but a beast driven by irrepressible sexuality. The key, then, to combating this stereotype lies in the repression of sexuality, in the confinement of desire to the constricted realm of the respectable marriage. Doing her part to dispel the Jezebel myth, Irene plays the role of the eminently respectable, asexual mother/wife. In focusing her energies and identity on her husband and sons, she deflects attention away from her own sexual nature. ⟨. . .⟩

It is unclear whether Larsen's suggestion of a lesbian relationship as an alternative to Irene's repressive marriage reflects a sexual decision she made or contemplated in her own life. However, her literary experimentation with non-traditional sexuality mirrors a larger trend in 1920s' Harlem, where lesbianism and particularly female bisexuality received a great deal of attention as naughty but exciting options for adventurous, "modern" women. As Lillian Faderman details in her recent book *Odd Girls and Twilight Lovers*, a visible black lesbian subculture was established in Harlem early in the century. Furthermore, large numbers of whites flocked to Harlem in the '20s "to experience homosexuality as the epitome of the forbidden." The perception of upper Manhattan as a center of laissez-faire sexuality drew both blacks and whites who wished to observe or participate in sexual practices deemed immoral by the white establishment. ⟨. . .⟩

Just as a romance with Clare would provide an alternative to Irene's emotionally empty existence, so leading a homosexual life in Brazil would free Brian from his own unsatisfying role in bourgeois Harlem society. In Brazil he would face less pressure to " 'care for ladies.' " He could express more openly his attraction to other men; he could, in fact, engage in sexual activity that would not be the " 'joke' " that straight sex is to him. He would be free of his unwanted role as sexual overlord to his wife, and free to determine for himself the role a man should play in sexual and social relationships. No longer the "empowered" yet burdened provider for a family, he would also no longer be the segregated subordinate in a white man's world. Brian's Brazil provides an alternate vision of an Afro-centric sphere in which a man need not provide for a woman and where men may love each other freely. This, surely, is a radical vision on Larsen's part.

> David L. Blackmore, " 'That Unreasonable Restless Feeling': The Homosexual Sub-texts of Nella Larsen's *Passing*," *African American Review* 26, No. 3 (1992): 478–79, 481

◈ *Bibliography*

Quicksand. 1928.

Passing. 1929.

An Intimation of Things Distant: Collected Fiction. Ed. Charles R. Larson. 1992.

Terry McMillan
b. 1951

TERRY L. MCMILLAN was born October 18, 1951, in Port Huron, Michigan. Her parents, Edward McMillan and Madeline Washington Tillman, were uneducated laborers who had to support six children. This task was made more difficult by the fact that Edward McMillan was an alcoholic; his death when his daughter was sixteen created still more hardship for the family. Terry McMillan took a job at a library that year, which she credits with introducing her to literature.

After graduating from high school, McMillan traveled to Los Angeles to attend a community college; she later transferred to the University of California at Berkeley. While in college she discovered black literature and also met and befriended writer and critic Ishmael Reed, who enabled her to publish her first short story, "The End," in 1976. She graduated from Berkeley with a B.A. in journalism in 1979 and then briefly attended film school at Columbia University before dropping out. For the next few years she supported herself by word processing while attempting to publish various short stories and eventually being accepted into the Harlem Writers Guild.

In 1983, McMillan was accepted at the MacDowell artists colony and then the Yaddo writers colony, where she quickly produced the first draft of *Mama*, a highly autobiographical novel about a poor family's struggles to survive. When the novel was published in 1987, McMillan, dissatisfied with her publisher's efforts, decided to promote the novel on her own, sending over 3,000 letters to bookstores and universities and establishing her reputation as an excellent reader and speaker. Her successful debut garnered her a National Endowment for the Arts Fellowship in 1988 and was followed by *Disappearing Acts* in 1989. The novel concerns a rocky relationship between a well-educated woman and her construction-worker boyfriend, Franklin Swift. While a commercial and critical success, it resulted in a $4.75 million defamation suit against McMillan filed by Leonard Welch, a former lover and the father of McMillan's only child, Solomon Welch, who maintained that the novel and specifically the character of Franklin

Swift were created solely to denigrate his character. The New York Supreme Court ruled in McMillan's favor in April 1991.

McMillan edited an anthology, entitled *Breaking Ice: An Anthology of Contemporary African-American Fiction*, in 1990 and contributed a critical essay to *Five for Five: The Films of Spike Lee* in 1991. In 1992, she published her most popular book, the best-selling *Waiting to Exhale*, a novel about four black women who are searching for suitable mates. The novel, written out of McMillan's frustrations with her own singleness, created a sensation and led to a number of lucrative paperback, movie, and foreign rights deals.

McMillan taught at the University of Wyoming at Laramie from 1987 to 1990, then as a tenured professor at the University of Arizona from 1990 to 1992. She currently lives with her son in Danville, California, where she is working on a film adaptation of *Waiting to Exhale*.

▣ *Critical Extracts*

CAROLYN SEE   Mildred is a black woman, and this ⟨*Mama*⟩ is a "black" novel, but in the most profound sense that's not the point. In America, where one in every two marriages ends in divorce, where women earn 59 cents for every dollar men earn, something like 50% of all American families are eventually going to be involved with aspects either of matriarchy or poverty. The author's artistic question here is—how does that dynamic work? Can children raised that way *live*? ⟨. . .⟩

Freda, that oldest girl who had to give up her Christmas presents and act as a substitute mama to the younger kids whenever her own mama went under, opts for education as her way out. She moves to Los Angeles, finds a bachelor apartment with a glittery ceiling, and proceeds by fits and starts through the university system.

But there's a moment—up in Marin County, when she and some handsome gent lounge in a hot tub, buzzing on cocaine—when the reader realizes that Freda and her mama are caught in the same trap. And it's not just men, and not just white society. It's alcohol and drugs and the wish to use sex as oblivion, a way not to notice the demands of the outside world. These are the patterns that Mildred and Freda share.

The story here, then, is what happens to people when they're locked out of mainstream life. Terry McMillan only mentions in one sentence that white journalists in New York aren't exactly waiting on pins and needles for a penniless black woman to come and join their ranks. The racism, the "oppression" she's addressing comes from far, far back, and it's been completely internalized. If you didn't deserve to have electric lights in your house when you were a kid, how can you deserve freedom, happiness and love when you've grown up?

The end here should not be given away, but the author suggests, almost as a Zen exercise, that the first way for the locked-out to break from the prison of their souls is to love each other; that if all those who are "locked out" could turn to each other for comfort and love and support, then it might be the tight, white, Establishment patriarchy that might end up, in fact, locked in.

Carolyn See, "Down-and-Out Family, Out of the Mainstream, Wants In," *Los Angeles Times*, 23 February 1987, p. V4

VALERIE SAYERS   Terry McMillan's new novel is a love story waiting to explode. The lovers of *Disappearing Acts* are both intelligent and good-looking, both possessed of dreams—but Zora Banks is an educated black woman and Franklin Swift is an unschooled black man. It's Brooklyn, it's 1982, and it's clear from page 1 that the two of them are sitting in a mine field and something's going to blow.

Ms. McMillan's first novel, *Mama,* was original in concept and style, a runaway narrative pulling a crowded cast of funny, earthy characters. *Disappearing Acts* is also full of momentum, and it's a pleasurable, often moving novel. In this intricate look at a love affair, Ms. McMillan strikes out in a whole new direction and changes her narrative footing with ease. But *Disappearing Acts* is also a far more conventional popular novel than *Mama* was. Despite its raunchy language and its narrative construction (Franklin's voice and Zora's alternate), its descriptions, its situations, even its generic minor characters are often predictable. I say this with some surprise, because it seems to me that Terry McMillan has the power to be an important contemporary novelist. ⟨. . .⟩

Zora's voice, though generally likeable, has a bland quality (Franklin's son says she "talk like white people"), and her narrative is sometimes written in a pop-magazine style that has her forever reminding her readers how handsome Franklin is. ⟨. . .⟩

⟨. . .⟩ Franklin Swift is smart, bigoted, passionate, loving, generous, mean-spirited, ignorant, intractable, forgiving, resentful. His voice is far grittier than Zora's and it's genuine. In addition, Ms. McMillan takes some real chances not only with Franklin's voice but with his life. Summarized, his history makes him sound like a loser: he's a high school dropout who's played with drugs and seen the inside of a prison; a man who despises his mother and his wife; a father who sees and supports his two children sporadically; a lover who sometimes asks for sex in a repellent, coarse whine; an expectant father so frustrated by his dealings with the white construction world that he hits a pregnant Zora—and later does worse. Much worse.

The miracle is that Ms. McMillan takes the reader so deep into this man's head—and makes what goes on there so complicated—that his story becomes not only comprehensible but affecting. The reader comes to see why Zora loves him, and why she kicks him out. Franklin is a more compelling character than Zora because he's allowed his moments of childishness and even wickedness: he's a whole person. Ms. McMillan's portrayal of this man may well be controversial (anybody looking for a successful, strong-but-gentle African-American male won't find him here), but it's undeniably alive.

Valerie Sayers, "Someone to Walk Over Me," *New York Times Book Review*, 6 August 1989, p. 8

DAVID NICHOLSON   For the past decade or more, books by black women have appeared in such numbers as to constitute almost a separate genre within an all too frequently ghettoized American literature. Surely, however, this second novel by Terry McMillan ⟨*Disappearing Acts*⟩ must be one of the few to contain rounded, sympathetic portraits of black men and to depict relationships between black men and black women as something more than the relationship between victimizer and victim, oppressor and oppressed.

For that, and for daring to create a heroine who, though disappointed in love, does not condemn all men or retreat to militant homosexuality, McMillan deserves applause. She has refused to perpetuate the well-worn conventions of black women's writing. And, in fact, she may have created a whole new category—the post-feminist black urban romance novel.

The novel concerns the two-year affair of Franklin Swift, a high-school dropout in his 30s who works intermittently doing construction, and Zora Banks (yes, she *is* named after the novelist, anthropologist and free spirit of the Harlem Renaissance), a junior high school music teacher who wants to become a singer. ⟨. . .⟩

⟨. . .⟩ Their biggest problem ⟨. . .⟩ is the difference in their backgrounds.

That last device is, of course, one of the oldest in literature, but the specifics here are of particular relevance to black Americans. Professional black women complain of an ever-shrinking pool of eligible men, citing statistics that show the number of black men in prison is increasing, while the number of black men in college is decreasing. Articles on alternatives for women, from celibacy to "man-sharing" to relationships with blue-collar workers like Franklin, have long been a staple of black general interest and women's magazines. ⟨. . .⟩

Despite the "equal time" given Franklin and the sympathetic way in which he is portrayed, this is, I think, a women's novel. I can't imagine most men liking it, in part because of the hard truths Zora and her friends have to tell (in the female equivalent of lockerroom bull sessions) about men they've known. Mostly, though, it's that there is a sweetness about *Disappearing Acts;* it is really an old-fashioned love story, albeit a sincere one. ⟨. . .⟩

For all that is good about this novel, however, I like it more for what it represents than for what it achieves, and I think McMillan deserves congratulations for what she has attempted, not for what she has accomplished.

David Nicholson, "Love's Old Sweet Song," *Washington Post Book World,* 27 August 1989, p. 6

THULANI DAVIS   Now that the '90s are at hand, it's inevitable that someone will announce a new generation of writers, folks who'll be the bridge to the next century. (WOW!) The "new generation" of African-American writers, novelist Terry McMillan said not too long ago, are "different from a generation before" because "they are not as race oriented, and they are not as protest oriented." I wondered at first who she was talking about. The novelists being published right now are, for the most part, around 40. Most of them began getting published 20 years ago, but those who were the talk of the '70s seem wildly different—and I mean wildly—from the crew McMillan is describing. The young writers back then were full of the anger, rhythms, sexuality, and wicked humor of jazz, r&b, and the '60s. I doubt if anyone would have guessed that the next generation was going to be less "race oriented." ⟨. . .⟩

If four novels published in the past few months, including one by McMillan, are any indication, there *is* a crop of African-American fiction coming in the '90s, written by 40ish folk, that's less interested in race and protest. It speaks in the practiced tongue of white mainstream literature. Melvin Dixon, Marita Golden, Tina McElroy Ansa, and McMillan show in their work a silent—in some cases maybe unconscious—struggle with assimilation. Each of their books describes some part of the lonely, self-involved journey of the middle-class African American who has access to some little piece of the Dream and is as deeply ensconced in American mass culture as in our boisterous yet closely held black world. ⟨. . .⟩

Even though Zora and Franklin ⟨of *Disappearing Acts*⟩ are last-week contemporary, they are also like classic folklore characters come to life in Brooklyn. She's the wily black woman of yore, smart-talking Eve who's always got a little something on the rail for the lizard, as we used to say. She's also a sophisticated shopper, who likes fancy cheeses and bottled water, and she says shit all the time. Zora has all the pulls and tugs of feminism versus the feminine that a modern black woman who's read Walker and Shange is supposed to have. She's not unlike Zora Neale Hurston's sassy folk women—characters *Cosmo* would never dare to pop-psychoanalyze.

Complicated as Franklin is supposed to be, he is a savvy urban John Henry—he don't take no tea fo' the fever. An intellectual Tina Turner meets a hardhat Ike. They are both bricks and though they may chip each other, they ain't never gonna blend. They live and work in New York City, but are in a very insulated world; their problems are completely personal. Their relationship is doomed by mutual expectations and ended by an outburst of gratuitous male violence. Let's just say it wasn't needed for the love affair to fall apart.

These two are as they are; like other folk heroes, they don't change much, or drag skeletons out of the closet, and they learn their lessons the hard way. They've been created by years of past mythologizing, drawn their images from popular culture, black and white. They are black, sho' nuff—the last thing I would say about McMillan's people is that they ain't black—but they're black in big, bold strokes. And that means her work will continue to raise questions among African Americans about the fuzzy line between realism and popular misconception. And at the same time, McMillan is, as she said, less race-conscious. She confines herself to the day-to-day life struggle, as told from behind the mask Claude McKay so poignantly described. McMillan uses, almost exclusively, the performance side of black character, emphasizing the most public, most familiar aspects of us. If you smell a little song and dance in the self-sufficient ribaldry, it's there.

Thulani Davis, "Don't Worry, Be Buppie: Black Novelists Head for the Mainstream," *Voice Literary Supplement* No. 85 (May 1990): 26, 29

TERRY McMILLAN   As a child, I didn't know that African-American people wrote books. I grew up in a small town in northern Michigan, where the only books I came across were the Bible and required reading for school. I did not read for pleasure, and it wasn't until I was sixteen when I got a job shelving books at the public library that I got lost in a book. It was a biography of Louisa May Alcott. I was excited because I had not really read about poor white folks before; her father was so eccentric and idealistic that at the time I just thought he was crazy. I related to Louisa because she had to help support her family at a young age, which was what I was doing at the library.

Then one day I went to put a book away, and saw James Baldwin's face staring up at me. "Who in the world is this?" I wondered. I remember feeling embarrassed and did not read his book because I was too afraid. I couldn't imagine that he'd have anything better or different to say than Thomas Mann, Henry Thoreau, Ralph Waldo Emerson, Nathaniel Hawthorne, Ernest Hemingway, William Faulkner, etc. and a horde of other mostly white male writers that I'd been introduced to in Literature 101 in high school. I mean, not only had there not been any African-American authors included in any of those textbooks, but I'd never been given a clue that if we did have anything important to say that somebody would actually publish it. Needless to say, I was not just naïve, but had not yet acquired an ounce of black pride. I never once questioned why there were no representative works by us in any of those textbooks. After all, I had never heard of any African-American writers, and no one I knew hardly read *any* books. ⟨. . .⟩

Not once, throughout my entire four years as an undergraduate, did it occur to me that I might one day *be* a writer. I mean, these folks had genuine knowledge and insight. They also had a fascination with the truth. They had something to write about. Their work was bold, not flamboyant. They learned how to exploit the language so that the readers would be affected by what they said and how they said it. And they had talent.

I never considered myself to be in possession of much of the above, and yet when I was twenty years old the first man I fell in love with broke my heart. I was so devastated and felt so helpless that my reaction manifested itself in a poem. I did not sit down and say, "I'm going to write a poem about this." It was more like magic. I didn't even know I was writing a poem until I had written it. Afterward, I felt lighter, as if something had happened to lessen the pain. And when I read this "thing" I was shocked because I didn't know where the words came from. I was scared, to say the least, about what I had just experienced, because I didn't understand what had happened. ⟨. . .⟩

⟨. . .⟩ I ended up majoring in journalism because writing was "easy" for me, but it didn't take long for me to learn that I did not like answering the "who, what, when, where, and why" of anything. I then—upon the urging of my mother and friends who had graduated and gotten "normal" jobs—decided to try something that would still allow me to "express myself" but was relatively safer, though still risky: I went to film school. Of course what was inherent in my quest to find my "spot" in the world was this whole notion of affecting people on some grand scale. Malcolm and Martin caused me to think like this. Writing for me, as it's turned out, is philanthropy. It didn't take years for me to realize the impact that other writers' work had had on me, and if I was going to write, I did not want to write inconsequential, mediocre stories that didn't conjure up or arouse much in a reader. So I had to start by exciting myself and paying special attention to what I cared about, what mattered to me.

Film school didn't work out. Besides, I never could stop writing, which ultimately forced me to stop fighting it. It took even longer to realize that writing was not something you aspired to, it was something you did because you had to.

Terry McMillan, "Introduction," *Breaking Ice: An Anthology of Contemporary African-American Fiction*, ed. Terry McMillan (New York: Viking, 1990), pp. xv–xviii

JACQUELINE TRESCOTT   As a novelist McMillan explores black family relationships through a yeasty jumble of contemporary hardships and blessings. As an essayist she reveals the feelings of one black woman's questions about single parenthood, the lack of male friendships, the dissatisfactions of wanting to be physically perfect. Once she elicited an echo of Amens across the country's phone lines with these words on black men: "They're like an itch we can't reach and won't be satisfied until we scratch it."

For the last few weeks, she has been on the road, discussing *Breaking Ice: An Anthology of Contemporary African-American Fiction,* which she edited. ⟨. . .⟩ In the wake of its praise, she has been indulging in the joy of introducing some lesser-known writers to a wider audience. ⟨. . .⟩

Breaking Ice was born out of a need to correct the publishing industry's neglect of black writers, to provide a handy reference book for some of the writing of the 1970s and 1980s and to share some of the good words she was reading. The anthology contains the works of esteemed veterans such as John A. Williams, Paule Marshall, Alice Walker and Amiri Baraka but also the lesser-known work of Barbara Neely, Steven Corbin, Doris Jean Austin and Randall Kenan.

"There are very few areas where you will see our work on a continuous basis," McMillan says. Three years ago when she was teaching at the University of Wyoming, Laramie, she was bothered by an edition of a short story collection. "It just hit me, there are no black writers, no Third World writers," she says. "I am like, 'hold it a minute.' " Her anger led to research and a book proposal drawing from the 30 non-household names that "popped into my head."

Why do black writers continue to be overlooked, except for the burst of enthusiasm for black female writers during the last decade and the occasional male entry?

"Lack of respect," says McMillan. "In some ways it is laced with racism but not always. . . . Right now that doesn't happen to be the case with me because my work is getting a lot of attention. A lot of people at readings ask, 'Terry, how did you get to be so successful?' I haven't thought of myself as successful until you people remind me of it. I say to be honest with you I think the white folks chose me as the flavor of the year. Next year it could be someone else." ⟨. . .⟩

Attention to McMillan's work enabled her to push for the anthology. ⟨. . .⟩ And she has edited a work that, like her fiction, grabs the hand and leads to discovery. Arranged in alphabetical order, the book does not have the traditional groupings of humor, science fiction or folk tale categories.

"I wanted it to be democratic, I wanted it to reflect the diversity of our experiences. That is why it is gay, lesbian, erotic, science fiction," she says. What emerged during those two decades are stories of love, identity, family, age and transition. The themes of protest are retreating, she says. "There are no stories about anger or rage unless the character was angry. Not when the writer was angry."

Jacqueline Trescott, "The Urban Author, Straight to the Point," *Washington Post*, 17 November 1990, pp. D1, D4

CHARLES R. LARSON   In the climactic scene of Terry McMillan's wickedly acerbic third novel, *Waiting to Exhale*, four African-American women—Gloria, Savannah, Bernadine and Robin, all between the ages of 34 and 38—celebrate the birthday of the youngest by drinking five bottles of champagne and talking about their on-going problems with men. All of them are single and/or recently divorced and "waiting to exhale"—yearning for the ideal mate who takes your breath away, although he never seems to materialize.

Furthermore, these women are all economically independent, horny and explicit in their feelings. Among other things, they conclude that the problem with black men is that they are "with white women," "gay," "ugly," "stupid," "in prison," "unemployed," "crackheads," "short," "liars," "unreliable," "irresponsible," "too possessive," "dogs," "shallow," "stuck in the sixties," "arrogant," "childish," "wimps" and too "old and set in their ways."

McMillan's dialogue is raunchy and wild, half black street speech and half one-liners. It's as if we're listening to four foul-mouth stand-up comediennes—all of them lashing out blindly at MEN. ⟨. . .⟩

While the dialogue sparkles throughout, the F-word appears so frequently that one has the feeling that McMillan is trying to one-up Spike Lee (whose films are alluded to a number of times). Indeed, McMillan seems to have written her novel with one eye on Hollywood and the other on the sisterhood of educated, articulate, independent black women who are very successful in their professions but frustrated and neurotic about the fact that there are so few black men they consider their equals.

This problem of mating is, however, about the only true lament of this otherwise very funny novel. Because of her biting comic tone, McMillan's work is distanced from that of a number of her contemporaries (Toni Morrison, Alice Walker, Marita Golden, for example). Although *Waiting to Exhale* is rooted in ethnicity, that ethnicity is never angry, bitter or bleak. One of McMillan's characters says, "I don't have anything against most white folks." The issue is gender, not race, and, above all, the question of sisterhood. ⟨. . .⟩

When Lorraine Hansberry wrote *A Raisin in the Sun* back in 1959, one critic accused her of writing a Jewish play about people who happened to be black. I can hear readers on the beach this summer laughing away and saying something like that about *Waiting to Exhale*.

These aren't black women; they're most women at a certain point of no return. And that may make you think about race—if not gender—in a totally different light.

> Charles R. Larson, "The Comic Unlikelihood of Finding Mr. Right," *Chicago Tribune Books*, 31 May 1992, pp. 6–7

CAROLYN SEE   It's inappropriate to compare Terry McMillan's third novel, *Waiting to Exhale*, to the works of other contemporary black women writers, like Alice Walker, Toni Morrison, Bebe Moore Campbell. This work isn't lofty, luminous or particularly "brilliant."

It also isn't right to stick McMillan in a box with elegant black *guy* writers, like charming Charles Johnson or grouchy Ishmael Reed. McMillan's new work is part of another genre entirely, so new it doesn't really have a name yet. This genre has to do with women, triumph, revenge, comradeship.

McMillan's immediate literary predecessor is, oddly enough, Olivia Goldsmith, who, last March, gave us *The First Wives Club*. There, four (white) women, having been dumped by their brutal, insolent, materialistic husbands, banded together and found justice—not by ruining their husbands, who weren't worth the effort, but by learning to live well on their own terms: to become, like that legendary lady in Chaucer's *Canterbury Tales*, their own women, well at ease.

McMillan sets up four middle-class black women, living in the highly symbolic town of Phoenix (because all of them will rise up, glorious, from the ashes of their present lives). This quartet is not oppressed greatly—or at all—by the problem of race. "White folks" wander around the periphery of this story like sad, soft, wiggly worms.

McMillan's plucky females are beleaguered, put upon, bugged, by black men—their misdeeds, their absences, their lies, their treachery. It's a tough life for a smart, pretty black woman. Maybe the only way to fight the system-as-it-exists is to unite to conquer. ⟨. . .⟩

These women help each other, cheer each other up, turn nightmare nights into daytime laughs. *Waiting to Exhale* has been marked to be a commercial success and it should be (it debuted June 7 at No. 5 on the bestseller list). Like *The First Wives Club*, it is a paean to the sisterhood of all women and should put the fear of God into any husband squirreling money away in numbered Swiss accounts against his upcoming divorce.

Carolyn See, "A Novel of Women: Triumph, Revenge and Comradeship," *Los Angeles Times*, 22 June 1992, p. E2

DANIEL MAX   Terry McMillan, at age 40, might just be as far as you can get from the traditional image of a tweedy novelist. She wears stylish clothes, lives in a plush Southwestern-style house in Danville, near Oakland, and rolls off the amounts of money made or owed to her with the ease of an agent—book advances, foreign publishing contracts, movie option money, book club money, reserves held against returns. She has a walk-in closet with rows of designer dresses and negligees. And she collects earrings, favoring ones with great dangling hoops and pyramids. Big earrings are one of her signatures. Another is her white sun-roofed BMW that still bears Arizona plates, a vestige of her last teaching assignment, in Tucson. ⟨. . .⟩

McMillan frequently draws from her own life for her fiction. Critics often object to her simple characters and dialogue-driven plots. Nonetheless, they regard her as an important chronicler of 1990's black life. ⟨. . . *Waiting to Exhale's*⟩ emphasis on brand names—BMW, Coach leather, Calvin Klein and Perrier—has earned the author the title of "the black Judith Krantz," but this is indicative more of how unfamiliar whites are with successful blacks than of the novel's content. Except for Bernadine, who is truly affluent, these women are only solidly middle class—it is their delight in their success that makes them seem richer.

McMillan's relationship with the white world is marked by such misinterpretations. A mutual fascination framed by uneasy jousting prevails. "They keep talking about my energy or something," she says, suspecting a putdown. Touring the Capitol and the Supreme Court with a group of writers last year as part of the PEN/Faulkner prize ceremonies, she wandered around the echoing marble halls with a minority phalanx, the black essayist Al Young and the novelist Charles Johnson, as well as the Asian-American novelist Amy Tan, teasing all the while that she wanted to introduce herself to the suspicious white faces in suits as the pop singer Anita Baker, playing with their inability to distinguish among black faces. ⟨. . .⟩

McMillan walks an even trickier line with black intellectuals. Despite the harsh portrait she paints of them, some black men are surprisingly supportive. Spike Lee contributed a blurb for *Waiting to Exhale*. Ishmael Reed, who elsewhere has been vociferous in opposing male-bashing by black female writers, nevertheless is a friend of McMillan's and has helped her. But McMillan has done less well with black female novelists. Alice Walker, Toni Morrison and Gloria Naylor, names often on McMillan's mind, are nowhere to be found on her book jackets. ⟨. . .⟩

What this reveals, on one level, is McMillan's search for literary respect. McMillan can remember the length of the reviews of all her books. "Am I gonna get a boxed interview this time [in *The New York Times Book Review*]?" she asked before the publication of *Waiting to Exhale*. In fact she did not, symptomatic to her of a lack of appreciation from established literary circles: "The bottom line is that at this point I've applied five or six years in a row for a Guggenheim and I can't get one. The same is true for a box in *The Times*. You can't beg for respect."

Paradoxically, the most radical and perhaps most important aspect of McMillan's success may be her very conventionality. She writes the kind of popular books white authors have long written, but which black authors were discouraged from undertaking because publishing wisdom decreed that black people didn't buy books.

Daniel Max, "McMillan's Millions," *New York Times Magazine*, 9 August 1992, pp. 20, 22–24

FRANCES STEAD SELLERS   Most black women writers are associated with a recognizable tradition of serious, ideologically inspired black literature, written primarily for "concerned" whites and black intellectuals. McMillan, however, has little truck with ideology of any kind. She writes to entertain, by providing the type of sexy, popular novel that has been making Jilly Cooper and Danielle Steel rich for years.

Written for and about educated black women, *Waiting to Exhale* reflects the growing numbers of successful African-Americans who have fled the drugs and violence of the ghettoes for fashionable neighbourhoods, while trying to preserve a uniquely black cultural heritage. McMillan's characters believe in black solidarity. To act like a white is an act of betrayal. "White folks" hover disconcertingly on the novel's margins. 〈. . .〉

〈. . .〉 McMillan's generalized male-bashing has understandably alienated some black men. Her portrayal of women may be more sympathetic, but it is equally shallow. Her characters' preoccupation with deodorants, douches and dates soon grows wearisome. And the attention McMillan draws to male-female rifts within the African-American community seems at odds with the black solidarity she otherwise implicitly approves.

But whether her views are politically correct or not, McMillan has hit a nerve. Many African-American women identify with her heroines. Using the vibrant street-talk McMillan grew up speaking, her protagonists tackle sexual issues that most women can relate to.

It may in part be concern to avoid accusations of racism that has prevented some critics putting this book firmly where it belongs—among the glitzy, commercial women's novels. Its one true importance is that it appeals to a market that American publishers have previously overlooked—the new black middle class. But its literary merits are modest.

Frances Stead Sellers, [Review of *Waiting to Exhale*], *Times Literary Supplement*, 6 November 1992, p. 20

▨ *Bibliography*

Mama. 1987.

Disappearing Acts. 1989.

Breaking Ice: An Anthology of Contemporary African-American Fiction (editor). 1990.

Waiting to Exhale. 1992.

⬧ ⬧ ⬧

Paule Marshall
b. 1929

PAULE MARSHALL was born Paula Burke on April 9, 1929, the daughter of Samuel and Ada Burke. Her parents had emigrated from Barbados, and Paule grew up in West Indian neighborhoods in Brooklyn, New York. She kept close ties with Barbadian culture in both America and Barbados. She received a B.A. from Brooklyn College in 1953 and briefly pursued a master's degree at Hunter College while working as a librarian and a staff writer for *Our World* magazine. At the same time she began writing stories and articles for a variety of periodicals. She married Kenneth E. Marshall in 1950; they had one child and divorced in 1963.

Marshall's first novel, *Brown Girl, Brownstones* (1959), set in the West Indian neighborhoods of Brooklyn, tells of a young woman's struggle for identity in the West Indian subculture. Critics have characterized the novel as a *Bildungsroman* and compared it to Zora Neale Hurston's *Their Eyes Were Watching God*. It is marked by rich language, perhaps influenced by the oral traditions preserved in the West Indian community of her childhood, and sensitive character portrayal. The novel was a critical success but a commercial failure.

In 1960 Marshall was awarded a Guggenheim Fellowship to work on *Soul Clap Hands and Sing* (1961), her second book, a collection of tales bound generally by the theme of race. This volume, which won the Rosenthal Award from the National Institute of Arts and Letters, contains four long stories about African descendants in the United States, the Caribbean, and South America and their race relations with other immigrant groups. Marshall contrasts traditional African spiritual values with the commercialism and materialism of the New World.

Although Marshall received a Ford Foundation grant for 1964–65 and a National Endowment for the Arts grant for 1967–69, her next novel, *The Chosen Place, the Timeless People* did not appear until 1969. In this work Marshall examines, with the eye of an anthropologist, the changing society of a third-world Caribbean community as it emerges from under colonial rule.

In 1970 Marshall became a lecturer on creative writing at Yale University. She has served as guest lecturer at other universities, including Oxford, Columbia, Michigan State, and Cornell. In 1970 she married Nourry Menard. Her third novel, *Praisesong for the Widow* (1983), returns to the theme of the destructive power of materialism and exhibits Marshall's interest in mythology and historical memory. It won the Before Columbus Foundation Book Award in 1984. *Reena and Other Stories*, gathering tales written since 1962, also appeared in 1983.

Marshall's long-awaited fourth novel, *Daughters* (1991), is the complex tale of a New York woman of West Indian heritage struggling to come to terms both with racial tensions in the U.S. and with the family she left on a small island in the Caribbean. It too was generally well received by critics.

Marshall and her husband now live alternately in New York City and the West Indies.

◈ *Critical Extracts*

CAROL FIELD   Rarely has a first novel come to hand which has the poignant appeal and the fresh, fierce emotion of *Brown Girl, Brownstones*.

The "brown girl" of the book's title is Selina Boyce, daughter of Deighton and Silla, Negro immigrants from the island of Barbados. The "brownstones" are the once socially desirable houses in a section of Brooklyn, which this group has moved into. The story Mrs. Marshall tells so effectively is mainly about the Boyces, but touching their lives closely are a score of other characters who share their background and their problems.

Racial conflict and the anger and frustration it nurtures are part of this tale, but equally, if not more, important are the personal conflicts of men and women making roots in a new land, of men and women caught in duels of love and hate, of ambition, envy and failure. 〈. . .〉

This is an unforgettable novel written with pride and anger, with rebellion and tears. Rich in content and in cadences of the King's and "Bajun" English, it is the work of a highly gifted writer.

> Carol Field, "Fresh, Fierce, and 'First,' " *New York Herald Tribune Book Review*, 16 August 1959, p. 5

PHILIP BUTCHER   Writing from the inside, from a short lifetime of experience, Paule Marshall achieves in *Brown Girl, Brownstones* (1959) a remarkably perceptive and mature story of a West Indian family's pursuit of happiness in Brooklyn. Selina, the heroine, is a sensitive child who admires above all else her indolent but charming father, Deighton Boyce. Her world is composed of her West Indian neighbors and the tenants in her home, including the inevitable prostitute and a very old white woman, Miss Mary, who lives with the ghosts of the aristocrats who walked in elegance behind the brownstone façade in the days when it was new. Deighton Boyce is even more of a dreamer than demented Miss Mary, but his visions are of the future. Undisturbed by a lifetime of failure, he is comforted by the illusion that he will someday build a white house on a bit of land he has inherited in his native Barbados. The prevailing obsession for security and respectability drives his wife to sell the land to relieve their poverty in Brooklyn, but Deighton takes his revenge by spending all the money on presents and clothes and a golden trumpet. Later he is converted to the cult of Father Divine. Even in heaven—Father Divine's heaven— the malice of his plodding wife pursues him. He is deported when she discloses that he has entered the country illegally. Within sight of Barbados, which means for him not home but public confession of failure, Deighton slips from his ship and drowns. Possibly at last he gains permanent entry into heaven, having known hell and purgatory largely of his own making.

With the passing years Selina becomes further estranged from her older sister, who finds fulfillment and respectability in the Espicopal Church, and from her mother, who obtains much the same values from the Association of Barbadian Homeowners and Business Men. The municipal college offers Selina partial escape from the narrow interests of the Barbadian community. Her release from the image of her father and her advance to womanhood are signalled by a love affair with a Barbadian bohemian, whose failure as a painter stems from his subjection by a possessive mother. Although she is an intelligent girl and a conscientious student, college means little to Selina except for the modern dance group, of which she is the only colored member. After a triumphant recital she is brutally reminded of her race by a malicious parent. She loses her spineless lover when she turns to him for consolation, but she gains a sense of identification with her Jewish girl friend, her mother, and the whole West Indian tradition. In her new maturity Selina accepts all that is best in her heritage but rejects the chauvinism, the provincialism, and the petty materialistic ambitions. Like other Barbadian girls, she has worn from birth two silver bangles. As she prepares to leave Brooklyn she hurls one of them into the night. The other remains on her arm.

> Philip Butcher, "Younger Novelists and the Urban Negro," CLA Journal 4, No. 3 (March 1961): 201–2

IHAB HASSAN   Though her stories ⟨in *Soul Clap Hands and Sing*⟩ do not all claim America for a setting, Paule Marshall enriches our idea of Memory by gentle, lyrical brooding on the meaning of lives that have been already spent or shaped. Her four aged protagonists can neither clap nor sing. But they have some kindlings of rage, and the bitter dignity of knowledge through defeat. In this lies the unique quality of the book. ⟨. . .⟩

By far the best story is the last, "Brazil," a sharp yet moving account of a famous comedian about to retire. "O Grande Caliban," as everyone knows him (his true name and his identity seem lost forever), is Rio's implacable jester. A tiny man, he seems all his life a "Lilliputian in a kingdom of giants." "The world had been scaled without him in mind—and his rage and contempt for it and for those who belonged was always just behind his smile, in the vain, superior lift of his head, in his every gesture." Caliban's frenzied effort to reclaim his identity from the posters and cheering crowds, from the stupid, spoiled, blonde Amazon who is his partner, and even from his young, pregnant wife, takes him to the center of his personality and the terrifying slums of Rio. Here all is done with tact and great power.

The example of Caliban shows that an aged man may not be entirely a paltry thing. (Indeed, the sequence of stories in the book reveals a progressive vitality in the characters.) Paule Marshall does not bring new resources of form or startling sensibility to the genre. But she allows her poetic style to be molded in each case by the facts of her fiction; she has escaped the clichés that must doubly tempt every Negro author writing today; and she has given us a vision, precise and compassionate, of solitary lives that yet participate in the rich, shifting backgrounds of cultures near and remote. Her retrospective vision is really a forecast of what we may wake up, too late, to see. There is a need for a poetics of gerontology.

> Ihab Hassan, "A Circle of Loneliness," *Saturday Review*, 16 September 1961, p. 30

EDWARD BRAITHWAITE   Anglophone West Indian literature—certainly its novels—has been mainly concerned with two main
themes: the relationship of the author's *persona* or *personae* to his society,
found in general to be limiting and frustrating; and stemming from this, a
presentation of that society and an illustration of its lack of identity. West
Indian novelists have so far, on the whole, attempted to see their society
neither in the larger context of Third World underdevelopment, nor, with
the exception of Vic Reid, in relation to communal history. Perhaps this
has been artistically unnecessary. West Indian novels have been so richly
home centered, that they have provided their own universe, with its own
universal application. West Indian novelists, faced with the exciting if
Sisyphean task of describing their own society in their own terms, for the
first time, have had to provide for themselves a priority list in which, quite
naturally, a relating of their own encounter with their environment, society
and sensibility, has had to take pride of place. In addition, since most West
Indian novelists have become exiles in several centres of the metropolitan
West, their concern with a continuing and widening exploration of the
societies has been limited by distance, separation and the concerns of a
different milieu. They have, most of them, continued to write about the
West Indies, but a West Indies stopped in time at the snapshot moment of
departure.

The question, however, remains as to whether the West Indies, or anywhere else for that matter, can be fully and properly seen unless within a wider
framework of external impingements or internal change. The contemporary
West Indies, after all, are not simply excolonial territories; they are underdeveloped islands moving into the orbit of North American cultural and
material imperialism, retaining stubborn vestiges of their Eurocolonial past
(mainly among the elite), and active memories of Africa and slavery (mainly
among the folk). ⟨. . .⟩

This way of looking at West Indian writing has been prompted by a
reading of Paule Marshall's new novel, *The Chosen Place, the Timeless People*.
Had Paule Marshall been a West Indian, she probably would not have
written this book. Had she not been an Afro-American of West Indian
parentage, she possibly could not have written it either; for in it we find a
West Indies facing the metropolitan West on the one hand, and clinging
to a memorial past on the other. Within this matrix, she formulates her
enquiry into identity and change. And it is no mere externalized or exotic
investigation. Mrs. Marshall has reached as far into West Indian society as

her imagination, observation, and memory will allow. The questions raised and the answers suggested are, one feels, an integral part of her own development while being at the same—and for the first—time, a significant contribution to the literature of the West Indies.

The scope and value of this contribution is no accident. Paule Marshall's background has prepared and qualified her for it. Born of Barbadian parents in Brooklyn, she was brought up in a West Indian/Afro-American environment in New York which she explored in her first novel, *Brown Girl, Brownstones* (1959). Visits to the West Indies, and especially ancestral Barbados, revived and strengthened direct links with the Caribbean, as many of her stories illustrate, including one in *Soul Clap Hands and Sing* (1961). Now in *The Chosen Place, the Timeless People*, (1969), we have her first mature statement on the islands—or more precisely, on a tiny, hilly corner of Barbados she calls Bournehills (though there is Port-of-Spain during Carnival and something of the Maroons of Jamaica as well).

> Edward Braithwaite, "West Indian History and Society in the Art of Paule Marshall's Novel," *Journal of Black Studies* 1, No. 2 (December 1970): 225–27

LEELA KAPAI   *The Chosen Place* . . . weaves in the race issue subtly in the entire story. Harriet represents the spirit of the white world. She is only a step ahead of the Bentons of this world. When she fails to comprehend why a woman would sell the eggs to someone else rather than feed her own family, she takes it to be another backward streak of the incorrigibles. Her impotent anger and frustration come out vivid in the carnival scene where she realizes that the reign of people like her is over and a new generation is emerging. Her death seems to be a symbolic end of all that white America stands for and the ever-mourning waves of the ocean perform the ablution of the old sins of the past. Perhaps a new race of active men like Saul and sympathetic ones like Allen will create better understanding between the races.

This new world, Miss Marshall feels, will be created only though an acute awareness of the past. Saul echoes her thoughts explicitly: "It's usually so painful though: looking back and into yourself; most people run from it . . . But sometimes it's necessary to go back before you can go forward, really forward. And that's not only true for people—individuals—but nations as well . . ." Since Miss Marshall believes that without tradition one has no real existence, she has all her major characters go back to their ancient heritage.

Time and again, Paule Marshall brings us to the question of human relationships. Beyond the barriers of race, all men are the same; they share the same fears, the same loneliness, and the same hopes. And they cannot live as islands; the bridges of communication have to be built. She repeatedly stresses the act of "using each other." In the complexity of human relationships we use each other in strange ways. Selina's affair with Clive is a way of getting even with her mother, while Clive needs to relieve his youthful aspirations through Selina. While Merle and Saul use each other to assuage their hurts and pains, Reena's boyfriend associates with her to annoy his father. But then Reena confesses with candor that she too has used him "to get at that white world which had not only denied me, but had turned my own against me." Despite these varied uses, the truth is that we need to share ourselves with others, barring which the life is a barren wasteland. However, sharing is by no means easy, for it means adding to one's sorrows.

The Chosen Place . . . also deals with the question of Western aid to the so-called underdeveloped countries. One cannot help wondering if the aid is meaningful and fruitful when an outsider tries to impose a new way of life to obliterate the centuries-old systems and values. The conflict between the old and the new assumes such proportions that the entire purpose is lost. Several attempts to modernize Bournehills have failed because the Americans have never tried to understand the place. Saul succeeds because he accepts the existing way of life and builds upon it.

Leela Kapai, "Dominant Themes and Technique in Paule Marshall's Fiction," CLA *Journal* 16, No. 1 (September 1972): 54–55

PAULE MARSHALL   In order to talk about what I believe to be some of the important early influences which shape my work, it will be necessary to take a giant step back to that stage in life when, without being conscious of it, I began the never-ending apprenticeship which is writing. It began in of all places the ground floor kitchen of a brownstone house in Brooklyn. Let me try to recreate the setting for you. Picture if you will a large old-fashioned kitchen with a second-hand refrigerator, the kind they used to have back then in the thirties with the motor on top, a coal stove that in its blackness, girth and the heat it threw off during the winter overwhelmed the gas range next to it, a sink whose pipes never ceased their rusty cough and a large table covered in flowered oilcloth set like an altar in the middle of the room.

It was at this table that the faithful, my mother and her women friends, would gather almost every afternoon upon returning from their jobs as domestics—or to use their term for the work they did "scrubbing Jew floor." Their work day had begun practically at dawn with the long train ride out to the white sections of Brooklyn. There, the ones who weren't lucky enough to have a steady job would stand on the street corners waiting in the cold— if it was winter—for the white, mainly Jewish housewives to come along and hire them for a half day's work cleaning their houses. The auction block was still very real for them.

Later, armed with the few dollars they had earned, my mother and her friends would make the long trip back to our part of town and there, in the sanctuary of our kitchen, talk endlessly, passionately. I didn't realize it then but those long afternoon rap sessions were highly functional, therapeutic; they were, you might even say, a kind of magic rite, a form of juju, for it was their way to exorcise the day's humiliations and restore them to themselves. ⟨. . .⟩

Moreover, all that free-wheeling talk together with the sometimes bawdy jokes and the laughter which often swept the kitchen was, at its deepest level, an affirmation of their own worth; it said that they could not be either demeaned or defeated by the daily trip out to Flatbush. It declared that they had retained and always would a strong sense of their special and unique Black identity.

I could understand little of this at the time. Those mysterious elements I heard resonating behind the words, which held me spellbound, came across mainly as a feeling which entered me it seemed not only through my ears but through the pores of my skin (I used to get goose pimples listening to them at times) to become part of my blood. It sings there to this day. I couldn't define it then, but I know now that contained in that feeling were those qualities which Black people possess no matter where you find them in the hemisphere—and which to my mind make of us one people.

Paule Marshall, "Shaping the World of My Art," *New Letters* 40, No. 1 (Autumn 1973): 97–98, 104

BARBARA CHRISTIAN   The interrelatedness of complex shapes and settings is so fused in Marshall that her books are verbal sculptures.

Form and space and humanity and culture cannot be separated. Her words chisel features, crevices, lines, into the grand, seemingly formless mass of history. Certainly marked in *Brown Girl, Brownstones,* this sculpted effect is the dominant formal chracteristic of *The Chosen Place, the Timeless People.* The land is the people, the people the land. Yet complexity and individuality of character are not sacrificed to largeness of theme. The intricacy of detail is maintained, even extended, in Marshall's panoramic novel. ⟨. . .⟩ Marshall's analysis is powerful because she so profoundly loves her characters, and she insists, throughout her work, that social themes are distorted if not fused with the complexity of individual human beings. ⟨. . .⟩

Paule Marshall's works, as psychopolitical images, elucidate the people who affect their culture and are affected in turn by their creation. Because of this thrust, her works remind us that all of us compose our own experiences in our minds and that our individual shapes are kinetically poised in a unified sculpture called the universe; that we all are continuity and process, shape and space, and that our sculpted creations are ourselves; that we change our world by changing our shapes, yet our world will change whether or not we want it to. Marshall's novels manifest history as a creative and moral process, for she graphically describes how we compose our own experiences in our minds as well as in the objective world; how we as individuals and whole cultures decide upon the moral nature of an act, a series of acts, a history. Above all, her work shows us that creative writing must be immersed in an act of honesty and love. The new child will come, when it has a mind to.

> Barbara Christian, "Sculpture and Space: The Interdependency of Character and Culture in the Novels of Paule Marshall," *Black Women Novelists: The Development of a Tradition 1892–1976* (Westport, CT: Greenwood Press, 1980), pp. 134–36

DARRYL PINCKNEY   In exploring the stages of black women's lives, Marshall insists that the woman with enough nerve can win even when the deck is stacked and the other players are hostile. Nerve, here, means making radical choices, and though the liberating destinies Marshall gives to her heroines are often unconvincing, the attraction of her work lies in a deep saturation in the consciousness of her characters and the ability to evoke the urban or tropical settings in which they toil. Dorothy Parker, in a review of the first novel, complained about the title. The years have not improved Marshall's ear for titles. They are sentimental and heavy with obvious meaning. They do not do justice to the discipline of the writing or to Marshall's engagement with questions of heritage, assimilation, and the black woman's identity.

Marshall's heroines tend to be stubborn, alienated, and ripe for some sort of conversion. The leap of faith is presented as a matter of making up one's mind to heed an inner voice, whatever the cost. Unfortunately, these assured, preachy women are not as interesting as the flawed souls who surround them and hold them down. ⟨. . .⟩

Virginia Woolf once observed that when women come to write novels, they probably find themselves wanting to alter established values, to make important what is insignificant to men and to make trivial what men think essential. Marshall shares this subversive inclination and sometimes it brings satisfying results. But Woolf also warned against a distorting element that can enter the fiction of those who are painfully aware of their "disability," and in Marshall's case the distorting element is not only a simplistic view of culture but also a simplistic idea of strength. The women in her novels are meant to seem courageous, but they have more of the manic certitude of religious fanatics. They have an almost narcissistic appreciation of their own states of mind but little is revealed about the complicated forces against which they claim to struggle. This limited picture of the world is what sets Marshall's women apart from those of Zora Neale Hurston, whose women are more tolerant, forgiving, and, one might say, truly experienced.

Perhaps this one-dimensional approach comes from current strains in black feminism. To counter the image of the black woman as victim, a different picture is deemed necessary, one that inadvertently makes such words as "nurturing," "positive," and "supportive" unbearable. One is constantly aware of a manipulation of reality at work in Marshall's fiction and this causes us to distrust it.

Darryl Pinckney, "Roots," *New York Review of Books*, 28 April 1983, pp. 26, 29–30

SUSAN WILLIS   Marshall demonstrates deep political understanding in *Brown Girl, Brownstones* by showing that the desire to own property may well have represented an initial contestation of bourgeois white domination, but because property ownership is implicit in capitalist society, the moment of opposition was immediately absorbed and integrated into the context of American capitalism. As long as white property owners could move out to the suburbs, it mattered little—nor did it represent a transformation of the system—that black people might be establishing parallel property systems in the cities. Marshall shows great sensitivity in demonstrating how the desire for property is lived as a passion, whose result is the repression of sexuality and the transformation of a loving, supportive couple relationship into one defined by deceit and treachery. Marshall's great talent as a writer is to show how broad historical developments are lived by families—and particularly by women in their roles as daughters and mothers. When we read *Brown Girl, Brownstones*, we cannot help but be amazed at the power of Silla's desire to "buy house," to be a full citizen like her neighbors, who, on their way up and out of poverty, ape middle-class modes of behavior. We cannot help but be struck by the horrible dissension the mother's project unleashes, which has its culmination in Silla's betrayal of her husband and Selina's denunciation of her mother as a "Hitler." And finally, we cannot help but be dumbfounded at Silla's brutal denial of self—her self-sacrifice, never allowing herself a moment's frivolity; her toil, taking on long hours and difficult jobs; and finally her repression of sexuality. Her refusal to have sex with her husband seems all the more self-negating when we see Silla, as Marshall portrays her during a wedding reception, dancing with delightful abandon and deep sensuality. Caught up in the all-consuming obsession to save every nickel and dime and to convert her husband's piece of land in Barbados into a down payment on a New York brownstone, Silla becomes a living embodiment of compulsive desires, some of which (like her frugality and possessiveness) she probably inherited with her peasant origins, but all of which dovetail with the demands of capitalism. The beauty of Marshall's portrayal is to make us ever aware of Silla's deeply human passions, which have been repressed or distorted in her relentless drive to ascend to the middle class.

Susan Willis, "Describing Arcs of Recovery: Paule Marshall's Relationship to Afro-American Culture," *Specifying: Black Women Writing the American Experience* (Madison: University of Wisconsin Press, 1987), pp. 74–75

DARWIN T. TURNER   In *Brown Girl, Brownstones* (1959), ⟨. . .⟩ Marshall tells the story of a Black family whose problems are not uniquely those of Black Americans. The mother, Serena Boyce, has come to America in search of the American Dream: through hard work, discipline, and frugal management, she and her family will acquire property, respectability, and a new home. Her immigrant husband, Deighton Boyce, however, wants only to earn enough money to be able to return to his homeland, where he can flaunt his affluence before his neighbors. Torn between the values of these two, their daughter Selina must also experience the problems of a young woman growing to physical, intellectual, psychological, and cultural maturity.

In her focus on Selina's growth, Marshall seems to anticipate *Bildungsromans* of Black women. That is, despite a few notable exceptions, such as Zora Neale Hurston in *Their Eyes Were Watching God* (1937), most Black women authors who wrote about Black women protagonists before 1950 concentrated on their adult lives. Even in *The Street* (1946), Ann Petry sketched only enough of Lutie Johnson's early life to enable a reader to learn something about her values, their source, and her reason for an early marriage. Four years after *Brown Girl, Brownstones*, Mary Elizabeth Vroman, in *Esther* (1963), revealed her protagonist's intellectual and emotional development from the age of thirteen into her adult life. In *God Bless the Child* (1964), Kristin Hunter portrayed Rosie Fleming from the age of seven until her death as a young woman. In the 1980s, when readers familiar with Black literature automatically think of such novels as Toni Morrison's *Sula* (1974) or Alice Walker's *The Color Purple* (1982), a story exploring the maturing of a Black woman does not seem unusual. In 1959, however, Marshall was among the earliest to trace such development.

Darwin T. Turner, "Introduction," Soul Clap Hands and Sing by Paule Marshall (Washington, DC: Howard University Press, 1988), pp. xxii–xxiii

---

MISSY DEHN KUBITSCHEK   In her depictions of female quests, Marshall follows Hurston in making storytelling central. Listening to stories motivates some questers; telling stories helps to heal others; above all, the sense of community involved in the participatory interchange of teller and audience strengthens the questers' identities. In *Brown Girl*, with its adolescent quester, older characters generally tell stories to younger ones; in *Chosen Place*, the middle-aged exchange stories. Selina must absorb the narratives of her parents and their generation, and Merle must draw out and contribute to the flow of personal stories in her mostly middle-aged circle.

Merle's search for her daughter, however, implies subsequent participation in the intergenerational pattern: questers do not choose one pattern or the other, but participate in each at different stages in their lives or in different roles during the same stage. *Praisesong* exalts the intergenerational narrative by making it Avatara's vocation. Both her process in claiming it and her conception of storytelling's purposes, however, diverge from those of Marshall's earlier novels and from a large portion of other African-American fiction. All three of Marshall's novels emphasize the integral relationship of storytelling and the female quest. Collaboratively constructing stories, both tribal and individual, furthers the development of both community and individual. The quester must find an empowering, participatory audience to help her articulate her own destiny within its larger destiny.

Missy Dehn Kubitschek, "Paule Marshall's Witness to History," *Claiming the Heritage: African-American Women Novelists and History* (Jackson: University Press of Mississippi, 1991), pp. 70–71

SUSAN FROMBERG SCHAEFFER   Paule Marshall's *Daughters* is that rarity, a good *and* important book. It attempts to look at black experience in our hemisphere, to praise what progress has been made and to point to what yet needs to be done. In its willingness to take real stock, to find true answers to complex questions, it is a brave, intelligent and ambitious work.

Ms. Marshall examines the state of black life through Ursa Mackenzie, whose heritage—and perhaps nature—is dual. Her father, Primus Mackenzie, is a prominent official of a mythical Caribbean island, Triunion; he has been known since his youth as "the PM." Her mother is the American-born Estelle Harrison, who sends a very young Ursa back to the United States so that her child can learn "to talk the talk and walk the walk." Most of all, Estelle does not want Ursa to grow up to be a Triunion woman, one who waits hand and foot on her man and who has little independence of thought or deed. It is as if Estelle knows that her daughter will have a special role to play in determining the fate of black people in one or both of her countries. She is determined to make a difference. ⟨. . .⟩

Daughters seems to imply that the purpose of many unions should now be mutual struggle; struggle, if necessary, *against* each other but always toward an ideal. Black men, who entered the political and economic arenas earlier than black women, have greater temptations to contend with and are thus more likely to be seduced from their ideals. Through Primus and Estelle Mackenzie, Ms. Marshall shows us how the *women* can—and perhaps should—find themselves becoming men's consciences. ⟨. . .⟩

⟨. . .⟩ Women, Ms. Marshall shows us, spend more of their time than men with children, friends and family. They are less likely to be distracted from what was probably always their original goal: to be of use.

Yet even here, women are hampered by the inevitable facts of life: they love and are sexually attracted to their husbands and fathers, and, unless they can free themselves from the spells of men, they are of little use as consciences. And so, when Estelle decides to move against her husband, to keep him "on the straight and narrow," she cannot do it. It is at this point that Estelle calls upon her daughter to act when she cannot. ⟨. . .⟩

Many ideas dominate this wonderful novel, but perhaps the most important is that we have been on the wrong road, a "bypass road" that allows us to travel through life without seeing the urgent needs of others. You close *Daughters* feeling as if you have taken a dangerous trip that cannot leave you unchanged. Flawless in its sense of place and character, remarkable in its understanding of human nature, *Daughters* is a triumph in every way.

Susan Fromberg Schaeffer, "Cutting Herself Free," *New York Times Book Review*, 27 October 1991, pp. 3, 29

CAROL ASCHER   *Daughters*, Marshall's fourth novel, is her most ambitious, mature and sharply political. It begins as small as the personal distress of a black woman, Ursa Mackenzie, returning from an abortion to her Upper West Side studio apartment in New York City. Single, in her thirties, temporarily jobless, Ursa is too paralyzed to return the call on her answering machine from her dear friend Viney Davis. She can only wait uselessly in the darkening evening for a ring from Lowell Carruthers, who has no reason to extend their relationship beyond a biweekly dinner and a little "company through the night," since she never even told him she was pregnant. Nor can Ursa open the one letter that lies among her junk mail: it's from her father, Primus Mackenzie, a politician on the small Caribbean island of Triunion, and a man she has always loved dearly. ⟨. . .⟩

From this tiny, isolated New York apartment, *Daughters* moves slowly outward in ever-widening circles that come to encompass relations, friends, lovers and colleagues in both the Caribbean and greater New York. Finally, this fictional world extends backward half a century, more, back to slavery itself, at the same time as it moves a mere two months forward, to election week on Triunion. Through the issues confronting Ursa's father, *Daughters* makes clear the dependent nature of Triunion as it grows poorer and more crowded over the years. (An American warship, the *Woody Wilson*, stands in the harbor at every election, ensuring that no candidate with wild socialist ideas, such as Primus once had, will win.) At the same time, we see life as it is lived at the increasingly compromised center of political power. Like Marshall's other books, *Daughters* prompts one to reflect on the life choices given to an African-American woman or man in both the metropolis and the colonies. ⟨. . .⟩

Daughters is intimately observed, culturally rich, morally serious. Marshall loves her complex, imperfect characters, male and female; she loves the tragic, often comic, worlds they inhabit. It is this love that one feels drives her to write so seriously and fully, and that makes each new work feel like the return of an old friend.

Carol Ascher, "Compromised Lives," *Women's Review of Books* 9, No. 2 (November 1991): 7

Bibliography

Brown Girl, Brownstones. 1959.
Soul Clap Hands and Sing. 1961.
The Chosen Place, the Timeless People. 1969.
Praisesong for the Widow. 1983.
Reena and Other Stories. 1983.
Daughters. 1991.

Toni Morrison
b. 1931

TONI MORRISON was born Chloe Anthony Wofford in Lorain, Ohio, on February 18, 1931, the second of four children of George Wofford, a shipyard welder, and his wife Ramah Willis Wofford. After attending Lorain High School, she went to Howard University, where she earned a B.A. in 1953, with a major in English and a minor in classics. She joined the Howard University Players and in the summer toured the South with a student-faculty repertory troupe.

After securing an M.A. at Cornell in 1955, Morrison taught for two years at Texas Southern University, then in 1957 returned to Howard, where she became an instructor of English and married Harold Morrison, a Jamaican architect. In 1964 she divorced Morrison and returned with her two sons to Lorain; a year and a half later she became an editor for a textbook subsidiary of Random House in Syracuse. By 1970 she had moved to an editorial position at Random House in New York, where she eventually became senior editor. In this capacity she anonymously edited *The Black Book* (1974), a collection of documents relating to the history of black Americans. Morrison has taught black American literature and creative writing at two branches of the State University of New York (Purchase and Albany), as well as at Yale University, Bard College, and Trinity College, Cambridge. She is currently Robert F. Goheen Professor in the Council of the Humanities at Princeton University.

Toni Morrison began to write when she returned to Howard in 1957, and since then she has published several novels in which the problems of black women in the Midwest are a major theme. Her first novel, *The Bluest Eye* (1970), draws upon her childhood in Lorain by depicting the lives of several young women, one of whom, Pecola, comes to believe that blue eyes are a symbol of whiteness and, therefore, of superiority. *Sula* (1973), set in the mythical town of Medallion, Ohio, has an even tougher edge, addressing issues of both racial and gender equality in its portrayal of the contrasting lives of two young women, one of whom settles down to middle-class conformity and the other of whom, Sula, attempts to achieve freedom by flaunting these conventions.

Morrison's third novel, *Song of Solomon* (1977), is a rich evocation of history in its chronicle of a black family over nearly a century; it was both a popular and critical success, winning the National Book Critics Circle Award and the American Academy and Institute of Arts and Letters Award. *Tar Baby* (1981), set on an imaginary Caribbean island, was less well received. But with her fifth novel, *Beloved* (1987), Morrison came to be recognized as perhaps the leading black American writer of her generation. This dense historical novel about a fugitive slave, Sethe, and her descendents not only achieved best-seller status but won the Pulitzer Prize for fiction. *Jazz* (1992) is a less ambitious work but is nonetheless a poignant depiction of the lives of black Americans in a mythical "City" in the 1920s.

Morrison has also written a small body of nonfiction. In the 1970s she wrote several pieces on black American women for the *New York Times Magazine*. Simultaneously with the release of *Jazz* appeared a challenging monograph, *Playing in the Dark: Whiteness and the Literary Imagination* (1992), probing the role of black Americans as symbols of the "other" in white American literature. In 1993 Morrison was awarded the Nobel Prize for literature. She is currently at work on a revision of *The Bluest Eye* and a new novel, tentatively entitled *Paradise*.

Critical Extracts

L. E. SISSMAN   *The Bluest Eye* is not flawless. Miss Morrison's touching and disturbing picture of the doomed youth of her race is marred by an occasional error of fact or judgment. She places the story in a frame of the bland white words of a conventional school "reader"—surely an unnecessary and unsubtle irony. She writes an occasional false or bombastic line: "They were through with lust and lactation, beyond tears and terror." She permits herself some inconsistencies: the real name of Soaphead Church is given as both Elihue Micah Whitcomb and Micah Elihue Whitcomb. None of this matters, though, beside her real and greatly promising achieve-ment: to write truly (and sometimes very beautifully) of every generation of blacks—the young, their parents, their rural grandparents—in this country thirty years ago, and, I'm afraid, today.

L. E. Sissman, "Beginner's Luck," *New Yorker*, 23 January 1971, p. 94

JERRY H. BRYANT   Sula, Ms. Morrison's protagonist, has qualities I have seen in a fictional black female only recently. When she is 11 years old, she cuts off the tip of her finger to demonstrate to a gang of threatening boys what she can do to them if she can do that to herself. She swings a child around by the wrists and half intentionally lets him slip out of her grasp into the river, where he drowns. In the shadows of her porch, she watches in an "interested" way while her mother burns to death.

Most of us have been conditioned to expect something else in black characters—guiltless victims of brutal white men, yearning for a respectable life of middle-class security; whores driven to their profession by impossible conditions; housekeepers exhausted by their work for lazy white women. We do not expect to see a fierceness bordering on the demonic. ⟨. . .⟩

⟨. . .⟩ Morrison at first seems to combine the aims of the Black Freedom Movement and women's liberation. Sula and Nel discover when they are 11 years old "that they were neither white nor male, and that all freedom and triumph was forbidden to them." When they grow up, Nel slips on the collar of convention. She marries, has two children, becomes tied to her "nest," a slave to racism and sexism. Sula goes to the big city, gets herself an education, and returns a "liberated" woman with a strange mixture of cynicism and innocence: "She lived out her days exploring her own thoughts and emotions, giving them full rein, feeling no obligation to please anybody unless their pleasure pleased her . . . hers was an experimental life." ⟨. . .⟩

Morrison does not accept—nor does she expect us to accept—the unqualified tenets of either of the two current freedom movements. There is more to both society and the individual, and she subjects each of these to a merciless analysis. The result is that neither lends itself to a clear moral judgment. For all her selfishness and cruelty, Sula's presence elicits the best in people, diluting their usual meanness and small-spiritedness. Indeed, with Sula's death the "Bottom" dies, its black people rushing headlessly in a comi-tragedy of communal suicide.

Jerry H. Bryant, "Something Ominous Here," *Nation*, 6 July 1974, pp. 23–24

JOAN BISCHOFF   Henry James delineated one of the earliest and most memorable precocious female protagonists in depicting the title character in *What Maisie Knew*. The extent of little Maisie's understanding of the adult world has remained tantalizingly elusive for several generations of readers, while her innocent suffering has shone with terrible poignance. Now, it seems, a new American novelist is offering some contemporary twists of the Jamesian type. With the publication of *The Bluest Eye* in 1970 and *Sula* in 1974, Toni Morrison has laid claim to modern portrayal of the preternaturally sensitive but rudely thwarted black girl in today's society. *Sula* is more fully dominated by the title character, and Sula's characterization is the more complex; in both novels, however, the protagonist is forced into premature adulthood by the *donnée* of her life. Pecola's comprehension of her world is never articulated for either the other characters or the reader; Sula, too, remains a partial enigma both in and out of her narrative. But the pain that each experiences is made vivid and plain. Taken together, the two novels can—and I think must—be read as offering different answers to a single question: What is to become of a finely attuned child who is offered no healthy outlet for her aspirations and yearnings? Pecola escapes in madness; Sula rejects society for amoral self-reliance. For both, sensitivity is a curse rather than a blessing. Morrison's second novel, though richer in many ways, is essentially a reworking of the material of the first with an alternative ending. Though her characters' problems are conditioned by the black milieu of which she writes, her concerns are broader, universal ones. Her fiction is a study of thwarted sensitivity. ⟨. . .⟩

Both Morrison's novels find beauty in sensitive response and show its inevitable doom in a world in which only the hard, the cagey, and the self-interested can triumph. Although both Pecola and Sula fill essential roles in their communities, it is not the admirable in their characters that has an influence. Pecola serves as the bottom-most societal rung whose lowliness raises the self-esteem of everyone else, while Sula's acknowledged "evil" encourages others' righteous sense of comparative superiority. Sensitivity is lovely, but impractical, says Morrison. It is a pragmatic outlook, if not a particularly happy one.

Joan Bischoff, "The Novels of Toni Morrison: Studies in Thwarted Sensitivity," *Studies in Black Literature* 6, No. 3 (Fall 1975): 21, 23

REYNOLDS PRICE   Toni Morrison's first two books—*The Bluest Eye* with the purity of its terrors and *Sula* with its dense poetry and the depth of its probing into a small circle of lives—were strong novels. Yet, firm as they both were in achievement and promise, they didn't fully forecast her new book, *Song of Solomon*. Here the depths of the younger work are still evident, but now they thrust outward, into wider fields, for longer intervals, encompassing many more lives. The result is a long prose tale that surveys nearly a century of American history as it impinges upon a single family. In short, this is a full novel—rich, slow enough to impress itself upon us like a love affair or a sickness—not the two-hour penny dreadful which is again in vogue nor one of the airless cat's cradles custom-woven for the delight and job-assistance of graduate students of all ages.

Song of Solomon isn't, however, cast in the basically realistic mode of most family novels. In fact, its negotiations with fantasy, fable, song and allegory are so organic, continuous and unpredictable as to make any summary of its plot sound absurd; but absurdity is neither Morrison's strategy nor purpose. The purpose seems to be communication of painfully discovered and powerfully held convictions about the possibility of transcendence within human life, on the time-scale of a single life.

Reynolds Price, "Black Family Chronicle," *New York Times Book Review*, 11 September 1977, p. 1

SUSAN L. BLAKE   The "Song of Solomon" that provides the title of Toni Morrison's third novel is a variant of a well-known Gullah folktale about a group of African-born slaves who rose up one day from the field where they were working and flew back to Africa. In the novel, this tale becomes both the end of, and a metaphor for, the protagonist's identity quest: Macon Dead III, known as Milkman, finds himself when he learns the story of his great-granddaddy Solomon who could fly. From this story he himself learns to fly, metaphorically: "For now he knew what Shalimar [Solomon] knew: if you surrendered to the air, you could *ride* it."

In basing Milkman's identity quest on a folktale, Morrison calls attention to one of the central themes in all her fiction, the relationship between individual identity and community, for folklore is by definition the expression of community—of the common experiences, beliefs, and values that identify a folk as a group. The use of the folktale of the flying Africans in this quest seems to establish equivalence between Milkman's discovery of community and his achievement of identity, but paradoxes in the use of the folktale suggest a more complex relationship and help to define just what Morrison means by the concept of community, a concept which she vigorously endorses.

The flight of the transplanted Africans dramatizes the communal identity of Afro-Americans in several ways. It establishes "home" as the place of common origin and dissociates the Africans from the American plantation where their identity is violated. It dissociates them as well from American-born slaves, for only the African-born have the power to fly. At the same time, as the ability to fly distinguishes the Africans from their descendants, it represents an identity that the African-descended tellers of the tale believe they would have if they had not had another identity forced upon them by slavery. The tale thus represents a common dream, a common disappointment, and a group identity. As the object of Milkman's quest, it suggests a multi-leveled equivalence between individual identity and community. Simply as folktale, it is an artifact of Afro-American history; its content links Afro-American to pan-African history; it is localized to represent Milkman's family history. His discovery of the tale thus represents Milkman's discovery of his membership in ever more inclusive communities; his family, Afro-Americans, all blacks. ⟨. . .⟩

The multiple ways of seeing Milkman's discovery as a discovery of community suggest that *Song of Solomon* is an elaborate, and entertaining, expansion of the equation between identity and community. In fact, however, the end of Milkman's quest is not the discovery of community, but a solitary leap into the void. And its mythical foundation is not the typical tale of the Africans flying as a group to their common home, but a highly individualistic variant. Milkman's discovery does not result in any of the conventional indications of community. Although Milkman is reconciled with Pilate and the two of them return to Shalimar to bury the bones of her father, Pilate dies (as she has lived, protecting Milkman's life) as soon as the burial is accomplished.

Susan L. Blake, "Folklore and Community in *Song of Solomon*," *MELUS* 7, No. 3 (Fall 1980): 77–79

DARRYL PINCKNEY   The setting ⟨of *Tar Baby*⟩ is exotic—an imagined tropical island called Isle des Chevaliers, privately owned, found off Dominique. But, like the small towns in ⟨Morrison's⟩ previous books, it also has its allegorical lore. ⟨. . .⟩

The story is not entirely confined to this mysterious island. The characters in *Tar Baby* recall the mansions of Philadelphia, trailers in Maine, the cream-colored streets of Paris of their past lives. There are heated moments in Manhattan. A hamlet in northern Florida, an all black town called Eloe, turns out to be very much like Eatonville, Zora Neale Hurston's celebrated birthplace in the same region. Travel, in Morrison's earlier novels, tended to mean crossing the country. Here, there are frequent and anxious escapes to the reservations counter at Air France.

Something else has changed. The laboring poor of *The Bluest Eye*, the self-sufficient women and drifting men of *Sula*, the avaricious middle class and defiantly marginal citizens of *Song of Solomon*—they are gone, replaced, in *Tar Baby*, by the rich, their servants, their dependents, and the sans culottes who threaten their security. Though much is made of money, fashion, commodities as consciousness, and the experiences open to the privileged, the cultured, and those clever enough to hustle a piece of the action, the people living on Isle des Chevaliers, voluntary exiles all, seem to inhabit a world that is oppressively parochial and provincial. ⟨. . .⟩

Many of Morrison's previous concerns are here—having to do with the inner life of black women and especially the offhand, domestic violence and conjugal brutality that burn out daily life. Much of the recent fiction by Afro-American women contains these themes. Their message is new and arresting, as if, in the past, the worries of the kitchen or the bedroom were not sufficiently large to encompass the intense lives of black people in a racist society. But *Tar Baby*'s sense of such experience is inchoate, muffled. One wishes for the fierce concentration, the radical economy of the novels of Gayl Jones as they describe the inner world of black women in language that is harsh, disturbing, and utterly unsentimental.

Darryl Pinckney, "Every Which Way," *New York Review of Books*, 30 April 1981, pp. 24–25

GLORIA NAYLOR and TONI MORRISON   TM: ⟨. . .⟩ I

remember after *The Bluest Eye* having an extremely sad six or eight months. And I didn't know what it was because that was the first time I had ever written a novel. And I wasn't thinking about being a novelist then. I just wrote *that* and I thought that would be *that* and that would be the end of *that* 'cause I liked to read it and that was enough. But then I moved from one town to another, for one thing, and I was feeling, for this very sustained period, what can only be described now as missing something, missing the company I had been keeping all those years when I wrote *The Bluest Eye*, and I couldn't just write because I was able to write. I had to write with the same feeling that I had when I did *The Bluest Eye*, which was that there was this exciting collection of people that only I knew about. I had the direct line and I was the receiver of all this information. And then when I began to think about *Sula*, everything changed, I mean, all the colors of the world changed, the sounds and so on. I recognized what that period was when I finished *Sula*, and I had another idea which was *Song of Solomon*. When I finished *Song of Solomon*, I didn't have another idea for *Tar Baby* but then I knew that it arrives or it doesn't arrive and I'm not terrified of a block, of what people call a block. I think when you hit a place where you can't write, you probably should be still for a while because it's not there yet.

GN: Even a block with an idea itself? That doesn't frighten you?

TM: It doesn't bother me. And that brings me to the book that I'm writing now called *Beloved*. I had an idea that I didn't know was a book idea, but I do remember being obsessed by two or three little fragments of stories that I heard from different places. One was a newspaper clipping about a woman named Margaret Garner in 1851. It said that the Abolitionists made a great deal out of her case because she had escaped from Kentucky, I think, with her four children. She lived in a little neighborhood just outside of Cincinnati and she had killed her children. She succeeded in killing one; she tried to kill two others. She hit them in the head with a shovel and they were wounded but they didn't die. And there was a smaller one that she had at her breast. The interesting thing, in addition to that, was the interviews that she gave. She was a young woman. In the inked pictures of her she seemed a very quiet, very serene-looking woman and everyone who interviewed her remarked about her serenity and tranquility. She said, "I will not let those children live how I have lived." She had run off into a little woodshed right outside her house to kill them because she had been caught as a fugitive. And she had made up her mind that they would not suffer the way that she had and it was better for them to die. And her mother-in-law was in the house at the same time and she said, "I watched her and I neither encouraged her nor discouraged her." They put her in jail for a little while and I'm not even sure what the denouement is of her story. But that moment, that decision was a piece, a tail of something that was always around ⟨. . .⟩

Gloria Naylor and Toni Morrison, "Gloria Naylor and Toni Morrison: A Conversation," *Southern Review* 21, No. 3 (July 1985): 583–84

STANLEY CROUCH   *Beloved* ⟨. . .⟩ explains black behavior in terms of social conditioning, as if listing atrocities solves the mystery of human motive and behavior. It is designed to placate sentimental feminist ideology, and to make sure that the vision of black woman as the most scorned and rebuked of the victims doesn't weaken. Yet perhaps it is best understood by its italicized inscription: *"Sixty Million and more."* Morrison recently told *Newsweek* that the reference was to all the captured Africans, who died coming across the Atlantic. But sixty is ten times six, of course. That is very important to remember. For *Beloved*, above all else, is a blackface holocaust novel. It seems to have been written in order to enter American slavery into the big-time martyr contest, a contest usually won by references to, and works about, the experience of Jews at the hands of Nazis. As a holocaust novel, it includes disfranchisement, brutal transport, sadistic guards, failed and successful escapes, murder, liberals among the oppressors, a big war, underground cells, separation of family members, losses of loved ones to the violence of the mad order, and characters who, like the Jew in *The Pawnbroker*, have been made emotionally catatonic by the past.

That Morrison chose to set the Afro-American experience in the framework of collective tragedy is fine, of course. But she lacks a true sense of the tragic. Such a sense is stark, but it is never simpleminded. For all the memory within this book, including recollections of the trip across the Atlantic and the slave trading in the Caribbean, no one ever recalls how the Africans were captured. That would complicate matters. It would have demanded that the Africans who raided the villages of their enemies to sell them for guns, drink, and trinkets be included in the equation of injustice, something far too many Afro-Americans are loath to do—including Toni Morrison. In *Beloved* Morrison only asks that her readers tally up the sins committed against the darker people and feel sorry for them, not experience the horrors of slavery as they do. ⟨. . .⟩

But Morrison ⟨. . .⟩ can't resist the temptation of the trite or the sentimental. There is the usual scene in which the black woman is assaulted by white men while her man looks on; Halle, Sethe's husband, goes mad at the sight. Sixo, a slave who is captured trying to escape, is burned alive but doesn't scream: he sings "Seven-o" over and over, because his woman has escaped and is pregnant. But nothing is more contrived than the figure of Beloved herself, who is the reincarnated force of the malevolent ghost that was chased from the house. Beloved's revenge—she takes over the house, turns her mother into a servant manipulated by guilt, and becomes more and more vicious—unfolds as portentous melodrama. Whan Beloved finally threatens to kill Sethe, 30 black women come to the rescue. At the fence of the haunted property, one of them shouts, and we are given this: "Instantly the kneelers and the standers joined her. They stopped praying and took a step back to the beginning. In the beginning there were no words. In the beginning was the sound, and they all knew what that sound sounded like."

Too many such attempts at biblical grandeur, run through by Negro folk rhythms, stymie a book that might have been important. Had Morrison higher intentions when she appropriated the conventions of a holocaust tale, *Beloved* might stand next to, or outdistance, Ernest Gaines's *The Autobiography of Miss Jane Pittman* and Charles Johnson's *Oxherding Tale*, neither of which submits to the contrived, post-Baldwin vision of Afro-American experience. Clearly the subject is far from exhausted, the epic intricacies apparently unlimited. Yet to render slavery with aesthetic authority demands not only talent, but the courage to face the ambiguities of the human soul, which transcend the race. Had Toni Morrison that kind of courage, had she the passion necessary to liberate her work from the failure of feeling that is sentimentality, there is much that she could achieve. But why should she try to achieve anything? The position of literary conjure woman has paid off quite well. At last year's PEN Congress she announced that she had never considered herself American, but with *Beloved* she proves that she is as American as P. T. Barnum.

Stanley Crouch, "Aunt Medea," *New Republic,* 19 October 1987, pp. 41–43

SUSAN WILLIS   There is a sense of urgency in Morrison's writing, produced by the realization that a great deal is at stake. The novels may focus on individual characters like Milkman and Jadine, but the salvation of individuals is not the point. Rather, these individuals, struggling to reclaim or redefine themselves, are portrayed as epiphenomenal to community and culture, and it is the strength and continuity of the black cultural heritage as a whole that is at stake and being tested.

As Morrison sees it, the most serious threat to black culture is the obliterating influence of social change. The opening line from *Sula* might well have been the novel's conclusion, so complete is the destruction it records: "In that place, where they tore the night shade and blackberry patches from their roots to make room for the Medallion City Golf Course, there was once a neighborhood." This is the community Morrison is writing to reclaim. Its history, terminated and dramatically obliterated, is condensed into a single sentence whose content spans from rural South to urban development. Here, as throughout Morrison's writing, natural imagery refers to the past, the rural South, the reservoir of culture that has been uprooted— like the blackberry bushes—to make way for modernization. In contrast, the future is perceived of as an amorphous, institutionalized power embodied in the notion of "Medallion City," which suggests neither nature nor a people. Joining the past to the future is the neighborhood, which occupies a very different temporal moment (which history has shown to be transitional), and defines a very different social mode, as distinct from its rural origins as it is from the amorphous urban future.

It is impossible to read Morrison's four novels without coming to see the neighborhood as a concept crucial to her understanding of history. The neighborhood defines a Northern social mode rather than a Southern one, for it describes the relationship of an economic satellite, contiguous to a larger metropolis rather than separate subsistence economics like the Southern rural towns of Shalimar and Eloe. It is a Midwestern phenomenon rather than a Northeastern big-city category, because it defines the birth of principally first-generation, Northern, working-class black communities. It is a mode of the forties rather than the sixties or the eighties, and it evokes the many locally specific black populations in the North before these became assimilated to a larger, more generalized, and less regionally specific sense of black culture that we today refer to as the "black community."

Susan Willis, "Eruptions of Funk: Historicizing Toni Morrison," *Specifying: Black Women Writing the American Experience* (Madison: University of Wisconsin Press, 1987), pp. 93–95

TERRY OTTEN   In Toni Morrison's fiction characters one way or another enact the historical plight of blacks in American society. She offers no apology for her black female perspective. Though the black experience frames and informs her fictional narratives, it in no way reduces their universality. For all their complexity and diversity, the novels are woven together by common themes: the passage from innocence to experience, the quest for identity, the ambiguity of good and evil, the nature of the divided self, and especially, the concept of a fortunate fall. Morrison works the gray areas, avoiding simpleminded absolutes. Guitar tells Milkman at one point that "there are no innocent white people," but Milkman knows that there are no innocent blacks, either, least of all himself. Blacks as frequently as whites inflict extreme physical and psychological violence on blacks: the Breedloves torment each other, and Cholly rapes his daughter; Eva Peace burns her son, and Nel and Sula betray the other self; Milkman callously rejects Hagar, and Guitar kills Pilate; Son takes revenge on the childlike Cheyenne, and Jadine abandons Son; Sethe murders her daughter, and Beloved demands uncompromising payment—and of course much more. There is no doubt, though, that underlying all these manifestations of cruelty is the pernicious racism of American culture which wields its power to pervert and distort the moral center. Clearly, Morrison wants us to see the most insidious form of evil in the malevolent ability of racism to misshape the human spirit.

Terry Otten, *The Crime of Innocence in the Fiction of Toni Morrison* (Columbia: University of Missouri Press, 1989), p. 95

HAROLD BLOOM   Morrison, like any potentially strong novelist, battles against being subsumed by the traditions of narrative fiction. As a leader of African-American literary culture, Morrison is particularly intense in resisting critical characterizations that she believes misrepresent her own loyalties, her social and political fealties to the complex cause of her people. If one is a student of literary influence as such, and I am, then one's own allegiances as a critic are aesthetic, as I insist mine are. One is aware that the aesthetic has been a mask for those who would deny vital differences in gender, race, social class, and yet it need not be an instrument for the prolongation of exploiting forces. The aesthetic stance, as taught by Ruskin, Pater, and Wilde, enhances a reader's apprehension of perception and sensation. Such a mode of knowing literature seems to me inescapable, despite times like our own, in which societal and historical resentments, all with their own validity, tend to crowd out aesthetic considerations. Yet, as an artist, Morrison has few affinities with Zora Neale Hurston or Ralph Ellison, or with other masters of African-American fiction. Her curious resemblance to certain aspects of D. H. Lawrence does not ensue from the actual influence of Lawrence, but comes out of the two dominant precursors who have shaped her narrative sensibility, William Faulkner and Virginia Woolf. Faulkner and Woolf have little in common, but if you mixed them potently enough you might get Lawrence, or Toni Morrison.

Lest this seem a remote matter to a passionate reader of Morrison, I would observe mildly that one function of literary study is to help us make choices, because choice is inescapable, this late in Western cultural history. I do not believe that Morrison writes fiction of a kind I am not yet competent to read and judge, because I attend to her work with pleasure and enlightenment, amply rewarded by the perception and sensation that her art generates. Reading Alice Walker or Ishmael Reed, I cannot trust my own aesthetic reactions, and decide that their mode of writing must be left to critics more responsive than myself. But then I reflect that every reader must choose for herself or himself. Does one read and reread the novels of Alice Walker, or of Toni Morrison? I reread Morrison because her imagination, whatever her social purposes, transcends ideology and polemics, and enters again into the literary space occupied only by fantasy and romance of authentic aesthetic dignity. Extraliterary purposes, however valid or momentous they may be for a time, ebb away, and we are left with story, characters, and style, that is to say, with literature or the lack of literature. Morrison's five novels to date leave us with literature, and not with a manifesto for social change, however necessary and admirable such change would be in our America of Chairman Atwater, Senator Helms, President Bush, and the other luminaries of what we ought to go on calling the Willie Horton election of 1988.

Harold Bloom, "Introduction," *Toni Morrison*, ed. Harold Bloom (New York: Chelsea House, 1990), pp. 1–2.

WILFRED D. SAMUELS and CLENORA HUDSON-WEEMS ⟨. . .⟩ Morrison writes to and for blacks. She has no problems stating this fact. "When I view the world, perceive it and write it, it is the world of black people. It is not that I won't write about white people. I just know that when I'm trying to develop the various themes I write about, the people who best manifest these for me are the black people whom I invent. It is not deliberate or calculated or self-consciously black, because I recognize and despise the artificial black writing some writers do." As Morrison told Walter Clemons, however, this does not mean that whites cannot adequately respond to her works. "When I write, I don't try to translate for white readers . . . Dostoevski wrote for a Russian audience, but we're able to read him. If I'm specific, and I don't overexplain, then anybody can overhear me."

It is clear, then, that Morrison sees her work as speaking to a specific audience but as reaching beyond the bounds of that audience to the rest of humankind. ⟨. . .⟩ Morrison uses the black slave experience in America as a metaphor for the human condition, which is necessarily all-inclusive.

Wilfred D. Samuels and Clenora Hudson-Weems, *Toni Morrison* (Boston: Twayne, 1990), p. 140

DOROTHEA DRUMMOND MBALIA   *Tar Baby* is an assimilation and advancement of the primary theme of her three earlier novels. For the first time, Morrison frees her work from the narrow geographical boundaries of American society. Recognizing that people of African descent, no matter where they live, share a common identity, a common history, and a common oppression, she uses an island in the Caribbean as the dominant and pivotal setting for her novel. In doing so, Morrison reflects her own maturing consciousness of the fact that African people must seek a common solution to their plight. She herself states that "Black culture survives everywhere pretty much the same" and that "Black people take their culture wherever they go."

Furthermore, in *Tar Baby* Morrison creates a revolutionary protagonist, Son, who realizes that he cannot run away and leave a body. Having discovered first the importance of knowing one's history and one's relationship to his people, Son commits himself to sharing this knowledge with other Africans. Thus, by struggling to politically educate Therese, Gideon, Sydney, Ondine, and, in particular, Jadine—symbols of the larger Pan-African society—Son becomes a disciple for African people, a modern-day revolutionary. ⟨. . . But⟩ what Son fails to realize is that there are some Africans, like Jadine, who—because they share the aspirations of the ruling class and receive handouts from it—will refuse to struggle against capitalism even though they are conscious of the fact that it is the primary enemy of African people.

Despite its weaknesses, the novel's theme and narrative structure reflect Morrison's heightened class consciousness. Structurally, she has embraced the traditional African concept of collectivism, for each of the major characters, as well as the omniscient narrator, contributes to the organic world of the novel. The story is told, in effect, by taking individual threads and sewing them into a whole, a wholeness that she so ardently wishes for African people.

> Dorothea Drummond Mbalia, *Toni Morrison's Developing Class Consciousness* (Selinsgrove, PA: Susquehanna University Press, 1991), pp. 26–27

JANE MILLER   Within the first half-page of Toni Morrison's novel ⟨*Jazz*⟩, an 18-year-old girl has been shot dead by her middle-aged lover, and his wife has been manhandled from the funeral after attempting to cut the dead girl's face with a knife. Both events are witnessed and kept secret by a community which has reason to distrust the police and to look kindly upon a hitherto gentle, childless couple, whose sudden, violent sorrows they recognise and are able to forgive. And as the spring of that year, 1926, bursts a month or two later upon the 'City' of this extraordinary novel, its all-seeing gossip of a narrator is moved to declare—if only provisionally—that 'history is over, you all, and everything's ahead at last.'

The novel's theme tune is spun out from these contrasts and whirled through a series of playful improvisations by a storyteller who admits to being—and, as it turns out, expects the reader to be—'curious, inventive and well-informed'. It is impossible to resist the seductions of this particular narrative voice as it announces its own fallibilities, mourns its distance from some of the events it will therefore need to invent, boldly revises its own speculations, even as it recalls, replays, retrieves them for us before our very eyes and with our assumed complicity. For, of course, this voice also undertakes to guarantee both tale and telling as truth, history, music known and shared by all who have roots in the black urban communities of America in the Twenties. And for readers with quite other roots? Well, the voice is no more prepared than Morrison is herself to 'footnote the black experience for white readers'. As she put it in a recent interview: 'I wouldn't try to explain what a reader like me already knew.' ⟨...⟩

Jazz is a love story, indeed a romance. And romance and its high-risk seductions for young women come with special health warnings when it is poor young black women who might succumb to it. For romance has always been white, popular, capitalistic in its account of love as transactions voluntarily undertaken between class and beauty and money. But the romance which is a snare and a delusion has also spelled out a future for young women, a destiny, significance and pleasure—and particularly when there was little enough of those possibilities for them or for the men they knew. The older women of Morrison's novels know that sex can be a woman's undoing, that men, 'ridiculous and delicious and terrible', are always trouble. The narrator in *Jazz* is generous with warnings: 'The girls have red lips and their legs whisper to each other through silk stockings. The red lips and the silk flash power. A power they will exchange for the right to be overcome, penetrated.'

Morrison's writing of a black romance pays its debt to blues music, the rhythms and the melancholy pleasures of which she has so magically transformed into a novel. More than that, she has claimed new sources and new kinds of reading as the inspiration for a thriving literature.

Jane Miller, "New Romance," *London Review of Books*, 14 May 1992, p. 12

DENISE HEINZE   As an artist, Morrison negotiates a very complex matrix of reality in which she is both despised and revered, absent and present, ignored and sought after. The result is a double-visionary canon, a symbiosis of novel-writing in which Morrison has complete mastery over the fictive reality she creates. And by her creative mediation between the real and fictive worlds, she generates possibilities rather than records continued frustration and oppression. Morrison may not write from a stance of art as life, but she may be a psychological and spiritual Wizard of Oz for life as art. ⟨...⟩

By combining political consciousness with aesthetic sensibility, Morrison achieves a very delicate balance: without directly denouncing white society, she illustrates the demise of blacks who have adopted the corrupting influence of the white community. By indirection Morrison avoids the polarization of black and white humanity—one as inherently good, the other irrevocably corrupt—and thus allows all people to vicariously experience a rebirth through the black community. While her intent may be to valorize the black community and ignite both blacks and whites into political action, what she also wishes is to elevate through art the beautiful—and hence reclaimable—in the human condition.

Perhaps therein lies her appeal, for in denouncing the dominant culture she presents to an aging America alternatives that have always existed and are now emerging, but which have long been suppressed by the rhetoric of an entrenched ideology. Morrison's success as a great American writer is perhaps a function of two factors: (1) her ability to manipulate her insider/outsider status, for she both subverts and maintains, is exploited by and exploits the literary establishment, and (2) her recognition that her double-consciousness can never be, perhaps never should be, integrated into a single vision. Indeed, she is in the truly remarkable position of being able to articulate with near impunity two cultures—one black, the other white American. By orchestrating this sense of connectedness between cultures rather than attempting to dissolve the differences, Morrison's successful career appears to have transcended the "permanent condition" of double-consciousness that afflicts her fictional characters.

Denise Heinze, The Dilemma of "Double Consciousness": Toni Morrison's Novels (Athens: University of Georgia Press, 1993), pp. 8–10

◨ Bibliography

The Bluest Eye. 1970.
Sula. 1973.
The Black Book (editor). 1974.
Song of Solomon. 1977.
Tar Baby. 1981.
Beloved. 1987.
Race-ing Justice, En-gendering Power: Essays on Anita Hill, Clarence Thomas, and the Construction of Social Reality (editor). 1992.
Jazz. 1992.
Playing in the Dark: Whiteness and the Literary Imagination. 1992.

Lecture and Speech of Acceptance, upon the Award of the Nobel Prize for Literature.
      1994.
Conversations with Toni Morrison. Ed. Danille Taylor-Guthrie. 1994.

◈ ◈ ◈

Gloria Naylor
b. 1950

GLORIA NAYLOR was born on January 25, 1950, in New York City to Roosevelt
Naylor, a transit worker, and Alberta McAlpin Naylor, a telephone operator.
Her interest in writing dates from grade school, but upon graduating from
high school in 1968 she decided not to continue her education, instead
becoming a missionary for the Jehovah's Witnesses. Naylor spent the next
seven years proselytizing in New York, North Carolina, and Florida before
becoming disenchanted with the movement and returning to New York in
1975.

Naylor worked as a telephone operator in various hospitals in New York
City to support herself as she continued her education. After a brief attempt
to study nursing at Medgar Evers College, Naylor enrolled in the English
program at Brooklyn College, where she received her B.A. in 1981. The
next year she published *The Women of Brewster Place*, a "Novel in Seven
Stories" that describes the lives of a group of women living in a slum
neighborhood. The book was a critical success, and in 1983 Naylor won
the American Book Award for best first novel and a Distinguished Writer
Award from the Mid-Atlantic Writers Association. The book was also turned
into a successful television special (and an unsuccessful series) on ABC in
1989.

In 1985 Naylor published *Linden Hills*, a novel that is set in an upscale
black neighborhood within sight of Brewster Place. *Linden Hills* was inspired
by Dante's *Inferno*; in Naylor's novel middle- and upper-class blacks sacrifice
some part of their soul to attain upward mobility. *Linden Hills* was followed
by *Mama Day* (1988), a novel about a community on a small, isolated island
off the coasts of Georgia and South Carolina that was orginally settled by
an African-born fugitive slave. Most recently, Naylor published *Bailey's Cafe*
(1992), a magical realist novel that takes place in a mysterious post–World
War II cafe.

Since the publication of *The Women of Brewster Place*, Naylor has held
a variety of academic positions at various universities, including Princeton

University, the University of Pennsylvania, Brandeis University, and Cornell University. In addition, she received a fellowship from the National Endowment for the Arts in 1985 and a Guggenheim Fellowship in 1988. She recently completed a play adaptation of *Bailey's Cafe,* which opened in April 1994 at the Hartford Stage in Hartford, Conneticut, to good reviews. Naylor currently resides in the Washington Heights area of Manhattan.

◈ *Critical Extracts*

DOROTHY WICKENDEN   Like any ghetto, Brewster Place has its horrors and its desperate charms. A dead-end street, cut off from the city's main arteries by a brick wall, this neighborhood is inhabited by decaying apartment buildings, children who "bloom in colorful shorts and tops plastered against gold, ebony, and nut-brown arms and legs," and women who "pin their dreams to wet laundry hung out to dry." There are men who live here too, of course. They visit their women like nightmares, leaving behind them babies and bile. But Gloria Naylor's women, much like those of Toni Morrison and Alice Walker, are daunting even in desolation. Most of them find that through laughter and companionship they can make themselves virtually impregnable. ⟨. . .⟩

It won't come as a surprise to readers of contemporary fiction by black women that Gloria Naylor has few kind words to waste on members of the other sex: Yet *The Women of Brewster Place,* like Alice Walker's extraordinary *The Color Purple* ⟨. . .⟩—and unlike much current fiction by privileged white feminists—is not simply a self-indulgent celebration of female solidarity. Naylor and Walker write with equal lucidity about the cruelty that poverty breeds and the ways in which people achieve redemption. Nor is there a wariness about traditional women's roles. *The Women of Brewster Place* is a novel about motherhood, a concept embraced by Naylor's women, each of whom is a surrogate child or mother to the next.

Despite the simple elegance of Naylor's prose, there is a risk that the accumulation of horrific experiences may deaden some readers' senses before the novel builds to its devastating climax. Yet the spirit with which these women cope is, finally, more powerful than the circumstances of their lives.

Dorothy Wickenden, [Review of *The Women of Brewster Place*], *New Republic,* 6 September 1982, pp. 37–38.

GLORIA NAYLOR and TONI MORRISON   GN: You know,

it takes a lot to finally say that. That "Yes, I write. No, Mama, I'll never have a regular job for more than a year. This is what I do."

You know, there are moments with my work when I can achieve the type of atmosphere that's permeating this house and our conversation now. It's as if I've arrived in a place where it's all spirit and no body—an over-whelming sense of calm. But those moments are rare. Usually, I vacillate between an intense love of my work and "What in the hell am I doing this for?" There has to be an easier way to get the type of pain that I'm inflicting upon myself at this desk. But I guess I keep at it because of those times when I can reach that spiritual center. It's like floating in the middle of that river, and waves are all around you . . . I actually begin to feel blessed.

TM: It is a blessing. Any art form that can do that for you is a special thing. People have to have that sense of having moved something from one place to another and made out of nothing something. Having added something to something and having seen a mess and made it orderly or seen rigidity and given it fluidity. You know, something. And writing encompasses for me all there isn't.

GN: Do you even think that you've been chosen, knowing that you're always going to do this? Because I really feel as if it's sort of like a calling. Not a calling meaning anything special or different, because the men who come up there to clean your road perform a service to this planet just like an artist performs a service. But I really feel that for me it goes beyond just a gift to handle words, but that it was *meant* for me to be writing as opposed to other things that I'm talented enough to do and can do well when I put my mind to it. For example, I do teach and I enjoy it. But there's not the same type of pull—I think I would self-destruct if I didn't write. I wouldn't self-destruct if I didn't teach.

TM: You *would* self-destruct if you didn't write. You know, I wanted to ask you whether or not, when you finished The Women ⟨of Brewster Place⟩, did you know what the next book was? ⟨. . .⟩ When you finished The Women of Brewster Place, what was the time period and the emotional trek to Linden Hills?

GN: Well, two things were going on, Toni. One was that I wanted there to be a Linden Hills.

TM: Even before you finished . . .

GN: Yes, because I had a character in Brewster Place named Kiswana Browne who lived in Linden Hills. And my next dream—you know, the daydreams about what you want to do, the easy part of writing any book—was that I would love to do a whole treatment of her neighborhood. And at about that time, I was taking this course at Brooklyn College, "Great Works of Literature." And we had read *The Inferno* and I was overwhelmed by the philosophical underpinnings of the poem as well as the characters that Dante created. Then the idea came to me that I could try to sketch out this neighborhood along the lines of *The Inferno*. But it was a while before I could actually sit down and work on the book because there was fear, a little, because this was going to be a *real* novel. *Brewster Place* was really interconnected short stories and that type of work demands a shorter time span, a different emotional involvement. So it was in the summer of 1981 when I began to seriously sketch out what I might like to do with *Linden Hills* and it was a year later when I literally sat down and said, "Here is the emotional involvement. I have the idea and I'm going to go for it."

Gloria Naylor and Toni Morrison, "Gloria Naylor and Toni Morrison: A Conversation," *Southern Review* 21, No. 3 (July 1985): 581–82

CATHERINE C. WARD   Gloria Naylor's second novel, *Linden Hills*, is a modern version of Dante's *Inferno* in which souls are damned not because they have offended God or have violated a religious system but because they have offended themselves. In their single-minded pursuit of upward mobility, the inhabitants of Linden Hills, a black, middle-class suburb, have turned away from their past and from their deepest sense of who they are. Naylor feels that the subject of who-we-are and what we are willing to give up of who-we-are to get where-we-want-to-go is a question of the highest seriousness—as serious as a Christian's concern over his salvation. ⟨. . .⟩

Naylor's tale is an allegory based on the physical and moral topography of Dante's *Inferno*. It covers four days in the life of a twenty-year-old black poet, Willie Mason, who lives in a poor neighborhood called Putney Wayne that lies above Linden Hills. Working temporarily as a handyman to earn money to buy Christmas presents, Willie passes through Linden Hills and, like Dante, analyzes the moral failures of the lost souls he encounters. By the time Willie escapes from the frozen lake at the bottom of Linden Hills and crosses to the safety of a nearby apple orchard, he has experienced a spiritual awakening. The "new" Willie has decided to give up his aimless drifting and to take charge of his life. He becomes, as his name implies, a decisive builder. He accepts responsibility for his life, he refuses to blame his problems on others or on fate, and he realizes that he can choose a middle way between the poverty of the ghetto and the depravity of Linden Hills.

Eight concentric drives cross Linden Hills. First Crescent Drive through Fifth Crescent Drive correspond to Circles One through Five in Dante's upper Hell. Below upper Linden Hills lies a more exclusive section, the Tupelo Drive area, which corresponds to the City of Dis. At the center of Linden Hills is the house of Luther Nedeed, surrounded by a frozen lake. Luther Nedeed is the fifth of his line; the original Luther Nedeed came from Tupelo, Mississippi, and founded the area in 1820. The Luther Nedeeds are the Satans or anti-Christs of Linden Hills. Each one has been both an undertaker and a real estate developer and thus has been able to control the residents in death as well as in life. ⟨. . .⟩

In Linden Hills up is down; the most prestigious lots are those lower down the hill. To gain one of those lots, which are never sold but are leased for 1001 years, each of the residents must give up something—a part of his soul, ties with his past, ties with his community, his spiritual values, even his sense of who he is. Like Dante's lost souls, the people of Linden Hills live on a circle that is appropriate to their "sins." Here most residents stay for the rest of their lives, locked in their wrong choices.

Catherine C. Ward, "Gloria Naylor's Linden Hills: A Modern Inferno," Contemporary Literature 28, No. 1 (Spring 1987): 67, 69–70

RITA MAE BROWN   God created the universe in six days. It took her longer, but Gloria Naylor has created her own universe in Mama Day.

The novel's title is the pet name of the most powerful figure in Willow Springs, a fictional Southern island. Miranda Day, born in 1895, is the great-aunt of Cocoa Day, a young, too-smart woman who moves to New York City.

Just why Cocoa would want to live among both the cold and the Yankees mystifies the residents of Willow Springs. Mama Day figures, observing the male inhabitants of the island, that there have to be better men in New York, even if they do talk funny. ⟨. . .⟩

Into this upside-down world ⟨of Willow Springs⟩ comes George Andrews, Cocoa's new husband. George's power comes from his logical Western mind. He is an engineer and values precision. He is also an orphan cut off from his roots, and therefore beguiled by Willow Springs where bloodlines can be traced through the centuries. ⟨. . .⟩

George is the linchpin of *Mama Day*. His rational mind allows the reader to experience the island as George experiences it. Mama Day and Cocoa are of the island and therefore less immediately accessible to the reader.

The turning point of the book comes when George is asked not only to believe in Mama Day's power but to act on it. Cocoa is desperately ill. A hurricane has washed out the bridge so that no mainland doctor can be summoned. Only Mama Day can show George the way to save his wife. He is told to go into the chicken coop and search in the northwest corner for the nest of an old red hen. He is to bring back to Mama Day what he finds there. He tries to do as he is told, but George needs a quantifiable result. He misses the symbolism of the eggs, of the old hen, and of the objects he must carry into the hen house. And so he "fails," but his action allows his wife to live even though the result of this task is horrible for him.

The formula for heterosexual salvation in conventional novels is for the man and woman either to understand one another and live happily ever after or to understand each other and realize they can't live together. The key is thinking, not necessarily feeling. Not so here. George must let go of his rigidity, his "male" mind. When he can't do that, he sacrifices himself on the altar of love. Success is a form of surrender: the opposite of the desire to control.

Rita Mae Brown, "Black Laughter in an Offshore Showoff Novel," Los Angeles Times Book Review, 6 March 1988, p. 2

LARRY R. ANDREWS   Female power and wisdom are vividly incarnated in Miranda, the title character ⟨of *Mama Day*. . . .⟩ Forced prematurely into a nurturing role in her family after her mother's suicide, Miranda eventually becomes not only a mother to her grandniece Ophelia but a "Mama" to the whole island community of Willow Springs. For decades she is not only the community's midwife but also its guardian of tradition and its central authority figure: "Mama Day say no, everybody say no." She is a powerful conjure woman with special gifts derived, in the community's view, from "being a direct descendant of Sapphira Wade, piled on the fact of springing from the seventh son of a seventh son." She feels the burdensome responsibility of her intuitive powers and her knowledge of nature and uses them only to advance the cause of life (making Bernice fertile or calling down lightning to punish the murderous Ruby).

Miranda's womanpower is thus presented as an expression of natural forces (note her gardening ability) and as an inheritance from the legendary ur-mother of the community. When Sapphira Wade liberated herself from her white husband and master, Bascombe Wade, in 1823, she initiated a tradition of female power as well as a religious tradition (Candle Walk) and strengthened the myth of the great conjure woman on hand at God's creation of the island. She was also legendary for bringing into the open the unresolved tensions between men and women. Miranda feels largely an unconscious sisterhood with Sapphira through various intuitive experiences of knowledge and power. For example, when she handles Sapphira's fabric while making a quilt for Ophelia, she has a sudden premonition that George will not be coming, and when she finds Bascombe's undecipherable ledger and Sapphira's bill of sale, she has vague dreams that lead to a way to save Ophelia's life. On the other hand, Miranda feels a more *conscious* bond of sisterhood with her mother. And her mother's madness and suicide, described partly as an escape from her husband, connect her mother and hence Miranda to Sapphira again.

Thus female power is *there* in the legendary past for the females of Willow Springs to learn, to accept, and to draw strength from in their own lives. As ⟨Susan⟩ Willis says, "For black women history is a bridge defined along motherlines." Sisterhood here is not a relationship that arises for the nonce as a *response to* a particular condition, such as oppression. It is a force that transcends particulars and is allied to nature itself. Miranda is the role model for the full acceptance and living of this power.

Larry R. Andrews, "Black Sisterhood in Gloria Naylor's Novels," *CLA Journal* 33, No. 1 (September 1989): 18–19

MICHAEL AWKWARD   The unity of form and content in Gloria Naylor's *The Women of Brewster Place* is, like that of its female-authored precursors, essentially related to its exploration of the redemptive possibilities of female coalescence. But because it is a work that consists of the narratively *disconnected* stories of individual women, such coalescence does not involve simply an individual protagonist's inside and outside as it does in *Their Eyes Were Watching God* and *The Bluest Eye*. Rather, it involves demonstrating— both by exhibiting essential psychological and circumstantial affinities between the women and by offering significant evidence of these women's recognition of such affinities—that the protagonists of the individual texts actually form, at the novel's conclusion, a community of women. As is the case in both of the texts on which this study has concentrated to this point, textual explorations of female unity in Naylor's novel are unmistakably related to the work's narrative strategies, strategies whose ends are under-scored by the novel's subtitle, "A Novel in Seven Stories": to demonstrate that the narratively disconnected texts of individual protagonists can be forged into a unified whole.

Naylor's narrative tasks are seemingly complicated by the means she chooses to demonstrate an achieved Afro-American's woman's community. In a novel in which unrealistic dreams are the source of much of the female characters' pain, the author's depiction of the scene of female coalescence— the women's unified efforts to tear down the wall that separates Brewster Place from the rest of the city—as the grief-inspired dream of one of these characters prevents a reading of Naylor's portrait of female nexus as either an actual narrative event or a realistic possibility. *The Women of Brewster Place*'s totalizing gesture, then, evidences the work's textual disjunctions. If Naylor's novel displays a unity of form and content, it is a unity based on a common *disunity*, on a shared failure to achieve wholeness.

> Michael Awkward, "Authorial Dreams of Wholeness: (Dis)Unity, (Literary) Parent-age, and *The Women of Brewster Place*," *Inspiriting Influences: Tradition, Revision, and Afro-American Women's Novels* (New York: Columbia University Press, 1989), p. 98

JILL L. MATUS   The inconclusive last chapter ⟨of *The Women of Brewster Place*⟩ opens into an epilogue that ⟨. . .⟩ teases the reader with the sense of an ending by appearing to be talking about the death of the street, Brewster Place. The epilogue itself is not unexpected, since the novel opens with a prologue describing the birth of the street. So why not a last word on how it dies? Again, expectations are subverted and closure is subtly deferred. Although the epilogue begins with a meditation on how a street dies and tells us that Brewster Place is waiting to die, *waiting* is a present participle that never becomes past. "Dawn" (the prologue) is coupled neither with death nor darkness, but with "dusk," a condition whose half-light underscores the half-life of the street. Despite the fact that in the epilogue Brewster Place is abandoned, its daughters still get up elsewhere and go about their daily activities. In a reiteration of the domestic routines that are always carefully attended to in the novel—the making of soup, the hanging of laundry, the diapering of babies—, Brewster's death is forestalled and postponed. More importantly, the narrator emphasizes that the dreams of Brewster's inhabitants are what keep them alive. *"They get up and pin those dreams to wet laundry hung out to dry, they're mixed with a pinch of salt and thrown into pots of soup, and they're diapered around babies. They ebb and flow, ebb and flow, but never disappear." They* refers initially to the "colored daughters" but thereafter repeatedly to the dreams. The end of the novel raises questions about the relation of dreams to the persistence of life, since the capacity of Brewster's women to dream on is identified as their capacity to live on. The street continues to exist marginally, on the edge of death; it is the "end of the line" for most of its inhabitants. Like the street, the novel hovers, moving toward the end of its line, but deferring. What prolongs both the text and the lives of Brewster's inhabitants is dream; in the same way that Mattie's dream of destruction postpones the end of the novel, the narrator's last words identify dream as that which affirms and perpetuates the life of the street.

> Jill L. Matus, "Dream, Deferral, and Closure in *The Women of Brewster Place*," *Black American Literature Forum* 24, No. 1 (Spring 1990): 49–50

BARBARA CHRISTIAN   It is precisely the fact that Naylor's two neighborhoods ⟨Brewster Place and Linden Hills⟩ *are* black that causes them to perceive so clearly their difference. Importantly, Naylor locates their similarities and differences in a historical process. Both Brewster Place and Linden Hills have been created by racism, or more precisely, as a result of the effects of racism on their founders. Linden Hills is literally carved out of a seemingly worthless soil by an ex-slave, Luther Nedeed, who in the 1820s had the secret dream of developing "an ebony jewel," a community of successful blacks who could stave off the racism of America and exhibit through their fine houses that members of the race can be powerful. In contrast, Brewster Place is "the bastard child of clandestine meetings" between local white politicians, at first to satisfy expected protests from the Irish community over the undeserved dismissal of their too-honest police chief. Later, Brewster Place becomes the neighborhood of successive waves of European immigrants, unwanted Americans who finally become, over time, the black poor.

The origin of communities and their historical development are as critical to the structure of Naylor's novels as they are to ⟨Paule⟩ Marshall's and ⟨Toni⟩ Morrison's. These two writers—Marshall particularly in *Brown Girl, Brownstones*, Morrison particularly in *Sula*—begin their narrative not with the introduction of their characters but with the history of their characters' natal communities. ⟨. . .⟩ The differences between these authors' respective treatments, however, is instructive, for Marshall's West Indian immigrants see their brownstones as places they can eventually own, as a step up, while Naylor's blacks of Brewster Place are at a dead end. Morrison's ex-slave earns his "bottom" as payment from his ex-master and is cheated in the process, for he is given the worst land in the area. But Naylor's Nedeed carefully *chooses* his site, outwitting everyone who sees his plateau as having no value.

Although Naylor characterizes one neighborhood as held together by women and the other as controlled by a family, she stresses that both are started by men for the purpose of consolidating power. The intentions of these men are evident in the geographical choices they make. Nedeed's choice of "a V-shaped section of land," "the northern face of a worthless plateau" indicates his direction. Not only is his site so clearly visible; even more important, its V-shape allows his land to be self-enclosed yet situated in the world. And since Nedeed lives on the lowest level of "the hills," he stands as a sentry to his private development. The shape of Brewster Place too is self-enclosed, for a wall is put up, separating it from other neighborhoods and making it a dead end. Ironically, what is positive in one context is negative in another, depending on who has power. For black Nedeed uses his enclosed V-shape to select those who will be allowed to live near him, while the people of Brewster Place have a wall imposed on them by white city officials who want them separated from more "respectable" folk.

Barbara Christian, "Gloria Naylor's Geography: Community, Class, and Patriarchy in *The Women of Brewster Place* and *Linden Hills*," *Reading Black, Reading Feminist: A Critical Anthology*, ed. Henry Louis Gates, Jr. (New York: Meridian, 1990), pp. 351–52

BARBARA SMITH   In "The Two" ⟨in *The Women of Brewster Place*
. . .⟩, Naylor sets up the women's response to their ⟨lesbian⟩ identity as an
either/or dichotomy. Lorraine's desire for acceptance, although completely
comprehensible, is based upon assimilation and denial, while Naylor depicts
Theresa's healthier defiance as an individual stance. In the clearest statement
of resistance in the story, Theresa thinks: "If they practiced that way with
each other, then they could turn back to back and beat the hell out of the
world for trying to invade their territory. But she had found no such sparring
partner in Lorraine, and the strain of fighting alone was beginning to show
on her." A mediating position between complete assimilation or alienation
might well evolve from some sense of connection to a Lesbian/gay community. Involvement with other Lesbians and gay men could provide a reference
point and support that would help diffuse some of the straight world's power.
Naylor mentions that Theresa socializes with gay men and perhaps Lesbians
at a bar, but her interactions with them occur outside the action of the
story. The author's decision not to portray other Lesbians and gay men, but
only to allude to them, is a significant one. The reader is never given an
opportunity to view Theresa or Lorraine in a context in which they are the
norm. Naylor instead presents them as "the two" exceptions in an entirely
heterosexual world. Both women are extremely isolated and although their
relationship is loving, it also feels claustrophobic. ⟨. . .⟩ Lorraine's rejection
of other Lesbians and gay men is excruciating, as is the self-hatred that
obviously prompts it. It is painfully ironic that she considers herself in the
same boat with Black people in the story, who are heterosexual, most of
whom ostracize her, but not with black people who are Lesbian and gay.
The one time that Lorraine actually decides to go to the club by herself,
ignoring Theresa's warning that she won't have a good time without her,
is the night that she is literally destroyed. ⟨. . .⟩

Whatever their opinions, it is not the women of the neighborhood who
are directly responsible for Lorraine's destruction, but six actively homopho-
bic and woman-hating teenage boys. Earlier that day Lorraine and Kiswana
Browne had encountered the toughs who unleashed their sexist and homo-
phobic violence on the two young women. Kiswana verbally bests their
leader, C. C. Baker, but he is dissuaded from physically retaliating because
one of the other boys reminds him: " 'That's Abshu's woman, and that big
dude don't mind kickin' ass.' " As a Lesbian, Lorraine does not have any
kind of "dude" to stand between her and the violence of other men. Although
she is completely silent during the encounter, C. C.'s parting words to her

are, "I'm gonna remember this, Butch!" That night when Lorraine returns from the bar alone, she walks into the alley which is the boy's turf. They are waiting for her and gang-rape her in one of the most devastating scenes in literature. ⟨. . .⟩

⟨. . .⟩ Although the Lesbian characters in "The Two" lack authenticity, the story possesses a certain level of verisimilitude. The generalized homophobia that the women face, which culminates in retaliatory rape and near murderous decimation, is quite true to life. Gay and Lesbian newspapers provide weekly accounts, which sometimes surface in the mainstream media, of the constant violence leveled at members of our communities. What feels disturbing and inauthentic to me is how utterly hopeless Naylor's view of Lesbian existence is. Lorraine and Theresa are classically unhappy homosexuals of the type who populated white literature during a much earlier era, when the only options for the "deviant" were isolation, loneliness, mental illness, suicide, or death.

Barbara Smith, "The Truth That Never Hurts: Black Lesbians in Fiction in the 1980s," *Wild Women in the Whirlwind: Afra-American Culture and the Contemporary Literary Renaissance,* ed. Joanne M. Braxton and Andrée Nicola McLaughlin (New Brunswick, NJ: Rutgers University Press, 1990), pp. 227–30

JACQUELINE BOBO and ELLEN SEITER   ⟨The television special⟩ *The Women of Brewster Place* runs close to the codes of the television melodrama (especially of soap operas and made-for-television movies), but at the same time is very different. There are three notable features appearing in the television adaptation that the novel *The Women of Brewster Place* shares with other works by black women writers ⟨. . .⟩: an exploration of the sense of community among black women, an indictment of sexism, and an emphasis on the importance of black women supporting each other. In *The Women of Brewster Place,* the black community is used for survival rather than individual advancement and upward mobility. Although the programme tells the story of seven women, the first and longest story establishes Mattie Michael (the Oprah Winfrey character) as a pivotal figure—functioning much as the 'tentpole character' does in soap opera. Mattie's story covers about eighteen years, beginning with her first and only pregnancy. Through good fortune, hard work and the friendship of an older woman, Mattie achieves one of her dreams of success: she becomes a home owner. Miss Eva's and Mattie's house is represented neither as a cold and alienating bourgeois prison in the tradition of family melodrama on film (and of avant-garde feminist films such as *Jeanne Dielmann*), nor as the flimsy, obviously artificial, temporary set of American soap operas. Rather, the characters' aspirations to the comforts and the aesthetics of cosy domestic space are dignified with many lingering takes of interiors in which an absence of dialogue focuses attention on the sounds and the rhythms of life within the home. These images contrast sharply with the cramped rooms without views on Brewster Place. At the end of the first episode, Mattie loses the house when her son, on a murder charge, skips bail and disappears. The rest of the story traces Mattie's descent, her fall from economic grace and her arrival at Brewster Place. By the end of the programme, we realize that Mattie's personal fall has permitted her move into a nexus of women friends and neighbours, and thus the beginning of the community—troubled though it may be—of Brewster Place.

This is a strikingly different structure from that of most Hollywood film narratives, in which images of community are for the most part entirely lacking, and narrative conventions are typically based on the autonomous, unconnected individual. *The Women of Brewster Place*, though, does not offer a utopian image of community: poverty, violence, and bigotry are permanent features, and these are shown to deform personal relationships and threaten women. Yet it contains striking instances of deeply held values that are starkly opposed to the values of the mainstream white culture and economy. For example, after Mattie has left her rat-infested apartment and searched futilely for another place to live, she and her infant son are taken in by Miss Eva to share her home. Miss Eva rejects the money that Mattie offers her for board, refusing to translate into market relations her gesture of help to a woman in need. Mattie, bewildered by this generosity, puts money in the cookie jar every week, but Miss Eva never takes it. Miss Eva shares all her material wealth and comfort with Mattie—literally a stranger off the street—without hesitation. It is almost impossible to conceive of this kind of act towards a person unrelated by blood in the universe of the white family melodrama.

Jacqueline Bobo and Ellen Seiter, "Black Feminism and Media Criticism: *The Women of Brewster Place*," *Screen* 32, No. 3 (Autumn 1991): 294–95

RICHARD EDER   Gloria Naylor's new novel ⟨*Bailey's Cafe*⟩ is devotional at heart, though it is told in contrasting shades of harsh, comic and magic realism. Its stories of ravaged urban blacks, most of them women, are savage and sardonic, but they float in a mystical lyricism. They are the stories of the regulars who frequent Bailey's, and they are told by the proprietor, doorkeeper and gritty good shepherd who both runs it and expounds it, along with his laconically nurturing wife, Nadine. It stands "on the margin between the edge of the world and infinite possibility," he tells us.

Naylor writes consummately well of the real world's edge. Her infinite possibility is shakier. It is cloudy or downright sentimental at times, though it can also be moving. Magic is a tricky proposition; when it doesn't transport you, it strands you. The seedy watering-place as a place of dreams—Saroyan's saloon in "The Time of Your Life," the End of the Line Cafe in *The Iceman Cometh*, Lanford Wilson's Hot L Baltimore and Bailey's place need a vigilant bouncer to keep bathos out. Bailey, like some of his predecessors, can grow distracted. ⟨. . .⟩

The horrors of our time—at war, and for blacks in the cities—defy practical remedy. And so, Bailey and Nadine ⟨. . .⟩ move into the partly grounded, partly floating Cafe. It is a place of kindness but it is more than a refuge. It is a place for stories and for healing—not healing as a cure but as a power to endure—by primal power. Much of this power, which suggests female shamanic traditions from Africa and the Caribbean, is lodged in Eve. She runs a boarding house—as real and supernatural as the Cafe— that is a brothel too, and a convent. Many of the brutalized women, whose story Bailey tells, live there. Their "gentleman callers" cannot buy them. They must, however, buy flowers from Eve to present to them; and each woman has her own totemic flower.

The Eve figure, her flowers and ancient female mysteries, impart a certain forced wonder, and over-dosed and over-sweet exhortation; though Naylor gives her fierceness and resourcefulness as well. Some of the women's stories, such as that of the Ethiopian child, Mariam, who gives birth at the Cafe although she is a virgin; and disappears in a wall of water that her parched longings have summoned up, show similar indulgence.

In others, the sheer strength and color of the story more than make up for a spot of undigested uplift here and there. "Josie" tells of a righteous woman who is both undone and transfigured by abuse. ⟨. . .⟩

When she sits in the cafe, her dream of a just and gracious life shines so strongly that she imparts grace to her shaking coffee mug. And when a kind and comic iceman recognizes her light and wants to marry her, she imagines making a perfect home with him. And in an impressive twist, Naylor suddenly suggests imagination as a kingdom more powerful than reality.

Richard Eder, "Grounds for the City," *Los Angeles Times Book Review*, 30 August 1992, p. 3

◈ *Bibliography*

The Women of Brewster Place: A Novel in Seven Stories. 1982.
Linden Hills. 1985.
Mama Day. 1988.
He's a Russian Jew. 1992.
Bailey's Cafe. 1992.

⊞ ⊞ ⊞

Ann Petry
b. 1912

ANN PETRY was born Ann Lane on October 12, 1912, in Old Saybrook, Connecticut. Her father was a pharmacist who operated his own drugstore, so that the Lanes were generally accepted by the white population of Old Saybrook in spite of the fact that they were only one of two black families in the small town. Several other members of Ann's family were also pharmacists. Ann began writing stories and poems while at Old Saybrook High School, from which she graduated in 1929; she then decided to pursue the family career by attending the College of Pharmacy of the University of Connecticut. She received a Ph.G. degree in 1931 and worked for seven years at her family's pharmacies in Old Saybrook and Lyme.

In 1938 Ann married the mystery writer George D. Petry; they have one daughter. Petry moved to Harlem, writing advertising copy for the *Amsterdam News* from 1938 to 1941 and being a reporter for the *People's Voice* from 1941 to 1946 while writing short stories in her spare time. Her first published story was "Marie of the Cabin Club," appearing in the *Afro-American* for August 19, 1939, under the pseudonym Arnold Petri. In 1943 she enrolled in a writing course at Columbia University; shortly thereafter, she was publishing stories in the *Crisis*, *Opportunity*, *Phylon*, and other journals. Petry's nonliterary life was also busy, as she formed a political group, Negro Women, Inc., lent assistance to a Harlem elementary school, and acted in an American Negro Theater production.

One of Petry's stories, "On Saturday the Siren Sounds at Noon," came to the attention of Houghton Mifflin, which invited her to apply for one of its literary fellowships. The synopsis and first five chapters of what would become Petry's first novel, *The Street*, won her the Houghton Mifflin Literary Fellowship. The novel was published in 1946 and received highly favorable reviews as a sensitive portrayal of a black woman's life in Harlem. The next year she published *Country Place*, a novel about small-town life in Connecticut; although all the major characters are white, Petry draws heavily upon her early life in Old Saybrook for many social and topographical details. In 1953 her third novel, *The Narrows*, appeared. Dealing with an interracial affair between a black man and a white woman in Connecticut, it is perhaps Petry's most complex and ambitious novel.

In the late 1940s Petry began to turn her attention to children's works, and she has produced *The Drugstore Cat* (1949), *Harriet Tubman: Conductor of the Underground Railroad* (1955), *Tituba of Salem Village* (1964), and *Legends of the Saints* (1970). Both her earlier and her later stories for adults were collected in *Miss Muriel and Other Stories* (1971).

Ann Petry left Harlem and returned to Old Saybrook in 1948, where she continues to reside with her husband.

▨ *Critical Extracts*

JAMES W. IVY   In person Mrs. Petry is of medium height, pleasant manners and intercourse, and possessed of a sense of companionable good humor. She has a creamy-brown complexion; alert, smiling eyes; and a soft cultivated voice. We entered at once into the intimacy of talk and the first thing I wanted to know was how she had come to write her first published story ("On Saturday the Siren Sounds at Noon").

"Did you have any particular message in that story? What were you trying to show?"

"Nothing in particular. I wrote it simply as a story. But it came to be written in this way. One Saturday I was standing on the 125th Street platform of the IRT subway when a siren suddenly went off. The screaming blast seemed to vibrate inside people. For the siren seemed to be just above the station. I immediately noticed the reactions of the people on the platform. They were interesting, especially the frantic knitting of a woman seated on a nearby bench.

"I began wondering," continued Mrs. Petry, "how this unearthly howl would affect a criminal, a man hunted by the police. That was the first incident. The second was a tragedy I covered for my paper. There was a fire in Harlem in which two children had been burnt to death. Their parents were at work and the children were alone. I imagined their reactions when they returned home that night. I knew also that many Harlem parents, like

Lilly Belle in the story, often left their children home alone while at work. Imaginatively combined the two incidents gave me my story." ⟨. . .⟩

I then asked her about her recently published novel, *The Street*.

"In *The Street* my aim is to show how simply and easily the environment can change the course of a person's life. For this purpose I have made Lindy Johnson an intelligent, ambitious, attractive woman with a fair degree of education. She lives in the squalor of 116th Street, but she retains her self-respect and fights to bring up her little son decently.

"I try to show why the Negro has a high crime rate, a high death rate, and little or no chance of keeping his family unit intact in large northern cities. There are no statistics in the book through they are present in the background, not as columns of figures but in terms of what life is like for people who live in over-crowded tenements.

"I tried to write a story that moves swiftly so that it would hold the attention of people who might ordinarily shy away from a so-called problem novel. And I hope that I have created characters who are real, believable, alive. For I am of the opinion that most Americans regard Negroes as types— not quite human—who fit into a special category and I wanted to show them as people with the same capacity for love and hate, for tears and laughter, and the same instinct for survival possessed by all men."

James W. Ivy, "Ann Petry Talks about First Novel," *Crisis* 53, No. 1 (January 1946): 48–49

ARNA BONTEMPS   The young woman's fight against the corrupting influences of this crowded little world, her effort to safeguard her son and to keep herself unsoiled, is the challenging theme Miss Petry has chosen for her novel ⟨*The Street*⟩. She could scarcely have found a more important human problem in our urban life today. She has treated it with complete seriousness in a story that will bear a lot of thoughtful reading.

As a novelist Miss Petry is an unblushing realist. Her recreation of the street has left out none of its essential character. It is a part of her achievement, however, that the carnal life of the slum never seems to be hauled in for its own sake. Even the earthy language, like something overheard on a truck or in a doorway, fails to draw attention to itself; in every case it seems to blend into the situation. It will not be for such details that *The Street* will be read and discussed.

Arna Bontemps, "Tough, Carnal Harlem," *New York Herald Tribune Weekly Book Review*, 10 February 1946, p. 4

WRIGHT MORRIS   Her first novel, *The Street*, published several years ago, attracted well-deserved praise—and, though it dealt with the familiar elements of the Negro-problem novel, it seemed to point the way to a brilliant creative future. But *The Narrows* reads like the first draft of an ambitious conception that has not been labored into imaginative life. It indicates what the author might have done but did not do. The forces that have lowered the craft of fiction have made it more difficult, not less, to write the book that will cry havoc and be heard. Miss Petry can do it, but it will take more brooding labor—and less space.

Wright Morris, "The Complexity of Evil," *New York Times Book Review*, 16 August 1953, p. 4

MARY ROSS   Ann Petry is a native New Englander with generations of New Englanders behind her. She started her career in chemistry. But the New England life of which she writes, in a small Connecticut city two hours' drive from New York, could be equally alien to the founding fathers and the suave commuters and summer people who now bowl along its highways. The "chemistry" of this remarkable novel ⟨*The Narrows*⟩ is something not learned in science books. ⟨. . .⟩

Mrs. Petry, using a theme that might have been merely sensational, builds a novel that has depth and dignity. There is power and insight and reach of imagination in her writing. Most white readers will find themselves in a world that has been closed to them, a world with its own beauty and strength and honor and humor, as well as its pathos and frustration. *The Narrows* is not an apologia for the Negro nor anything so simple as an indictment of the white race. It has no concern with posing or solving a "problem." It is a novel that stands on its own feet and it is an unusual and stirring experience. I have not read Ann Petry's earlier novel, *The*

Street, but I shall do so as soon as I can, and I shall look forward to her future work eagerly.

Mary Ross, "Depth and Dignity, Pathos and Humor," *New York Herald Tribune Book Review*, 16 August 1953, p. 3

ANN PETRY   In recent years, many novels of social criticism have dealt with race relations in this country. It is a theme which offers the novelist a wide and fertile field; it is the very stuff of fiction, sometimes comic, more often tragic, always ironic, endlessly dramatic. The setting and the characters vary in these books but the basic story line is derived from *Uncle Tom's Cabin*; discrimination and/or segregation (substitute slavery for the one or the other) are evils which lead to death—actual death or potential death. The characters either conform to the local taboos and mores and live, miserably; or refuse to conform and die.

This pattern of violence is characteristic of the type for a very good reason. The arguments used to justify slavery still influence American attitudes toward the Negro. If I use the words intermarriage, mixed marriage, miscegenation, there are few Americans who would not react to those words emotionally. Part of that emotion can be traced directly to the days of slavery. And if emotion is aroused merely by the use of certain words, and the emotion is violent, apoplectic, then it seems fairly logical that novels which deal with race relations should reflect some of this violence.

As I said, my first novel was a novel of social criticism. Having written it, I discovered that I was supposed to know the answer to many of the questions that are asked about such novels. What good do they do is a favorite. I think they do a lot of good. Social reforms have often received their original impetus from novels which aroused the emotions of a large number of readers. *Earth and High Heaven*, *Focus*, and *Gentleman's Agreement* undoubtedly made many a person examine the logic of his own special brand of anti-Semitism. The novels that deal with race relations have influenced the passage of the civil rights bills which have become law in many states.

Ann Petry, "The Novel as Social Criticism," *The Writer's Book*, ed. Helen Hull (New York: Barnes & Noble, 1956), pp. 38–39

DAVID LITTLEJOHN   Mrs. Petry has—this first must be
granted—an uncomfortable tendency to contrive sordid plots (as opposed
to merely writing of sordid events). She seems to require a "shocking" chain
of scandalous doings, secret affairs, family skeletons revealed, brutal crimes,
whispered evil, adulterous intrigue on which to cast her creative imagination,
in the manner of the great Victorians or the tawdry moderns. So wise is
her writing, though, so real are her characters, so total is her sympathy,
that one can often accept the faintly cheap horrors and contrivances. Even
if not, though, he can dispense with them. It may seem odd to suggest
reading a novel while skipping the plot; but it can be done. And if one
allows himself to be overexcited by these intrigues (it *is* hard to escape their
clutches, but one should), he misses, I think, the real treasures of Ann
Petry's fiction.

There is, first, more intelligence in her novels, paragraph for paragraph,
than in those of any other writer I have mentioned; solid, earned, tested
intelligence. This woman is sharp. Her wisdom is more useful, even, more
durable, than the brilliant, diamond-edged acuteness of Gwendolyn Brooks.

This wisdom, secondly, reveals itself in a prose that is rich and crisp, and
suavely shot with the metallic threads of irony. It is a style of constant
surprise and delight, alive and alight on the page. It is so charged with sense
and pleasure you can taste it—and yet never (almost never) is it mere
"display."

And out of the female wisdom, the chewy style, grow characters of shape
and dimension, people made out of love, with whole histories evoked in a
page. There is not one writer in a thousand who owns so genuine and
generous and undiscriminating a creative sympathy. Ann Petry *becomes* each
character she mentions, grants each one a full, felt intensity of being, the
mean and the loving, the white and the black, even when they come and
go in only fifty words. ⟨. . .⟩

This, to me, the intelligence, the style, and above all the creative sympathy, is what sets Ann Petry apart from this second rank of American Negro
novelists, sets her, in fact, into a place almost as prominent and promising
as that of the bigger three. She is not, of course, writing "about" the race
war, any more than most of the last eight or ten novelists mentioned are.
This is a delusion fostered either by publishers, playing up a profitable
approach, or by the fake guilty egocentricity of white readers, who presume
that all books by Negroes must somehow be about them. But if an American
Negro can, despite all, develop such an understanding of other people as

Ann Petry's—and more prodigious still, *convey* that understanding—then let her write what *Peyton Place*-plots she will, she is working toward a genuine truce in the war.

> David Littlejohn, *Black on White: A Critical Survey of Writing by American Negroes* (New York: Grossman Publishers, 1966), pp. 154–56

ALFRED KAZIN   By contrast with Mr. ⟨Henry⟩ Van Dyke and/or the majority of black novelists, Ann Petry seems old-fashioned, so surprisingly "slow" in her narrative rhythm that you wonder if the title story in *Miss Muriel and Other Stories* took place in another century. Mrs. Petry's timing is as different from most contemporary black writing as is her locale, which in the best of these leisurely paced stories is a small upstate New York town where a pharmacist and his family are the only Negroes. Their life centers entirely around the drugstore itself. The longest and most successful of these stories, "Miss Muriel," tells of an eccentric elderly white shoemaker in the town, Mr. Bemish, who, to the astonishment and terror of the Negro family, falls in love with Aunt Sophronia. There is no "Muriel" in the story; the title is a sad joke about an old Negro who asked for "Muriel" cigars and was sternly told that *he* would have to ask for them as "Miss Muriel." But the feeling behind the "joke" is so strong in the small, isolated black family that poor Mr. Bemish not only doesn't get Aunt Sophronia, but is driven out of town for falling in love with a black lady.

This reversal of roles is typical of Mrs. Petry's quiet, always underplayed but deeply felt sense of situation. The other stories aren't as lovingly worked out as "Miss Muriel"—which is an artful period piece that brings back a now legendary age of innocence in white-black relationships. Several stories are just tragic situations that are meant to touch you by that quality alone. A famous black drummer loses his adored wife to a pianist in his band, but the drumming must go on; a Harlem old-clothes man falls in love with the oversized statue of a dark woman he calls "Mother Africa"; a Negro teacher is unable to stand up to a gang of young students and flees town, ashamed of not having played a more heroic part; a Negro woman at a convention is insulted by a white woman, and realizes in the morning, on learning that the other woman died of a heart attack during the night, that she might have saved her. These delicate points are characteristic of Mrs. Petry's quietly firm interest in fiction as moral dilemma. Clearly, her sense of the

Negro situation is still "tragic." Her stories are very far from contemporary
black nationalist writing, and by no means necessarily more interesting. But
they are certainly different.

> Alfred Kazin, "Brothers Crying Out for More Access to Life," *Saturday Review*, 2
> October 1971, pp. 34–35

MARGARET B. McDOWELL   As in all her work, Petry excels
in *The Narrows* in her use of concrete detail, her ability to dramatize a
situation, and her ear for exact dialogue. She is a master at transcribing the
details of a given milieu as she recreates, for example, the sound of the river
lapping against the dock at night, the feeling that fog generates as it rolls
up the street from the river, the smell of beer from the saloon across from
Abbie's brick house, and the glare of sunlight on the River Wye. To help
convey the sense of plenitude in the social scene that she recreates in her
novel, she appeals to the auditory sense of her reader, as when Mamie
Powther sings her plaintive blues throughout the novel.

Each place, object, and fragment of dialogue becomes important in creating the realistic milieu, but certain aspects of the Narrows generate abstract
associations. The cemetery becomes segregated, as if the dead must not
mingle across racial lines. A myriad of placards proclaiming rooms for rent
and a growing number of drifters sleeping under Abbie's big tree suggest
the increasingly transient nature of the population. The River Wye, though
a beautiful stream, draws the desperate to suicide. In its growing pollution,
the river symbolizes, to a degree, the economic exploitation of the area.
The naming of the Last Chance saloon promises fellowship as well as food
and drink for the survival of the down-and-outer, but the name also implies
an impending finality to those who need more than food and drink. It offers
no further opportunities for the repressed of society to attain for themselves
security, love or justice. Its neon sign is ugly and cheap, its owner's temper
flares in murderous violence, and it is linked with lucrative prostitution and
gambling enterprises which exploit the poor while providing them with
specious pleasure. The Treadway estate—remote from the Narrows—is also
symbolic. It is the site for an annual festival for the workers in a munitions
plant, but the celebration is an impersonal gesture which expresses no true
concern of the employers for their workers. The laborers, in turn, gossip

viciously about Camilla Treadway's presence on the dock at Dumble Street at midnight when she was allegedly threatened with rape.

The motor cars of the Treadways—the Rolls-Royce and their fleet of Cadillacs—are symbolic of power. Camilla's automobiles make possible the anonymity which she and Link achieve by driving to Harlem. Camilla's impulsive, reckless driving suggests her instability. Treadway automobiles, in a more sinister context, facilitate the kidnaping of Link and the hauling away of his body. Bill Hod's secondhand Cadillacs represent the rewards of his shady dealings, many of which exploit his Black brothers and sisters, while F. K. Jackson's funeral limousine (with its whiskey bottle for the weary and its case of long black gloves and lace veil, available for any bereaved woman to wear for a half hour of proper mourning) reflects how superficial and conventional the rites of grief are to the capitalist entrepreneur.

> Margaret B. McDowell, "*The Narrows*: A Fuller View of Ann Petry," *Black American Literature Forum* 14, No. 4 (Winter 1980): 137

BERNARD W. BELL   Petry, like Himes and Wright, is adept at character delineation, but her protagonists are cut from a different cloth than those of her major contemporaries. Rather than sharing the pathology of a Bigger Thomas or Bob Jones or Lee Gordon, Lutie Johnson and Link Williams are intelligent, commonplace, middle-class aspiring blacks, who, despite the socialized ambivalence resulting from racism and economic exploitation, are not consumed by fear and hatred and rage. Petry's vision of black personality is not only different from that of Himes and Wright, but it is also more faithful to the complexities and varieties of black women, whether they are big-city characters like Mrs. Hedges in *The Street* or small-town characters like Abbie Crunch in *The Narrows*. Ann Petry thus moves beyond the naturalistic vision of Himes and Wright to a demythologizing of American culture and Afro-American character.

> Bernard W. Bell, "Ann Petry's Demythologizing of American Culture and Afro-American Character," *Conjuring: Black Women, Fiction, and Literary Tradition*, ed. Marjorie Pryse and Hortense J. Spillers (Bloomington: Indiana University Press, 1985), p. 114

JAMES DE JONGH   Ann Petry's *The Street* (1943), Ralph Ellison's *Invisible Man* (1952), and James Baldwin's *Go Tell It on the Mountain* (1952)

⟨. . .⟩ are the three novels of this period to rise above typical expression of the emerging ghetto and incorporate the new Harlem of the 1930s and 1940s with transcendent and enduring literary artistry. *The Street* is a keenly observed portrait of the emerging ghetto of Harlem in the early 1940s, and a vivid perceptual rendering as well. The omniscient narrator of *The Street* identifies so convincingly with the perspective of the particular character from whose point of view each specific portion of the story is told that the illusion of a flow of intimate, overlapping autobiographies is sustained without compromising the impartial authority of the narrative voice. Consequently, Petry's third-person narrative reads with the intimacy and perceptual emphasis of a first-person narration. ⟨. . .⟩ Perceptual interpretation of Harlem in *The Street* is reserved almost exclusively for Lutie Johnson, the novel's protagonist. Lutie's view of Harlem is the one that counts in *The Street*, for her struggle to rebuild her family is waged against the malevolent phenomenon of Harlem itself. The microcosmic form of one block of 116th Street is a personage in its own right, and Lutie's true antagonist. ⟨. . .⟩

Lutie tries to make money with her modest voice, when Boots, a Harlem bandleader, is attracted to her. She is unaware that the bandleader is himself little more than a pawn of the malevolent forces of Harlem, embodied by Mrs. Hedges and Junto, two benignly placid puppetmasters whose bizarre relationship constitutes one of the most inventive details in *The Street*. Mrs. Hedges is a gigantic black woman, whose scars from a fire confine her to a comfortably furnished first-floor apartment in the building to which Lutie moves. Junto is a physically unprepossessing white man, who first ran across Mrs. Hedges when he was starting out as a junk dealer in Harlem and recognized her to be one of the few people of any race with a "self-will" comparable to his own. Junto is not squeamish in any way about Mrs. Hedges's scarred and unwomanly figure. To him, she is uniquely attractive, but her own sensitivity about her appearance has made any physical intimacy impossible. Instead Junto and Mrs. Hedges have sublimated their intense feelings into a curious business relationship. From her apartment in a building owned by Junto, Mrs. Hedges has spent her time looking at the life of the street and, with the insights gained from ceaseless observation, has directed Junto to the best investments in Harlem—places where people dance, drink, and make love, in order to forget their troubles. Together the couple monopolize a substantial portion of Harlem's infrastructure, each profiting in respective ways from Harlem by pacifying the pain of the very oppressions that they conspire to create and sustain. His bar, called the Junto, creates an oasis of warmth in winter and of coolness in summer by giving black men the illusion of dignity and younger black women the illusion of possessing the fine things they lack. One of Mrs. Hedges's few pleasures is presenting beautiful, compliant young black women to Junto as symbolic substitutes for herself. After he tires of each stand-in, Junto sets the woman up in one of his classier houses for white clients, and Mrs. Hedges offers up another surrogate to their odd passion. For much of the novel, Lutie is the unwitting target of this bizarrely touching relationship. Mrs. Hedges identifies Lutie for such a role early in the novel and is content to watch and wait, defending Lutie from physical harm while secretly using Harlem to break Lutie's spirit. Only gradually, as circumstances conspire to force her to submit, does Lutie begin to understand that Harlem and Junto are facets of each other. Junto makes Harlem bearable, while Harlem makes the Junto indispensable and profitable. Harlem has become less an instrument of black hopes and aspirations, and more a means of limiting and controlling blacks. As Junto's net closes around her, Lutie kills in desperation and flees Harlem in despair, abandoning the young son whose future was the principal motivation for her struggle with life on the street in the first place.

> James de Jongh, *Vicious Modernism: Black Harlem and the Literary Imagination* (New York: Cambridge University Press, 1990), pp. 89–92

DIANNE JOHNSON   A particularly distinguished historical novel is *Tituba of Salem Village*. Set in Salem Village, Massachusetts in 1692, this historical fiction recreates some of the events surrounding and leading up to the infamous Salem witch trials. More specifically, it recreates the story of Tituba Indian, a slave brought to Massachusetts from Barbados, who was one of the first three women to be condemned as being a "witch." What she is, in reality, is an artist, though she is not a singer, or painter, or writer. But she does have talent, which she hones, which she perfects and practices, and which is misinterpreted and misunderstood. She is, in fact, a master of herbal medicine and the art of healing.

Petry meticulously includes details which inform this particular world view, a world view in which Tituba is nurtured and of which she is and always remains a part. The first clue that the reader has that Tituba is part of a non-western world is when the narrator talks about the thunderstone that was given to her by an old man:

> As long as she kept it with her, she would have a part of the island with her. The old man who had given it to her had told her that if she ever thought her life was in danger, she was to unwrap the thunderstone and hold it in her hand. If she felt it move in her hand, it was a sign that she would live. She wasn't sure that she believed this, but she wouldn't want to lose the thunderstone.

This last sentence is crucial. In effect, the second half negates the doubt expressed in the first half. Tituba is, in fact, entrenched in this particular culture. ⟨. . .⟩

⟨. . .⟩ Lillian Smith asserts that "historical fiction must be a fusion of story and period if it is to enrich and enlarge our picture of the past to the extent that it becomes part of our experience." And this is precisely what Petry accomplishes. She powerfully draws the interconnectedness between color, one's identity (servants referred to as Black first, then by name), religion, culture, and historical era. I have focused here on African/Black characters. But in fact, their blackness in and of itself is not the single focal point of the novel. On the other hand, their blackness is an integral component of their very beings. And in recreating their stories, in their respective and particular time periods, the author integrates this into a composite portrait.

Dianne Johnson, *Telling Tales: The Pedagogy and Promise of African American Literature for Youth* (Westport, CT: Greenwood Press, 1990), pp. 53–55

NELLIE Y. McKAY   In addition to its focus on a female protagonist, *The Street* is significantly different from its male counterparts in that while Petry lashes out uncompromisingly at racism, classism, and sexism, she undercuts the conventions of the naturalistic novel by refusing to make Lutie a mere victim of her social environment. Nor does this step on the part of the author lessen the impact of the oppression of that environment. Lutie may well have had greater success in achieving her goals had she been less innocent of the politics of race, class, and gender. Her uncritical acceptance of white middle-class values and the capitalist tenets of the American dream make her an easy prey for the greed and sexism of the black and white men who surround her. In addition, Lutie serves herself poorly by separating from any support she might have had from the black community and those values that have insured black survival in America since the first slaves arrived on its shores. Preoccupied with her ambitions for herself and her son to escape the poverty and disillusionment of black ghetto life and wholly uncritical of the white models to which she is exposed, she has no friends or relatives with whom she seeks association, attends no church, and in her attitudes, denies the possibilities of communal sources of strength. Consequently, she was vulnerable to the greed, anger, and sexism of those who were capable of destroying her.

> Nellie Y. McKay, "Ann Petry's *The Street* and *The Narrows*: A Study of the Influence of Class, Race, and Gender on Afro-American Women's Lives," *Women and War: The Changing Status of American Women from the 1930s to the 1950s*, ed. Maria Diedrich and Dorothea Fischer-Hornung (New York: Berg, 1990), pp. 134–35

KEITH CLARK   While something of an anachronism in the 1990s, the African-American protest novel of the 1940s and 1950s maintained a symbiotic relationship with the mythic American Dream: It decried a history of American racism which made achieving the Dream a chimera for blacks. While Richard Wright is considered the "father" of the genre, and *Native Son* (1940) its quintessential document, Ann Petry emerged as another strident voice—a progenitor or native daughter. While her novel *The Narrows* (1953) deviated somewhat, it nevertheless continued the Wrightian tradition. Link Williams, the protagonist, differs superficially from Bigger in that he has attained a Dartmouth education and enjoys relative freedom from economic hardships; it would *appear* that he has the means to acquire the bootstraps over which Bigger can only ruminate. However, Link's "success" cannot shield him in an America which insists upon his inhumanity. When he breaks the taboos of class and race by having an affair with a white New England heiress, his violent murder becomes ritual—an inexorable response to a black stepping out of his "place." While Petry's "New England" novel echoes *Native Son* thematically, more ostensibly it also foregrounds the black *male* as the victim of an America which denies African-Americans their very personhood. But in *The Street* (1946), Petry recasts the Herculean quest for the American Dream in an unequivocally female context. Indeed, the novel represents the "distaff" side of the African-American literary tradition, emerging as a groundbreaking work in its examination of the black women's pursuit of happiness. Not only does Petry depict how women pursue the Dream in traditionally "American" terms, but, more deftly, she illustrates how black women subvert the quest for the American Dream and fulfill their own version of it.

Given the spurious nature of the American Dream, one would assume that the African-American writer would vigorously expose its shortcomings—for instance, the myopic measuring of "success" in monetary and material terms. But the tendency has not been so much to attack the Dream as to *protest* whites' insistence on treating blacks as outsiders and interlopers. Indeed, the hue and cry of the Biggers and the Walter Lee Youngers emanate from their staunch loyalty to the hallowed Constitution, which stipulates that "all men are created equal"; they cry only because they want their slice of the pie. As Richard Yarborough points out, "Despite severe disappointments, . . . Afro-Americans have generally been among the most fervent believers in the American Dream."

Lutie Johnson, the protagonist in *The Street*, embodies the female version of the archetypal quest. Patterning her life after Benjamin Franklin's, Lutie embarks on an expedition she hopes will bestow the trappings of success upon herself and Bub, her eight-year-old son. However, Lutie's odyssey from Jamaica, New York, to Lyme, Connecticut, to Harlem bestows upon her little more than disillusionment. Ultimately, what Calvin Hernton calls the "three isms"—racism, capitalism and sexism—launch an implacable assault on Lutie, precipitating the novel's tragic conclusion.

While it would be tempting to view the novel as a treatise on how men, black and white, collude to destroy the All-American black girl, Petry's text discourages this sort of naturalistic preoccupation with character as subject and object. Instead, one might view this seminal examination of the black woman's search for the Dream as a mosaic—much like Alice Walker's tropological quilt—that includes other women, other stories, and other voices. In addition to presenting Lutie and her blind adherence to American values, Petry depicts two black female characters who circumvent the quest: Mrs. Hedges, who operates a bordello in the apartment building where Lutie lives and who also oversees the day-to-day events on "the street," and Min, the downtrodden and subservient companion of William Jones, the building superintendent.

Far from being minor characters, Mrs. Hedges and Min embody what I see as a history of black women *subverting* the vacuous Dream myth through an almost innate ability to secure their own space despite the twin scourges of racism and sexism. Existing in a milieu where the Dream's core assumptions belie their lived realities, these black women *undermine* the myth, altering it to ensure both economic survival and varying degrees of emotional stability. And because "traditional" principles have been the bane of black people since America's inception, questions involving "morality" of how these women survive become ancillary ones given their predatory, hostile environment.

Superficially, Mrs. Hedges and Min adhere to the ideals of "hard work" and "ingenuity" in a country where "anything is possible." However, these women more accurately replicate techniques used by such archetypal African-American trickster figures as Charles Chesnutt's Uncle Julius or black folklore's Peetie Wheatstraw in (re)inventing lives independent of the white American Dream. While denied opulent lifestyles and material objects, Petry's "minor" women attain life's basic necessities, and, given their tenuous existences, they (re)construct their own "dream" by tapping into a tradition of what Peter Wheatstraw in *Invisible Man* calls " 'shit, grit and motherwit.' " Thus, *The Street* transcends the boundaries of the *"roman-à-these,"* the thesis presumably being that white racism extinguishes all black hope. The denizens of Petry's Harlem face a world more Darwinian than Franklinian, and they act according to their individual circumstances.

> Keith Clark, "A Distaff Dream Deferred? Ann Petry and the Art of Subversion," *African American Review* 26, No. 3 (Fall 1992): 495–97

Bibliography

The Street. 1946.

Country Place. 1947.

The Drugstore Cat. 1949.

The Narrows. 1953.

Harriet Tubman, Conductor on the Underground Railroad. 1955.

Tituba of Salem Village. 1964.

The Common Ground: A Talk Given at the Central Children's Room of the New York Public Library. c. 1964.

Legends of the Saints. 1970.

Miss Muriel and Other Stories. 1971.

⊠ ⊠ ⊠

Alice Walker
b. 1944

ALICE MALSENIOR WALKER was born on February 9, 1944, in Eatonton, Georgia, the eighth child of sharecroppers Willie Lee and Minnie Tallulah (Grant) Walker. When she was eight she was blinded in her right eye after being accidentally shot with a BB gun by one of her brothers. She attended Spelman College from 1961 to 1963, then left to travel in Africa. She transferred to Sarah Lawrence College, where she received a B.A. in 1965. About this time she underwent a severe trauma in which she aborted a pregnancy and came close to suicide. In response to these events she took to writing, producing her first published short story, "To Hell with Dying," and the poems that would form her first collection of poetry. She married civil rights lawyer Melvyn Rosenman Leventhal in 1967; they had one child before their divorce in 1976.

During the late 1960s Walker participated in the civil rights movement in Mississippi. She wrote an essay, "The Civil Rights Movement: What Good Was It?," that won an *American Scholar* essay contest. She worked with Head Start programs in Mississippi and later served as writer in residence at Tougaloo College and Jackson State University.

Alice Walker has written several volumes of poetry, including *Once* (1968), *Revolutionary Petunias and Other Poems* (1973), *Good Night, Willie Lee, I'll See You in the Morning* (1979), *Horses Make a Landscape More Beautiful* (1984), and, most recently, *Her Blue Body Everything We Know: Earthling Poems 1965–1990 Complete* (1991). They have received considerable praise, particularly from the black and feminist communities.

Walker is, however, primarily known as a novelist. Her first novel, *The Third Life of Grange Copeland* (1970), depicts three generations in the life of a poor farm family. It was praised for the sensitivity with which the characters were drawn, but it received little attention from either popular or academic circles. In 1970 Walker discovered the work of Zora Neale Hurston, whom she would be instrumental in raising to the status of a major American author. Hurston's influence can be seen in many of the short stories Walker was writing in this period. Her second novel, *Meridian* (1976), is considered by many to be the best novel of the civil rights era. *The Color Purple* (1982), an epistolary novel concerning the growth to maturity of a poor black woman in an oppressive, brutish society, launched Walker to mainstream critical success and best-seller popularity. It received the 1983 Pulitzer Prize and the American Book Award, and was made into an Academy Award–nominated film by Steven Spielberg.

In 1989 Alice Walker published her fourth novel, *The Temple of My Familiar*, a work that resurrects some characters from *The Color Purple* but whose major action takes place in Africa. This novel was on the whole poorly received for its implausibility (a goddess informs the characters of the origin of women) and the stridency of its ideological message. Her fifth novel, *Possessing the Secret of Joy* (1992), however, fared better with reviewers. It deals with female circumcision and genital mutilation, the subject of a nonfiction book Walker published the next year in collaboration with Pratibha Parmar, *Warrior Masks*.

In addition to poetry and novels, Walker has written two volumes of short stories, *In Love and Trouble: Stories of Black Women* (1973) and *You Can't Keep a Good Woman Down* (1981); a biography of Langston Hughes for children; and a book of criticism and social commentary, *In Search of Our Mothers' Gardens: Womanist Prose* (1983). A selection of her essays, *Living by the Word*, appeared in 1988.

Walker has been a lecturer at Wellesley College and the University of Massachusetts, a writer in residence at the University of California at Berkeley, and the Fannie Hurst Professor of Literature at Brandeis University. She has also served as a contributing editor of *Ms.* magazine. Since 1978 she has lived in San Francisco.

Critical Extracts

ALICE WALKER   Perhaps my Northern brothers will not believe me when I say there is a great deal of positive material I can draw from my "underprivileged" background. But they have never lived, as I have, at the end of a long road in a house that was faced by the edge of the world on one side and nobody for miles on the other. They have never experienced the magnificent quiet of a summer day when the heat is intense and one is so very thirsty, as one moves across the dusty cotton fields, that one learns forever that water is the essence of all life. In the cities it cannot be so clear to one that he is a creature of the earth, feeling the soil between the toes, smelling the dust thrown up by the rain, loving the earth so much that one longs to taste it and sometimes does.

Nor do I intend to romanticize the Southern black country life. I can recall that I hated it, generally. The hard work in the fields, the shabby houses, the evil greedy men who worked my father to death and almost broke the courage of that strong woman, my mother. No, I am simply saying that Southern black writers, like most writers, have a heritage of love and hate, but that they also have enormous richness and beauty to draw from. And, having been placed, as Camus says, "halfway between misery and the sun," they, too, know that "though all is not well under the sun, history is not everything."

No one could wish for a more advantageous heritage than that bequeathed to the black writer in the South: a compassion for the earth, a trust in humanity beyond our knowledge of evil, and an abiding love of justice. We inherit a great responsibility as well, for we must give voice to centuries not only of silent bitterness and hate but also of neighborly kindness and sustaining love.

Alice Walker, "The Black Writer and the Southern Experience" (1970), *In Search of Our Mothers' Gardens: Womanist Prose* (San Diego: Harcourt Brace Jovanovich, 1983), pp. 20–21

MARK SCHORER   She is not a finished novelist. She has much to learn. Fortunately, what she has to learn are the unimportant lessons, that is, those that *can* be learned: some economy, formal shaping, stylistic tightening, deletion of points too repetitiously insisted upon, the handling of time, above all development rather than mere reversal of character. The important fictional qualities that she commands, those that she was born with, she has supremely.

Mark Schorer, "Novels and Nothingness," *American Scholar* 40, No. 1 (Winter 1970–71): 172

JERRY H. BRYANT   My initial reaction to the first several stories of *In Love & Trouble* was negative. Miss Walker's search for ways to be new and different struck me as too willful and strained. I felt the same way about her earlier novel, *The Third Life of Grange Copeland*, whose style seemed too fine for the rough subject—the way two black men, a son and a father, try to degrade and destroy each other. But as I read on through these thirteen stories, I was soon absorbed by the density of reality they convey. They contain the familiar themes and situations of conventional black political and sociological fiction. There are black revolutionaries who read books and meet in small study groups, radical lady poets who read before black student audiences shouting "Right on!," and sharecroppers victimized by white landlords. But we see all these from genuinely new angles, from the point of view of the black woman or man totally absorbed in the pains of their inner life rather than the point of view of the protester or the newspaper headline. ⟨. . .⟩

But what I like most about these stories is what Miss Walker seems to like most about her people, the ones who are themselves, naturally and unself-consciously, and live by putting what they have to "everyday use," the title of one of her stories. She is best, therefore, not when she is depicting revolutionary consciousness or sophisticated awareness of the most recent rules of race relations, but when she is getting inside the minds of the confused, the ignorant, the inward-turning character, when she lets stand the mysterious and the ambiguous, and gives up explaining by doctrine the nature of her characters' lives. She can put a lump in the reader's throat even when she is a little sentimental. But what she can do most powerfully is make me feel the heat of her characters' lives, smell their singed bodies going up in literal and figurative flames of their own making. That is when I lose touch with myself as critic and interpreter and enter Miss Walker's created world of love and trouble.

Jerry H. Bryant, "The Outskirts of a New City," *Nation*, 12 November 1973, pp. 501–2

GREIL MARCUS   At its best, ⟨. . .⟩ the tone of ⟨*Meridian* is⟩ flat, direct, measured, deliberate, with a distinct lack of drama. ⟨. . .⟩ And the tone is right; it's not the plot that carries the novel forward but Meridian's attempt to resolve, or preserve the reality of, the questions of knowledge, history, and murder that Miss Walker introduces early on. The astonishing dramatic intensity that Walker brought to *The Third Life of Grange Copeland* would in *Meridian* blow those questions apart.

But such questions lead all too easily to high-flown language and to pretensions that fictional characters cannot support, which is why most "philosophical" novels are impossible to reread. Miss Walker does not always avoid this trap; though her tendency is to insist on the prosaic, to bring philosophy down to earth, Meridian at times seems to be floating straight to Heaven. The book tries to make itself a parable—more than a mere novel—or trades the prosaic for an inert symbolism that would seem to be intended to elevate the story but instead collapses it. In an early chapter, Meridian, age seven, finds a gold bar and rushes with it to her parents; they ignore her. She buries the gold (her unrecognized gifts) and finally forgets about it (and it will be years until she finds her gifts again). In college, as Meridian lies sick in bed, a halo forms around her head. Back in the South after the meeting in New York, she works alone persuading people, one at a time, to register to vote, organizing neighborhoods around local issues, and staging symbolic protests, which she calls, wonderfully, her "performances." This is beautifully presented and utterly convincing; each incident is memorable, shaped as a story in itself. But after every "performance" Meridian falls to the ground, paralyzed, and must be carried like a corpse back to wherever she is living. A hundred years ago, an author would simply have made Meridian an epileptic if we were meant to guess that she was sainted. ⟨. . .⟩

Meridian is interesting enough without all this—without symbolism and "higher meanings" that are one-dimensional and fixed. There is no mystery in these symbols—as there is in Meridian's ability to get through to Southern blacks, or in the questions of the rebel, murder, and limits—and a symbol without mystery, without suggestive power, is not really a symbol at all. But most of the book's scenes have the power its symbols lack, and its last chapters rescue Meridian's questions from a holy oblivion.

Greil Marcus, "Limits," *New Yorker*, 7 June 1976, p. 135

TRUDIER HARRIS   Walker's use of folk material is less prominent in her novel *The Third Life of Grange Copeland* (1970), but it is apparent. Folk material becomes significant in defining the relationship between

Grange and Ruth, his granddaughter. It is a way to seal the bond between them and to identify their unity against a hostile and un-understanding world. Even Josie, Grange's wife, is shut out of the bantering between Ruth and Grange, as she will later be physically excluded from their presence. Grange tells Ruth tales and generally entertains her on the nights when they sit around peeling oranges and shredding coconut in their Georgia farmhouse.

Although Grange knows "all the Uncle Remus stories by heart" and can produce even more exciting ones about John the trickster, he is not a mindless teller of tales solely for the sake of entertainment. Walker attributes to him the analytical ability that is often only implied in historical storytellers. Grange does not accept the benign Uncle Remus as historically accurate or even as having common sense. He criticizes Uncle Remus's stance and re-interprets it with political connotations and renewed emphasis on social awareness, especially black social awareness. ⟨. . .⟩ It is obvious from Grange's attitude that Walker does not view the folk culture as something separate from life, but as an integral part of one's existence. The change Grange would impose on Uncle Remus is synonymous with the changes that take place in the novel. From sharecropping with its shuffling, head-bowing, acquiescing days, Walker moves Grange and his family into the Sixties and the days of Martin Luther King. Marching, voting, and statesmanship do indeed replace the tendency to minstrelize.

Grange also tells Ruth stories about "two-heads and conjurers; strange men and women more sensitive than the average spook," but he laments that "folks what can look at things in more than one way is done got rare." Grange's feelings are again commensurate with the theme of change that Walker explores in the novel. ⟨. . .⟩

Alice Walker is assuredly in the literary and historical traditions of the recording and creative use of black folk materials. Like ⟨Charles W.⟩ Chesnutt, she uses such material for social commentary. But her environment allows more freedom of usage than did Chesnutt's; where he had to embed his statements about slavery in an elaborate framing device and filtered them through the eyes of a white Northerner, Walker can be obvious, blatant, and direct about social injustices. Like ⟨Zora Neale⟩ Hurston, Walker reflects a keen insight into the folk mind. As Hurston reflected the nuances of relationships between men and women in *Their Eyes Were Watching God* (1937) through the use of the folk culture, so too does Walker use this culture to reflect relationships between the characters in *The Third Life of Grange Copeland*.

Trudier Harris, "Folklore in the Fiction of Alice Walker: A Perpetuation of Historical and Literary Traditions," *Black American Literature Forum* 11, No. 1 (Spring 1977): 7–8

ROBERT TOWERS   In *The Color Purple* Alice Walker moves backward in time, setting her story roughly (the chronology is kept vague) between 1916 and 1942—a period during which the post-Reconstruction settlement of black status remained almost unaltered in the Deep South. Drawing upon what must be maternal and grandmaternal accounts as well as upon her own memory and observation, Miss Walker, who is herself under forty, exposes us to a way of life that for the most part existed beyond or below the reach of fiction, and that has hitherto been made available to us chiefly through tape-recorded reminiscences: the life of poor, rural Southern blacks as it was experienced by their womenfolk. Faulkner, to be sure, touches upon it in his rendering of the terrified Nancy in "That Evening Sun," but her situation, poignant though it is, comes to us largely through the eyes and ears of the white Compson children; similarly, the majestic figure of Dilsey in *The Sound and the Fury* is, for all its insight, sympathy, and closeness of observation, a white man's portrait of a house servant, idealized and, one imagines, subtly distorted by the omission of those moments of sickening rage (as distinct from exasperation) which must have been an ingredient in Dilsey's complex attitude toward the feckless and demanding family that employs her. The suffering, submissive women in Wright's *Native Son* are no doubt authentically portrayed—but again from a man's point of view; furthermore, they are city dwellers, poor but still different from the dirt-poor countryfolk. ⟨. . .⟩

I cannot gauge the general accuracy of Miss Walker's account or the degree to which it may be colored by current male-female antagonisms within the black community—controversial reports of which from time to time appear in print. I did note certain improbabilities: it seems unlikely that a woman of Celie's education would have applied the word "amazons" to a group of feisty sisters or that Celie, in the 1930s, would have found fulfillment in designing and making pants for women. In any case, *The Color Purple* has more serious faults than its possible feminist bias. Alice Walker still has a lot to learn about plotting and structuring what is clearly intended to be a realistic novel. The revelations involving the fate of Celie's lost babies and the identity of her real father seem crudely contrived—the stuff of melodrama or fairy tales. ⟨. . .⟩

Fortunately, inadequacies which might tell heavily against another novel seem relatively insignificant in view of the one great challenge which Alice Walker has triumphantly met: the conversion, in Celie's letters, of a subliterate dialect into a medium of remarkable expressiveness, color, and poignancy. I find it impossible to imagine Celie apart from her language; through it, not only a memorable and infinitely touching character but a whole submerged world is vividly called into being. Miss Walker knows how to avoid the excesses of literal transcription while remaining faithful to the spirit and rhythms of Black English. I can think of no other novelist who has so successfully tapped the poetic resources of the idiom.

Robert Towers, "Good Men Are Hard to Find," *New York Review of Books*, 12 August 1982, pp. 35–36

GERALD EARLY   ⟨. . .⟩ *The Color Purple* remains an inferior novel not because it seems so self-consciously a "woman's novel" and not because it may be playing down to its mass audience, guilty of being nothing more than a blatant "feel-good" novel, just the sort of book that is promoted among the nonliterary. *The Color Purple* is a poor novel because it ultimately fails the ideology that it purports to serve. It fails to be subversive enough in substance; it only *appears* to be subversive. Indeed, far from being a radically feminist novel, it is not even, in the end, as good a bourgeois feminist novel as *Uncle Tom's Cabin*, written 130 years earlier. Its largest failure lies in the novel's inability to use (ironically, subversively, or even interestingly) the elements that constitute it. Take, for instance, these various Victorianisms that abound in the work: the ultimate aim of the restoration of a gynocentric, not patriarchal family; the reunion of lost sisters; the reunion of mother and children; the glorification of cottage industry in the establishment of the pants business; bequests of money and land to the heroine at novel's end; Celie's discovery that her father/rapist is really a cruel stepfather; the change of heart or moral conversion of Mr. Albert, who becomes a feminized man at the end; the friendship between Shug Avery and Celie, which, despite its overlay of lesbianism (a tribute to James Baldwin's untenable thesis that nonstandard sex is the indication of a free, holy, thoroughly unsquare heterosexual heart), is nothing more than the typical relationship between a shy ugly duckling and her more aggressive, beautiful counterpart, a relationship not unlike that between Topsy and Little Eva. Shug convinces Celie that she is not black and ugly, that somebody loves her, which is precisely what Eva does for Topsy. For Walker, these clichés are not simply those of the Victorian novel but of the *woman's* Victorian novel. This indicates recognition of and paying homage to a tradition; but the use of these clichés in *The Color Purple* is a great deal more sterile and undemanding than their use in, say, *Uncle Tom's Cabin*. Together, for Walker, these clichés take on a greater attractiveness and power than for the female Victorian, since they are meant to represent a series of values that free the individual from the power of the environment, the whim of the state, and the orthodoxy of the institution. The individual still has the power to change, and that power supersedes all others, means more than any other. Human virtue is a reality that is not only distinct from all collective arrangements except family; in the end, it can be understood only as being opposed to all collective arrangements. But all of this is only the bourgeois fascination with individualism and with the ambiguity of Western family life, in which bliss is togetherness while having a room of one's own. ⟨. . .⟩

What Walker does in her novel is allow its social protest to become the foundation for its utopia. Not surprisingly, the book lacks any real intellectual or theological rigor or coherence, and the fusing of social protest and utopia is really nothing more than confounding and blundering, each seeming to subvert the reader's attention from the other. One is left thinking that Walker wishes to thwart her own ideological ends or that she simply does not know how to write novels. In essence, the book attempts to be revisionist salvation history and fails because of its inability to use or really understand history.

Gerald Early, "*The Color Purple* as Everybody's Protest Art," *Antioch Review* 44, No. 3 (Summer 1986): 271–73

LAUREN BERLANT   *The Color Purple*'s strategy of inversion, represented in its elevation of female experience over great patriarchal events, had indeed aimed to critique the unjust practices of racism and sexism that violate the subject's complexity, reducing her to a generic biological sign.

But the model of personal and national identity with which the novel leaves us uses fairy-tale explanations of social relations to represent itself: this fairy tale embraces America for providing the Afro-American nation with the right and the opportunity to own land, to participate in the free market, and to profit from it. In the novel's own terms, American capitalism thus has contradictory effects. On one hand, capitalism veils its operations by employing racism, using the pseudonatural discourse of race to reduce the economic competitor to a subhuman object. In Celie's parental history, *The Color Purple* portrays the system of representation characteristic of capital relations that *creates* the situation of nationlessness for Afro-Americans.

But the novel also represents the mythic spirit of American capitalism as the vehicle for the production of an Afro-American utopia. Folkpants, Unlimited is an industry dedicated to the reproduction and consumption of a certain system of representation central to the version of Afro-American "cultural nationalism" enacted by *The Color Purple*. But Folkpants, Unlimited also participates in the profit motive: the image of the commodity as the subject's most perfect self-expression is the classic fantasy bribe of capitalism. The illogic of a textual system in which the very force that disenfranchises Afro-Americans provides the material for their national reconstruction is neither "solved" by the novel nor raised as a paradox. The system simply stands suspended in the heat of the family reunion on Independence Day.

What saves Celie and Nettie from disenfranchisement is their lifelong determination to learn, to become literate: Nettie's sense that knowledge was the only route to freedom from the repressive family scene gave her the confidence to escape, to seek "employment" with Samuel's family, to record the alternative and positive truth of Pan-African identity, to face the truth about her own history, to write it down, and to send it to Celie, against all odds. Writing was not only the repository of personal and national hope; it became a record of lies and violences that ultimately produced truth.

Lauren Berlant, "Race, Gender, and Nation in *The Color Purple*," *Critical Inquiry* 14, No. 4 (Summer 1988): 857–58

J. M. COETZEE   Readers of *The Color Purple* will remember that part of the book—the less convincing part—consists of letters from Miss Celie's missionary sister about her life in Africa.

The Temple of My Familiar again bears a message from Africa, but this time in a far more determined manner. The message reaches us via Miss Lissie, an ancient goddess who has been incarnated hundreds of times, usually as a woman, sometimes as a man, once even as a lion. Less a character than a narrative device, Lissie enables Alice Walker to range back in time to the beginnings of (wo)man.

Here are just three of the ages in human evolution that Lissie lives through:

First, an age just after the invention of fire, when humanfolk live in separate male and female tribes, at peace with their animal "familiars." Here Lissie is incarnated as the first white-skinned creature, a man with insufficient melanin, who flees the heat of Africa for Europe. Hating the sun, he [invents] an alternative god in his own image, cold and filled with rage.

Next, an age of pygmies, when the man tribe and the woman tribe visit back and forth with each other and with the apes. This peaceful, happy age ends when men invent warfare, attack the apes and impose themselves on women as their sole familiars. Thus, says Ms. Walker (rewriting Rousseau and others), do patriarchy and the notion of private property come into being.

Third, the time of the war waged by Europe and monotheistic Islam against the Great Goddess of Africa. The instrument of the warfare is the slave trade (Lissie lives several slave lives). Its emblem is the Gorgon's head, the head of the Goddess, still crowned with the serpents of wisdom, cut off by the white hero-warrior Perseus.

These episodes from the past of (wo)mankind give some idea of the sweep of the myth Alice Walker recounts, a myth that inverts the places assigned to man and woman, Europe and Africa, in the male-invented myth called history. In Ms. Walker's counter-myth, Africa is the cradle of true religions and civilization, and man a funny, misbegotten creature with no breasts and an elongated clitoris. ⟨. . .⟩

History is certainly written by people in positions of power, and therefore principally by men. The history of the world—including Africa—is by and large a story made up by white males. Nevertheless, history is not just storytelling. There are certain brute realities that cannot be ignored. Africa has a past that neither the white male historian nor Ms. Walker can simply invent. No doubt the world would be a better place if, like Fanny and Suwelo, we could live in bird-shaped houses and devote ourselves to bread making and massage, and generally adopt Fanny's mother's gospel: "We are all of us in heaven already!" Furthermore, I readily concede that inventing a better world between the covers of a book is as much as even the most gifted of us can hope to do to bring about a better real world. But whatever new worlds and new histories we invent must carry conviction: they must be possible worlds, possible histories, not untethered fantasies; and they must be born of creative energy, not dreamy fads.

> J. M. Coetzee, "The Beginnings of (Wo)man in Africa," *New York Times Book Review*, 30 April 1989, p. 7

ALICE HALL PETRY   Walker's disinclination for exposition, and the concomitant impression that many of her stories are outlines or fragments of longer works, is particularly evident in a technique which mars even her strongest efforts: a marked preference for "telling" over "showing." This often takes the form of summaries littered with adjectives. In "Advancing Luna," for example, the narrator waxes nostalgic over her life with Luna in New York: "our relationship, always marked by mutual respect, evolved into a warm and comfortable friendship which provided a stability and comfort we both needed at that time." But since ⟨. . .⟩ the narrator comes across as vapid and self-absorbed, and since the only impressions she provides of Luna are rife with contempt for this greasy-haired, Clearasil-daubed, poor-little-rich-white-girl from Cleveland, the narrator's paean to their mutual warmth and friendship sounds ridiculous. No wonder critic Katha Pollitt stated outright that she "never believed for a minute" that the narrator and Luna were close friends. Even more unfortunate is Walker's habit of telling the reader what the story is about, of making sure that he doesn't overlook a single theme. For example, in "The Abortion," the heroine Imani, who is just getting over a traumatic abortion, attends the memorial service of a local girl, Holly Monroe, who had been shot to death while returning home from her high school graduation. Lest we miss the point, Walker spells it out for us: "every black girl of a certain vulnerable age *was* Holly Monroe. And an even deeper truth was that Holly Monroe was herself [i.e., Imani]. Herself shot down, aborted on the eve of becoming herself." Similarly transparent, here is one of the last remarks in the story "Source." It is spoken by Irene, the former teacher in a federally-funded adult education program, to her ex-hippie friend, Anastasia/Tranquility: " 'I was looking toward "government" for help; you were looking to Source [a California guru]. In both cases, it was the wrong direction—*any* direction that is away from ourselves is the wrong direction.' " The irony of their parallel situation is quite clear without having Irene articulate her epiphany in an Anchorage bar. Even at the level of charactonyms, Walker "tells" things to her reader. We've already noted the over-used "he"/"she" device for underscoring sex roles, but even personal names are pressed into service. For example, any reasonably perceptive reader of the vignette "The Flowers" will quickly understand the story's theme: that one first experiences reality in all its harshness while far from home, physically and/or experientially; one's immediate surroundings are comparatively "innocent." The reader would pick up on the innocence of nearsightedness even if the main character, ten-year-old Myop, hadn't been named after myopia. Likewise, "The Child Who Favored Daughter" is actually marred by having the father kill his daughter because he confuses her with his dead sister named "Daughter." The hints of incest, the unclear cross-generational identities, and the murky Freudian undercurrents are sufficiently obvious without the daughter/Daughter element: it begins to smack of Abbott and Costello's "Who's on First?" routine after just a few pages. Alice Walker's preference for telling over showing suggests a mistrust of her readers, or her texts, or both.

Alice Hall Petry, "Alice Walker: The Achievement of the Short Fiction," *Modern Language Studies* 19, No. 1 (Winter 1989): 21–22

CHARLES R. LARSON   Fiction and conviction make strange bedfellows. Nor am I convinced that novels that resurrect characters from a writer's earlier work are likely to be as imaginative and as artful as the result of the initial inspiration. But one does not have to read many pages of *Possessing the Secret of Joy* to realize that Alice Walker has not foisted her subject—female circumcision—upon us; instead, this writer of bold artistry challenges us to feel and to think. Here is a novel—and a subject—whose time has surely come. ⟨. . .⟩

The novel's ironic beginning is patently romantic. There is joy in Tashi and Adam's initial lovemaking, in spite of their conflicting backgrounds. Because of her conversion to Christianity, Tashi has not been traditionally circumcised. And Adam, the African-American missionary's son, appears not to harbor the Puritan layers of guilt typical of missionaries at the time—though Walker uses no dates, apparently the 1920s or '30s—the story begins.

What, in fact, can possibly diminish their happiness? The marriage appears destined to become a union of their complementary spirits and yearnings for togetherness.

But then Tashi wavers. As Adam's future wife, in America, shouldn't she attempt to retain as much of her African culture as possible? Should she be circumcised? The operation, she feels, will join her to her sisters, "whom she envisioned as strong, invincible. Completely woman. Completely African." ⟨. . .⟩

⟨. . .⟩ How is it possible, ⟨Tashi⟩ asks herself, that the person who administered her own excision ⟨. . .⟩ could be a woman? The question takes her back to Africa, to her Olinka people, and to the resolution of her fate. Though it would be unfair to reveal the end of her story—Tashi's final act of defiance—a part of her understanding of her ordeal can be noted: "The connection between mutilation and enslavement that is at the root of the domination of women in the world." It's a chilling realization, not simply related to Tashi's own culture, but central to images of female victimization worldwide. Tashi says: "It's in all the movies that terrorize women . . . The man who breaks in. The man with the knife . . . But those of us whose chastity belt was made of leather, or of silk and diamonds, or of fear and not of our own flesh . . . we worry. We are the perfect audience, mesmerized by our unconscious knowledge of what men, with the collaboration of our mothers, do to us."

Charles R. Larson, "Against the Tyranny of Tradition," Washington Post Book World, 5 July 1992, pp. 1, 14

DONNA HAISTY WINCHELL   The Alice Walker of the 1980s and early 1990s comes across as a woman at peace with herself. She has spent half a literary lifetime tracing women's search for self, including her own. Ironically, her harshest critics have focused on her portrayal not of women, but of men. One regret that she has is that such criticism merely succeeds once more in drawing attention away from injustices done to women. Another is that people tend to see only the negative behavior of her male characters.

Walker told Oprah Winfrey in 1989, "Why is it that they only see, they can only identify the negative behavior? . . . I think it's because it's the negative behavior, the macho behavior, that they see as male behavior and that when the men stop using that behavior, when the men become gentle, when the men become people you can talk to, when they are good grandparents, when they are gentle people, they are no longer considered men and there is an inability even to see them." Critics don't often "see," or at least don't remember, that near the end of *The Color Purple*, a reformed Albert asks Celie to marry him again, this time in spirit as well as flesh. They forget that Grange Copeland comes back from his "second life" in New York a new and responsible man—and a loving grandfather. Truman Held takes on the burden that Meridian finally puts down when she walks away, refusing to be a martyr. And Suwelo in *Temple of My Familiar* grows from using Carlotta's body without considering her pain to recognizing that she is far more than blind flesh, that indeed all women are. At the end of the novel, he has left university teaching and is learning carpentry, although he suffers pangs of guilt over the requisite slaughter of trees.

Walker already saw a "new man" beginning in some of her poetry from the 1970s. At first, she thought that new man would be one who, like Christ, put love in front and the necessary clenched fist behind, as she explains in "The Abduction of Saints." However, by the time she wrote the dedication to the 1984 volume that contains this poem, *Good Night, Willie Lee, I'll See You in the Morning*, she had set a slightly different standard for the new man. Her ideal man's rebellion now takes a more subtle form; he doesn't need fists. She calls him simply "the quiet man." Walker considers such a new, nurturing man essential for the survival of the planet.

Donna Haisty Winchell, *Alice Walker* (New York: Twayne, 1992), pp. 132–33

▩ *Bibliography*

Once. 1968.

The Third Life of Grange Copeland. 1970.

Five Poems. 1972.

Revolutionary Petunias and Other Poems. 1973.

In Love and Trouble: Stories of Black Women. 1973.

Langston Hughes, American Poet. 1974.

Meridian. 1976.

The Women's Center Reid Lectureship, November 11, 1975: Papers (with June Jordan). 1976.

*I Love Myself When I Am Laughing . . . and Then Again When I Am Looking
    Mean and Impressive: A Zora Neale Hurston Reader* (editor). 1979.

Good Night, Willie Lee, I'll See You in the Morning. 1979.

Beyond What. 1980.

You Can't Keep a Good Woman Down. 1981.

The Color Purple. 1982.

In Search of Our Mothers' Gardens: Womanist Prose. 1983.

While Love Is Unfashionable. 1984.

Horses Make a Landscape Look More Beautiful. 1984.

The Alice Walker Calendar for 1986. 1985.

To Hell with Dying. 1987.

From Alice Walker. 1988.

Living by the Word: Selected Writings 1973–1987. 1988.

The Temple of My Familiar. 1989.

Finding the Green Stone. 1991.

Her Blue Body Everything We Know: Earthling Poems 1965–1990 Complete.
    1991.

Possessing the Secret of Joy. 1992.

Warrior Masks: Female Genital Mutilation and the Sexual Blinding of Women
    (with Pratibha Parmar). 1993.

Everyday Use. Ed. Barbara Christian. 1994.

⊞ ⊞ ⊞

Harriet E. Wilson
c. 1828–c. 1863

HARRET E. ADAMS WILSON was born Harriet Adams in 1827 or 1828, as the U.S. census of 1850, taken on August 24, 1850, gives her age as twenty-two. On her marriage license her birthplace is given as Milford, New Hampshire. Nothing is known of her life prior to 1850. Her autobiographical novel, *Our Nig*, suggests that she was taken from her home at an early age. The 1850 census lists her as residing with a white family—Samuel Boyles, a carpenter; his wife, Mary Louisa, and their seventeen-year-old son Charles. Harriet Adams was probably their indentured servant.

A letter by "Allida" appended to *Our Nig* states that Harriet Adams was taken to W———, Massachusetts, by an "itinerant colored lecturer" and that she became a domestic servant at the household of a Mrs. Walker and was also a straw-hat maker. The itinerant lecturer was probably Thomas Wilson, listed on his marriage license as a resident or native of Virginia; he took Harriet Adams back to Milford and married her there on October 6, 1851. The letter by "Allida" reports that the marriage went well at the beginning, but that the husband soon after ran away to sea. Harriet, already pregnant, felt obliged to go to the Hillsborough County Farm, a home for the poor; she gave birth to a son, George Mason Wilson, in May or June 1852.

"Allida" states that the husband then returned and that the family moved to some town in New Hampshire, where Thomas Wilson supported his family "decently well." But then Thomas left again, this time for good, and Harriet, her health failing, put her son in the County Farm; shortly afterward, however, he was taken into the home of a "kindly gentleman and lady."

The Boston city directory lists a Harriet Wilson, "widow," residing at various locations in northeastern Boston from 1855 to 1863. "Allida" states that Wilson's failing health compelled her to write her autobiography as "another method of procuring her bread." Wilson states in her preface that she wrote the novel in order to reclaim her son from his foster home. But

210

George Mason Wilson died of fever on February 15, 1860, at the age of seven years and eight months.

Our Nig; or, Sketches from the Life of a Free Black, although heavily autobiographical, is in fact a novel, probably the first novel published in the United States by a black American. (William Wells Brown's *Clotel* and Frank Webb's *The Garies and Their Friends* precede it, but they were published in England.) *Our Nig* was published anonymously (as "By 'Our Nig' ") but was copyrighted by Harriet E. Wilson and printed for the author on September 5, 1859, by a Boston printing company, George C. Rand & Avery. It tells the story of a white orphan, Mag Smith, who marries a black man named Jim and gives birth to two children. When Jim deserts Mag, she abandons her six-year-old child, Frado, leaving her at the home of a middle-class white family, the Bellmonts. Frado becomes an indentured servant and is brutally treated by Mrs. Bellmont and her daughter Mary, although she develops good relationships with Mr. Bellmont and his son James. At the age of eighteen Frado is able to leave the family and, in spite of ill health and a series of bad jobs, she develops skill as a needleworker. She then meets an itinerant lecturer named Samuel, whom she marries and with whom she has a son. But Samuel abandons her, and the novel ends with Frado fleeing from one town to another to escape slave-catchers and "professed abolitionists" who "didn't want slaves at the South, nor niggers in their own houses, North."

Of the later life of Harriet Wilson nothing is known. The 1860 census lists a Harriet Wilson as a resident in the household of a black couple, Daniel and Susan Jacobs, in Boston; but it gives her age as fifty-two and her birthplace as Fredericksburg, Virginia. It has been conjectured that Wilson deliberately falsified her vital statistics to the census taker in the shadow of the Fugitive Slave Act of 1850. Since she disappears from the Boston city directory after 1863, it is thought that she died then. *Our Nig* was virtually forgotten until Henry Louis Gates, Jr., rediscovered and reprinted it in 1983. It is now regarded as a landmark for being the first novel published in the United States by a black American, the first by a black woman, and a subtle and complex work in its own right.

❖ *Critical Extracts*

HENRY LOUIS GATES, JR.   Wilson's achievement is that she combines the received conventions of the sentimental novel with certain key conventions of the slave narratives, then combines the two into *one new form*, of which *Our Nig* is the unique example. Had subsequent black authors had this text to draw upon, perhaps the black literary tradition would have developed more quickly and more resolutely than it did. For the subtleties of presentation of character are often lost in the fictions of Wilson's contemporaries, such as Frances E. W. Harper, whose short story "The Two Offers" was also published in September 1859, and in the works of her literary "heirs."

Our Nig stands as a "missing link," as it were, between the sustained and well-developed tradition of black autobiography and the slow emergence of a distinctive black voice in fiction. That two black women published in the same month the first novel and short story in the black woman's literary tradition attests to larger shared cultural presuppositions at work within the black community than scholars have admitted before. The speaking black subject emerged on the printed page to declare himself or herself to be a human being of capacities equal to the whites. Writing, for black authors, was a mode of being, of self-creation with words. Harriet E. Wilson depicts this scene of instruction, central to the slave narratives, as the moment that Frado defies Mrs. Bellmont to hit her. The text reads:

> "Stop!" shouted Frado, "strike me, and I'll never work a mite
> for you;" and throwing down what she had gathered, stood like
> one who feels the stirring of free and independent thoughts.

As had Frederick Douglass in his major battle with overseer Covey, Frado at last finds a voice with which to define her space. ⟨. . .⟩

In the penultimate chapter of *Our Nig*, the narrator tells us that along with mastering the needle, Frado learns to master the word:

> Expert with the needle, Frado soon equalled her instructress; and
> she sought to teach her the value of useful books; and while one
> read aloud to the other of deeds historic and names renowned,
> Frado experienced a *new impulse*. She felt herself capable of
> elevation; she felt that this book information supplied an
> *undefined dissatisfaction* she had long felt, but could not express.

> Every leisure moment was carefully applied to self-improvement,
> . . . [emphasis added]

In these final scenes of instruction, Harriet Wilson's text reflects upon its own creation, just as surely as Frado's awakened speaking voice signifies her consciousness of herself as a subject. With the act of speaking alone, Frado assumes a large measure of control over the choices she can possibly make each day. The "free and independent thoughts" she first feels upon speaking are repeated with variation in phrases such as "a new impulse," and "an undefined dissatisfaction," emotions she experiences while learning to read. "This book information," as the narrator tells us, enables Frado to *name things* by reading books. That such an apparently avid reader transformed the salient and tragic details of her life into the stuff of the novel—and was so daring in rendering the structures of fiction—is only one of the wonders of *Our Nig*.

Henry Louis Gates, Jr., "Introduction," *Our Nig; or, Sketches from the Life of a Free Black* (New York: Random House, 1983), pp. lii–liv

---

MARGO JEFFERSON   *Our Nig* is part drama, part declaration and part documentary. Wilson sometimes tells her tale baldly; sometimes hurries it along, issuing stage directions and inserting exposition; sometimes crafts it with crisp scenes and dialogue shrewdly attuned to the rhythms and phrasings of class and character. Her tone changes continually—the result, I think, of the haste and pain with which she wrote, the mixed audience she anticipated with dread and the conflict between her gift for biting realism and her taste for genteel lyricism. She will be brusque, then fastidious; she will shift from melancholy to outrage and sarcasm. ⟨. . .⟩

The final chapters are poignant and dissonant. As Frado drags herself from destitution to subsistence and from town to town, "watched by kidnappers, maltreated by professed abolitionists, who didn't want slaves at the South, nor niggers in their own houses, North," the narrator's voice seems about to disappear beneath the weight of its burden. But Wilson draws herself up and abruptly presents a combined autobiographical and fictional ending.

Frado prevails: "Nothing turns her from her steadfast purpose of elevating herself." And, we are told in a tone that fuses a lady's claim to modesty with a free woman's right to privacy, she merits our help—"Enough has been unrolled to demand your sympathy and aid." The closing history of the Bellmonts is briskly supplied. Frado has outlived all but Jane and her husband, who perhaps signify her hopes for a better marriage. Then, in a sweeping Old Testament image, Wilson reduces even them to minor functionaries and elevates Frado to the stature of a chosen prophet and ruler.

> Margo Jefferson, "Down & Out & Black in Boston," *Nation*, 28 May 1983, pp. 676–77

IRA BERLIN   Despite its lurid sadism, *Our Nig* is more than an indictment of white racial brutality. While Frado is abused by her mistress, the men of the household—father and sons—provide friendship and protection; indeed, Wilson's account is laced with an undercurrent of unspoken interracial sexuality rarely found in antebellum fiction. To complicate the story further, the protective shield of white manhood is counterposed to the chicanery and deception of a smooth-talking black itinerant who ensures Frado's ruination, marrying, impregnating, and abandoning the friendless young woman and their child. In short, while Wilson places the stock characters of America's interracial drama on stage like so many set pieces, she also adds to the array new characters and thereby provides a more subtle, complex story than most sentimental novels of the day. In many ways, *Our Nig* is more complicated than any black novel before Charles Chesnutt's *The House Behind the Cedars* (1900). Indeed, the questions raised in *Our Nig* about the relation of black men and women in the 19th century and the antebellum black perspective on interracial marriage have hardly been addressed since the novel's publication.

> Ira Berlin, "America's First Black Novel," *Washington Post Book World*, 3 July 1983, pp. 1–2

MARILYN RICHARDSON   ⟨. . .⟩ there is ⟨. . .⟩ a certain religious ambiguity ⟨in *Our Nig*⟩. While Frado is clearly a person of strong spiritual leanings, she is, like Sojourner Truth or, later, Frances Harper, quick to recognize the hypocrisy of religious rationales for racial oppression and segregation. She is open to the teachings of the church on some issues, but she is uncertain about spending eternity in a heaven which might also harbor the likes of Mrs. Bellmont who, although a professed Christian, tells her captive servant that "if she did not stop trying to be religious, she would whip her to death."

Frado knows her mistress well. Like Margaret Walker, whose epic novel *Jubilee* gives the lie to every syllable written about black women by Margaret Mitchell, black women writers have, over the years, limned with a deft and unsparing touch the lives, foibles, strengths and weaknesses—warts and all—of those whites against whom they have struggled. In these works, white people are known and understood to their innermost recesses of mind and spirit, while they, in turn, are shown to perceive "their" blacks in terms of the broadest stereotypes and generalizations. That contrast underlies one of the classic recurring symbolic scenes in early black writing, male and female, the confrontation by which the black character claims, once and for all, a distinct sense of self.

There is in *Our Nig* just such a moment of resistance, when Frado finds the strength to stand her ground against Mrs. Bellmont's violence. " 'Stop!' shouted Frado, 'strike me and I'll never work a mite for you'; and throwing down what she had gathered [firewood], stood like one who feels the stirring of free and independent thoughts."

Marilyn Richardson, "The Shadow of Slavery," *Women's Review of Books* 1, No. 1 (October 1983): 15

BERNARD W. BELL   The point of view, narrative structure, and style ⟨of *Our Nig*⟩ also reveal the double-vision characteristic of the black American experience and the Afro-American novel. Although the story is told primarily by an omniscient, third-person, editorializing narrator, the titles of the first three chapters ("Mag Smith, My Mother," "My Father's Death," and "A New Home for Me") employ the first-person pronoun. The titles of the subsequent eight chapters do not continue this pattern, but the tension in aesthetic distance, suggesting the close identification on all levels of the author-narrator with her protagonist, returns in the opening sentence of chapter 12: "A few years ago, within the compass of my narrative, there appeared often in some of our New England villages, professed fugitives from slavery, who recounted their personal experience in homely phrase, and awakened the indignation of non-slaveholders against brother Pro." The ambivalence and irony here are that Wilson's narrative also recounts her personal experience with "slavery," which she fears will awaken "severe criticism" of her though, as she tells us in the preface, she has "purposely omitted what would most provoke shame in our good anti-slavery friends at home." ⟨. . .⟩

The ambivalence of the author-narrator culminates in the most explicit indictment in the novel of the treatment of blacks in New England by Northern white abolitionists: "Watched by kidnappers, maltreated by professional abolitionists, who didn't want slaves at the South, nor niggers in their own houses, North. Faugh! to lodge one; to eat with one; to admit one through the front door; to sit next one; awful!" This rhetorical strategy of a series of verbal forms, which shift abruptly without quotation marks from the descriptive mode of participial phrases to the dramatic with infinitive phrases enclosed by exclamations, underscores the anomaly of the protagonist's situation and the illuminating power of the author's double vision.

As important to the traditions of the Afro-American novel and feminist literature as the illuminating power of Wilson's double vision and her historical significance is her unique treatment of the theme and character of the tragic mulatto. Harriet Wilson not only introduces into American fiction the first interracial marriage in which the wife is white and husband African, but also develops the character of her mulatto protagonist, the couple's daughter, as an individual rather than a type. Frado's story is not about virtue in distress because of mixed blood and male oppression, but about the violation of human rights because of the hypocrisy of New England Christians and of the racial and class exploitation by some white middle-class women. Also, because Wilson was influenced more by the sophistication and sentimentality of the Euro-American literary tradition than by the Afro-American oral tradition and slave narratives, *Our Nig* clearly and convincingly illustrates that the conventions of both traditions contributed to the development of the early Afro-American novel.

Bernard W. Bell, *The Afro-American Novel and Its Tradition* (Amherst: University of Massachusetts Press, 1987), pp. 48–50

BLYDEN JACKSON   In the treatment of its theme, *Our Nig* disposes contradictorily to what it proposes. Racism undoubtedly was an ugly fact of life for Negroes in the North when *Our Nig* was written. Such racism explained William Wells Brown's ride in a baggage car of a train on which he had anticipated a passenger's reception. It accounted for the antipathy of whites to the spectacle of Frederick Douglass escorting, in no wise as a servant, the white Griffith sisters (who were from England) along a northern street. But Frado's troubles in the Bellmont household hardly seem attributable to her color. Jack Bellmont is her friend. So is his sister Jane and his father's sister, Aunt Abby, while Mr. Bellmont's urbanity toward her never falters. She has problems only with Mrs. Bellmont and Mary, both of whom all who know them regard as cut from the same mold as Cinderella's stepmother. Mr. Bellmont usually walks warily around Mrs. Bellmont, and Mary's schoolmates are overjoyed at any discomfiture to her. Frado has problems with Mrs. Bellmont and Mary not so much becasue she is black as because they are what they are. Moreover, when Frado first goes to school and the children are prepared to be unkind to her, the teacher, Miss Marsh, with commendable tact, so admonishes them that they suspend judgment on Frado until she eventually becomes a favorite with them. The workers on the Bellmont farm ⟨. . .⟩ are as enamored of Frado as her schoolmates. And Aunt Abby's minister experiences no difficulty in conducting himself with Frado according to the higher dictates of his calling.

Indeed, in *Our Nig*, Frado's major source of displeasure seems not to be racistic abuse of herself by others but dissatisfaction with her own color. She wants to be white. She asks James Bellmont, almost as soon as she meets him, why God has made her black and not white. She seeks assurance from others that blacks will go to heaven as well as whites. In her prayers she bemoans her color, always with the implication that she would prefer to be white. Wilson would not be the last black author to debilitate an attack on racism with an unwitting expression of a wish to be white. *Our Nig* illustrates, in one regard at least, racial protest gone awry. Autobiographical in form, it does invite comparison with the slave narrative, which it echoes in form and in such particulars as the helplessness of its protagonist and her ultimate termination of her indenture. And it is a better novel than the first novel written by a black American male. Of Frado and Clotel, Frado is the superior artifact.

Blyden Jackson, A *History of Afro-American Literature* (Baton Rouge: Louisiana State University Press, 1989), Vol. 1, pp. 362–63

CLAUDIA TATE   The lexical identity established between the novel's principal title—*Our Nig*—and its pseudonymous authorial signatory—"Our Nig"—inscribes a sophisticated mode of self-reflexive irony that extenuates direct public censure. The title and the signatory are locked in cyclic parody, like black people in tarface on the minstrel stage; as a result, the aspersion in the self-reflexive title circuitously finds its real target—the very people H. E. W. claimed she wished not to offend in her preface— "our good anti-slavery friends at home." Thus, the text calls attention to the fact that they were ultimately responsible for the quality of life for those free black people who lived among them. In other words, by displacing the well-known slave narrative signatory—Written by Him or Herself—with the diminutive form of a racist epithet—"Our Nig"—the text shifts northern readers' likely resentment of public censure to a deliberately constructed self-derisive humility. Hence, the text exhorts their verification of Frado's hardships and by implication those generally suffered by northern, free, black people by seeing herself from a white perspective. After all, as Wilson insisted with her title, Frado was *their* "nig." Inasmuch as national public opinion had relegated black people, free or slave, to white ownership, Wilson ironically referred to her re-created self as chattel in order to give her voice uncontested authority. As *their* "nig," she could tell her own story of racial abuse seemingly from their point of view and possibly arouse the sympathy of white readers as well as demonstrate that her life was not substantially different from those who were born in bondage. This authorial strategy would also allow her to abort much of the criticism from readers who might regard her story as atypical or exaggerated because technically she was not a slave. However, this epithet may have alienated potential black readers who might not have seen its doubly reflexive irony. The prominent inscription of so hated an epithet among black people may have given them cause to question the racial identity of the book's author, and they may have erroneously concluded that *Our Nig* was a masked white story about black inferiority.

Claudia Tate, "Allegories of Black Female Desire; or, Rereading Nineteenth-Century Sentimental Narratives of Black Female Authority," *Changing Our Own Words: Essays on Criticism, Theory, and Writing by Black Women*, ed. Cheryl A. Wall (New Brunswick, NJ: Rutgers University Press, 1989), pp. 113–14

BETH MACLAY DORIANI   The novel, like ⟨Harriet⟩ Jacobs's narrative ⟨*Incidents in the Life of a Slave Girl*, 1853⟩, ends with a series of appended letters as do many slave narratives, but Wilson defies the stereotype of the "heroic slave." In her narrative, the writers of the letters—"Allida," Margaret Thorne, and "C. D. S."—do not stop at testifying to the truth of the author's assertions or the goodness of her character. Unlike most slave narratives, these letters have a purpose beyond that of testimony: they appeal to the reader to buy the book, thereby aiding the author in her quest for economic independence. "I hope those who call themselves friends of our dark-skinned brethren," writes Thorne, "will lend a helping hand, and assist our sister not in giving, but in buying a book; the expense is trifling, and the reward of doing good is great." Of course, even at the outset of her narrative Wilson has revised slave narrative conventions by beginning with an account of her parentage, not her own birth. Unlike the "heroic slave," she has a clear and definite knowledge of her heritage and her role in society: she is an individual and not a type. She does not move "up" from slavery or oppression—as in the pattern of ascension that ⟨Robert B.⟩ Stepto describes for Afro-American narrative—but moves "within" the oppressive community, struggling for independence and selfhood within the confines of racism.

Her awareness of this role is most apparent in the way she concludes the novel. The lack of closure, an indicting revision of the white domestic novel, also challenges stereotypes of women. Like Jacobs—and unlike the "tragic mulatta"—she desires financial independence, but the lack of closure at the end of the novel indicates an ambiguity about her own success. Whether she will completely achieve that success depends upon the number of books the people of her racist world will buy. The narrator explicitly appeals to the reader in the novel's closing lines: "[S]he asks your sympathy, gentle reader. Refuse not. . . . Enough has been unrolled to demand your sympathy and aid." It is the poverty and oppression Wilson faces as a black woman that force her to "experiment," first by writing, and then by attempting to sell her story. Her novel lacks closure because her ultimate success is uncertain given the confines of racism. Having no guarantee of a house and home, Wilson must revise the sentimental convention of the happy ending. As an autobiographical act of a black woman, *Our Nig* can end only in uncertainty, if it is to have integrity.

Beth Maclay Doriani, "Black Womanhood in Nineteenth-Century America: Subversion and Self-Construction in Two Women's Autobiographies," *American Quarterly* 43, No. 2 (June 1991): 217–18

◼ Bibliography

Our Nig; or, Sketches from the Life of a Free Black, in a Two-Story White House, North. Showing That Slavery's Shadows Fall Even There. 1859.